Mark Kitto was a cap⸺ ⸺uards before he became a metals tra⸺ ⸺on and then China. His series of *that's* listing magazines became the most successful English language publications in China. On the verge of signing a groundbreaking deal that would make him the first authorized foreign publisher in the People's Republic of China, the Communist Party took over his business. He is still in a legal wrangle over Intellectual Property. Variously accused of being a spy, pornographer and terrorist, he retreated to Moganshan where he now lives with his wife and two children. The family runs a successful coffee-shop that is bringing foreigners back to the mountain for the first time since the Communists came in 1949.

China Cuckoo

How I Lost a Fortune
and Found a Life in China

Mark Kitto

CONSTABLE • LONDON

For Isabel and Tristan

Constable & Robinson Ltd
3 The Lanchesters
162 Fulham Palace Road
London W6 9ER
www.constablerobinson.com

First published in the UK by Constable,
an imprint of Constable & Robinson, 2009

UK ISBN: 978-1-84529-940-8

3 5 7 9 8 6 4 2

Printed in Great Britain by Clays Ltd, St Ives plc

Acknowledgements

Be careful what you wish for. It's a cliché, but like all clichés, it's true.

I used to daydream about ending my China career on a hillside above a tea plantation, in an old stone house with a verandah, and dogs, and a family of course. The dream was prompted by a visit to Hangzhou in the mid-nineties, a city surrounded by hills and tea plantations. I must have been reading Somerset Maugham at the time.

Today – a fair few years earlier than I expected – the dream is reality. The tea plantation is round the back of the hill, not below us, but my family and I – with two dogs and a housemaid – do live in an old stone house on a Chinese hillside, and the nearest city is Hangzhou.

For this – to me remarkable – twist of fate, I have the State Council of the Government of the People's Republic of China to thank. For all the irony, I am sincerely grateful. I hope, if or when they read this book, they will allow me to stay here.

I would like to thank the people of Moganshan for accepting me into their community. In all the years I have lived in China I have never felt so at home. Nor have I ever met such a close-knit community. I am very lucky.

I am also lucky to have a circle of friends in China and

v

further afield who have been generous in their support and advice during the writing of this book. Prominent amongst them and in no order as such: Adam Williams, Tess Johnston, Rena Krasno, Paul French, Jeremy Goldkorn, Alex Pearson, Nick Bonner, Bartle Bull, Grant Horsefield, Johnny Reed, Richard McGregor and John Warburton-Lee. For practical assistance with this book, including the generous contribution of photographs, I would like to thank Arthur Jones, Luo Tong, Luther Jones, Rodney Evans, Luke Cardew, Aline Shkurovich and Margaret Body. Closer to home, my wife Joanna has put up with a hell of a lot. Thank you. My thanks too to my friends who helped me through difficult times. Most of you get a mention in the pages that follow.

A certain Charles Blackmore has always claimed credit for setting me on my path to China. That's typical of him, and he knows what I think of the idea, but there are a few sand-grains of truth in it. So here's your acknowledgement, Charles. Thanks.

For really making it all happen, without the irony – and I do hope you read this one day – I must thank Mr Sun Xiao Feng of the Yangzhou Municipal People's Government News Office. Mr Sun, I owe you so much, and it will always be my regret that I could not repay you as we planned, back in those heady days.

My sincere gratitude to the team at Constable & Robinson; my highly perspicacious editor Becky Hardie, also Sam Evans, Andy Hayward, and Nick Robinson, and last but by no means least, my irrepressible agent, Benython Oldfield.

List of Illustrations

The view from the summit of Moganshan. © *Aline Shkurovich.*

Miao Qian, one of the villages on the lower slopes of the mountain. © *Rodney Evans.*

The guest cottage. © *Rodney Evans.*

'The Lodge', the family's coffee-shop. © *Rodney Evans.*

The viewing pagoda at Sword Pond. © *Rodney Evans.*

Mr Shi's wife crosses the stream above Sword Pond. © *Rodney Evans.*

The locals of San Jiu Wu village enjoy the cool evening air. © *Aline Shkurovich.*

Mark and Joanna Kitto. *Author's photograph.*

The Kitto family outside their coffee-shop. *Author's photograph.*

Joanna Kitto's parents enjoy the shade with their grandson. *Author's photograph.*

Moganshan in its heyday, circa 1930. *Author's photograph.*

Moganshan as it appears today. © *Aline Shkurovich.*

The crowd gather by the tennis-courts, possibly during a children's sports day in the 1930s. *Author's photograph.*

A group stands on the steps of Villa Victorella, 1937. *Author's photograph.*

Rena Krasno observes the remains of the villa, 2007. *Author's photograph.*

Family and friends sing carols outside the locked up church. *Author's photograph.*

The swimming-pool surrounded by spectators. *Author's photograph.*

Tristan Kitto looks on at the deserted swimming-pool. *Author's photograph.*

Mark Kitto is pictured in a promotional photo for *that's* magazines. *Author's photograph.*

The group of friends during a trip to Xinjiang province. *Author's photograph.*

Brent Beisher in the kitchen. *Author's photograph.*

The Zhejiang Province, shown in relation to the rest of China.

Contents

A detailed map of the Zhejiang Province.

Chapter One

The Hans on the Hill

Another resort within easy reach of Shanghai, and one that is, let it be whispered, highly popular among honeymooning couples, is the mountain resort of Mokanshan, which seems to exercise an appeal all of its own.

North-China Daily News Sunday Magazine, Summer Holiday Special Issue, 14 June 1936

The Lunar New Year is dead quiet in China, deader than a turkey on Christmas Eve. The entire vast country, the world's production house, grinds to a halt.

Like Christmas, the holiday is a family affair, and family is important in China. Everyone goes home, not back-from-work home, but real home, where grandparents live and ancestors' graves lie, possibly four days' journey by crowded train and bus. And then China stops. City streets are deserted, offices empty, building sites fall silent.

I had been in China for three years and should have known better, but the Lunar New Year in February 1999 caught me completely by surprise. All I had done for the past eight months was work. My business partner and I had moved to Shanghai to launch ourselves in magazine publishing and our

1

feet had not touched the ground since. Like the city itself, our business was booming, out of control. I had even spent Christmas Day at my desk. We had no time for holidays in Shanghai.

Late one cold winter evening I sat at the kitchen table in my tiny attic flat with a glass of whisky. Ten days of enforced idleness. What the hell was I going to do with myself?

Out of the blue I remembered the name Moganshan. Where I'd heard it I had no idea. I must have met someone who had been there, I supposed. The name brought to mind faded images of a neglected colonial backwater full of Western-style houses on a secluded mountaintop.

I fetched a tattered copy of the China *Lonely Planet* that the previous tenant had left on the bookshelf. I turned to the index. Moganshan was not listed.

After a painstaking search I found two short sentences tacked on to the end of 'Other Sights' in the chapter for Hangzhou, China's most popular domestic tourist city. I topped up my glass of whisky and read them slowly.

'Moganshan was developed as a resort for Europeans living in Shanghai and Hangzhou during the colonial era,' the first one said.

The second told me to get a minibus from Hangzhou West Bus Station for forty yuan, and that a double room in a hotel on the mountain might cost 250.

So Moganshan was still standing and I could get there via Hangzhou, two hours by train from Shanghai. That was enough to go on and I would have plenty of time. And it was something to do.

It was also possible I might have a companion.

Her English name was Crystal. She was Shanghainese,

tall, head-turning beautiful and I had met her a couple of days ago at the first party I ever went to in Shanghai that had nothing to do with my job. Her phone number was still in my pocket. As I lay back in bed that night I fantasized about a cosy sitting-room with a log fire in an old stone house on a wintry mountainside. It was an easy next step and a very pleasant one to paste Crystal into the picture.

On our third or fourth date, Crystal and I were both a little drunk from one too many martinis in that week's bar of the moment. It was the early hours and she had stopped off for a nightcap. Her long legs, wrapped in stretch-tight jeans, were tucked up beneath her on the thin cushions of the hardwood sofa in my sitting-room. She was wearing a white sweater, a sheepskin-lined hippie-type waistcoat and a pale pink muffler. Her cheeks were glowing from cold and alcohol. She looked gorgeous.

'Moganshan sounds interesting, don't you think?' I asked as I poured her a Bailey's, trying to sound casual yet all the time wondering frantically whether she would be going home that night. 'I mean, think of the history of the place. Wouldn't it be fascinating to see the houses where foreigners used to hang out in the old days?'

Crystal watched me with patience and a charming smirk. Why would a glossy Shanghainese want to go and dig around in an dusty old mountain village?

She took a sip of Bailey's and looked up, her eyes so desperately trying to appear neutral that they were patently mischievous. She wiped an imaginary drop of Bailey's from the corner of her mouth with a delicate finger.

'I'd love to come with you,' she said.

Before we could set off, Crystal had to perform the family

duties of the New Year Festival: eat dumplings with her parents, call on relatives and watch the Chinese equivalent of *The Sound of Music* on China Central Television One. I waited patiently, still not entirely believing my luck, and in my damp and draughty garret reread the two sentences in the *Lonely Planet*.

Three days into the marathon holiday – imagine Christmas lasting for ten days – Crystal made a break for it and met me at Shanghai South train station.

It was a cold and crisp February morning under a clear blue sky. There was nobody on the streets of Shanghai. Long stretches of the kerbside were coated red with the remains of firecrackers that had been draped over railings and let off on New Year's Eve. A longstanding ban on fireworks in the inner city had been lifted that year. The desolate roads looked like the aftermath of a bloody street battle. The silence was eerie.

After the outward calm on the streets it was a surprise to find the train station heaving with people. We were obviously not the only ones getting out of town. Leisure travel was just beginning to catch on in China, with the young at least. The station waiting room was packed with day trippers heading for Hangzhou and the city's scenic and rightly-famous West Lake.

Crystal and I were lucky to find places beside each other in a soft seat carriage. It was full of twenty-something Shanghainese, chattering loudly in the local dialect. Bags of sunflower seeds and dried fruit littered the tiny metal-framed tables. As we pulled out of the station a conductor ambled down the aisle with a trolley of soft drinks, then another who offered to book hotel rooms in Hangzhou, the next sold maps and first day covers, and finally a man appeared with

4

a wooden tray of nylon socks. He demonstrated the quality by scraping them with a metal brush under our noses. Muzak blared from speakers in the luggage racks.

Crystal and I ignored the din. We were too interested in each other. When I asked what her parents thought about her leaving home during the holiday, she told me they were used to her trips to Hangzhou with girlfriends. I did not press her for details.

The semi-urban sprawl that surrounds Shanghai on all sides except the sea droned past the train's grubby windows. The country is flat as a pancake. Grey clusters of farmers' cinder block houses gave way to fields of leafless mulberry bushes, green swathes of winter cabbages and bright splashes of pearl farms, the water's surface cluttered with ranks of white polystyrene floats. Scattered amongst the rural vistas enormous plots of earth had been cleared and concreted like new runways, waiting for a factory to land on them. Long strings of barges chugged along the waterways towards Shanghai, loaded so heavily with sand and gravel that their gunwales barely broke the surface above the tiny waves that splashed against them. The few barges heading up country were empty. All roads led to Shanghai. It was good to be going against the flow.

Mid-holiday Hangzhou station was utter mayhem. At the end of a dark passageway there was a row of shiny chrome exit barriers where we bottlenecked like cows passing through a branding pen. We squeezed through sideways and out into the concourse.

Unlicensed taxi drivers and hotel touts stood their ground in the middle of the human torrent. The desperation on their faces almost made you feel sorry. I brushed off a chubby middle-aged woman who was thrusting a cling film-wrapped photograph of a dull brown bedroom in my face and we shuffled to one side. In a small eddy I pulled out the *Lonely Planet*.

'We need to find the West Bus Station,' I shouted to Crystal.

'I'll ask someone,' she replied, and glided across the stream of people towards a uniformed attendant.

'He says it's the North Bus Station for Moganshan,' she said, once she had struggled back to where I waited.

'Ah. Great start.'

'How shall we get there?' Crystal asked.

I looked at the logjam forming by the exit that led to the taxi rank. There would be no queue out there, only a scrum.

'Let's get a bus,' I suggested.

City buses are best avoided in my book and nowhere is this more true than China. But today there was no alternative. We found a bus whose driver told us he was going to the North Bus Station, he actually meant 'towards'. Half an hour later we stepped out at a crossroads in the outskirts of Hangzhou. The area looked like the suburbs of any Chinese city: broad brown streets, bicycle lanes behind knee high privet hedges and white-tiled apartment blocks surrounding dirty factories. The driver nodded up one of the empty roads.

'You need to change here for the North Station,' he said as the doors clanked shut.

We started walking. There was no sign of another bus stop. But the sun was shining and our bags were not heavy. So we kept going.

A taxi appeared from nowhere and slowed beside us. The driver gave me the hangdog hopeful look that Chinese taxi drivers practise in the mirror every morning. I looked up and down the street to confirm I had no idea where we were, signalled him to pull over and bent down to the open passenger window. I had already made a decision.

'How much to Moganshan?' I asked.

He thought for a split second then replied 'Three hundred' without blinking.

'Done.'

I had an urgent appointment with a fireplace fantasy.

The driver took us the long way but neither of us knew or cared. We drove out of Hangzhou on a potholed, crumbling highway, the National Route 104. Once the city was behind us small hills appeared to the west. Many were being quarried for their stone that would become the gravel that went into the barges and then the foundations of Shanghai. Some were almost completely hollowed out. The summits would only be a vague memory for the older villagers who had climbed them in their youth. I thought of the Chinese fable about the foolish old man who tried to move a mountain single-handedly because it blocked his way. According to the story, the gods were so impressed by his determination that they moved it for him. Now the god Mammon was moving the mountains of Zhejiang to Shanghai.

Forty minutes from Hangzhou we turned off the 104 on to a country road lined with sycamore trees. The road wound into the hills along a broad valley of fallow rice paddy, crisp brown in the winter sun. Farmers in padded blue cotton jackets and fur-flapped hats putted towards us on smoke-belching three-wheeled tractors that looked like easy rider motorbikes crossed with lawnmowers. They were hauling towering stacks of bamboo. The bases of the trunks formed a cab over the driver's head while the wispy tops sashayed along the road behind. Somewhere inside the lumbering green brown mass was a trailer.

7

Then the valley closed in and we started climbing. I had butterflies in my stomach. We were getting close. My hopes were high but I had no idea what to expect. Perhaps we would only find ruins of the old villas, piles of rubble scattered across the hillside like Celtic stone circles. Or worse, a modern and cheesy tourist trap with a funfair beside a coach park and a cable car to the peak.

But the signs were promising. The scenery we glimpsed through the bamboo was beginning to look mountainous, remote. Green hills, ridge upon ridge of them, receded into the distance. The only signs of habitation were the small hamlets we glimpsed far below as we swept round the hairpin bends. At last the road traversed a final spur of the mountainside and we entered the village of Moganshan.

It took my breath away.

Tucked into a bowl on the side of the mountain was a European village. There was nothing fake or fabricated about it – unlike the Spanish villa complexes in the suburbs of Shanghai that look like film sets for spaghetti westerns. This was the real thing, solid and three-dimensional, as if transported stone by stone from the Alps or Provence or even North Wales, where I grew up.

A dense cluster of granite buildings under tiled and corrugated iron roofs lined a short street. More houses were scattered across the hillside, all grey stonework and sloping roofs, most of them with long verandas facing the plain below.

Apart from the Chinese characters across the walls of the hotels and restaurants, the bamboo we could see stretching away across the slopes and a single stubby pagoda perched below us, this was not China. A light dusting of snow completed the Alpine effect. Above us everything was white and the top of the mountain was shrouded in cloud. We had stepped back in time and into another country.

We paid the driver and explained there was no need to wait. We would be staying overnight. He stared over his shoulder in disbelief and patent disappointment that he was not getting a return fare. We stepped out of the car on to the snow and ice that had crusted along the edge of the road.

A woman wrapped up like a Siberian *babushka* stopped and stared. Crystal beckoned her over and asked if there were any hotels open.

'Everything frozen,' she replied, her voice itself sharp as ice. 'At least above here. No water, no heating. But you might find a room in that place and they can probably give you a thermos of hot water.' She pointed to one of the larger buildings on the street. It looked like an abandoned Victorian prison. We shook our heads but did not write it off. At least there was a bed somewhere.

'Let's look around,' I suggested. Crystal nodded. She smiled too. She seemed to be enjoying the adventure so far, which was a good sign.

From the village street we made our way up some verglas-covered steps that led to the cloud-covered ridge. At their top we came out on a single-track road. The only faint noise to disturb the silence was the dripping of snowmelt from the bamboo and the pine trees on to the crisp bamboo leaves that covered the ground. The drops landed with tiny thuds and cracks. No one was about.

We followed the road through the damp fog. Above and beside us spectral houses emerged from the shadows like so many landlocked *Marie Celestes*. Shuttered windows ignored us. Wet walls gave us the cold shoulder.

9

We came to a solid square house beside the road. It was closed up tight for the winter. A chimney ran up the outside of the wall facing the road and on the left a large first-floor balcony – second-floor in China or America – was supported by thick, tapered stone columns. I put my hand on Crystal's arm.

'This is the place,' I said. 'This is exactly the kind of house I want to stay in. You wouldn't believe how similar it is to the house where I grew up. I love it.'

'Shame it's shut,' Crystal replied with genuine sympathy.

Looking back over my shoulder, I took Crystal's hand and we made our way back down to Yin Shan Jie, Shady Mountain Street, and the only open restaurant. Huddled beside a small and rusty wood-burning stove, we ate fish-flavoured meat and bowls of rice. The only vegetable was winter cabbage. The waitress, who was also the cook, sat to one side, wrapped in a knee-length duvet jacket. She put up her fluffy-slippered feet and stared up at the wall-mounted television showing a local soap opera. We were the only clients, the only visitors in the whole village.

Crystal and I debated our options. Stay in the grim hotel over the road or go for another walk and then back to Hangzhou, somehow. We regretted dismissing the taxi driver so impetuously.

Then the woman who had first put us off stuck her head through the sliding glass door.

'Hey,' she shouted. 'There's someone here says you could stay at her place up on the ridge if you want. No water at all mind. Want to come meet her? She's over there.' She pointed to her right.

Keeping our hopes in check, we skidded on to the street

and down the short slope to an open space under the sprawling winter skeleton of a sycamore tree. It could have passed for a *place* in a southern French village. The woman waiting for us was five foot nothing. She was bundled up against the cold in a deep red padded jacket but bare-headed. Her scruffy hair was cut short above her round and rosy cheeked face. She spoke in a rush, stumbling over her words and ending every statement with a quizzical rise in pitch.

'Even the water in the toilet bowls is frozen?' she explained, as if we might not want to hear more. 'But I have blankets, and an electric heater. If you really want to stay up there you can come and have a look, if you like?'

'Do you have a fireplace?' I asked, trying not to mimic her.

'Yes we do. Never use it.'

'Let's go.'

She waddled ahead of us up the steep road. Her name was Mrs Han. We explained to her back that we had come from Shanghai looking for some peace and quiet. Mrs Han told her feet that we should have come in the summer, when everything was open.

We reached the crest of the ridge in the clouds again and retraced our steps, back towards my dream house.

'That's it,' said Mrs Han, pointing at the very same house.

I squeezed Crystal's hand through her glove.

Mrs Han pulled a bunch of keys out of her coat pocket, opened the front door, and we stepped into the wooden-floored hallway. It was colder than outside. We followed her up to the bedroom with the fireplace. Heavy quilts were folded at the foot of twin beds. There was not a speck of dust. The room seemed frozen in time, as if guests had left that morning and more were due any minute. The cold had kept it fresh and crisp. And there, at one end of the room, was a small, real fireplace, the high-sided type you find in the sculleries of Victorian town houses. It was hard to tear my eyes away from it.

I checked to see if the table between the beds was fixed to the wall. It moved. So the twins could be pushed together to make a double. Another small table and some comfortable bamboo chairs were squared away against the opposite wall. There was no other furniture, no rug on the cold floorboards. A glass door opened on to the balcony, which was shared with the next door room. I was staring at the fireplace again when Mrs Han wheeled in an electric radiator.

'This is perfect,' I told her. 'How much?'

She smiled. She must have put up a few honeymooning couples.

'Oh, we'll talk about that later,' she said and then asked: 'What would you like for supper?'

'Can we talk about that later too?'

'Of course.' She smiled again. 'And by the way, do you mind turning the heater off when you leave the room? Electricity is very expensive here.'

That afternoon we met Mr Han. He knocked and let himself in as I was uncorking a bottle of red wine. The camembert was warming on the radiator.

Mr Han looked mid-forties, well-preserved, dashing even. He had a matinee idol's clean-cut jaw and a high-bridged, straight and narrow nose. The way he swept away the long forelock that kept falling across his brow helped with the film star impression.

'Mr Han,' I asked, 'is there any chance of some firewood?' I nodded towards the small grate.

12

'Hmm.' He gripped his square chin. 'We've just had it painted.'

Sure enough, the fireplace was sparkling white. I did not attempt to work out why, nor try logic on Mr Han.

'We won't make a mess,' I said.

'OK, I'll get you some wood,' he replied, and disappeared.

Crystal had no idea how excited I was.

A minute later Mr Han charged back in with a bundle of twigs in one hand. 'Here,' he said, 'this should be fine.'

I watched with disappointment as he threw the bird's nest into the grate. It would never make a roaring fire.

I remembered Mrs Han's words about expensive electricity. I pulled her husband to one side.

'Mr Han,' I explained, 'if we can have a proper fire and I mean, you know, one that actually keeps us warm, then we won't need to use the *electric* heater.' I pointed at it as if it was made of gold and about to melt through the floorboards. He gripped his chin again and disappeared for longer this time.

Ten minutes later a pile of decent logs was piled up beside the chimney. The twigs made good kindling.

I poured the wine, sliced some cheese, shuffled a pack of cards and then we dived into bed. The fire blazed in the hearth. It was growing dark outside and my daydream was coming true. We stayed there for three days.

We drank wine by the fire, played cards, slept, made love and went for walks in the snow. The weather cleared and for the first time in almost a year I relaxed. My resentment at the obligatory holiday turned into guilty gratitude. I had forgotten how much simple pleasure there was in an aimless walk – through the woods and up to a rocky hilltop where we could sit and stare into the distance and discuss what to have for dinner. I had also forgotten the nervous thrill of starting a relationship. Moganshan was the perfect place for both.

One afternoon when we had returned from a long walk and were enjoying an intensely-physical siesta we were interrupted by Mrs Han. She hammered on the door. 'I've got a blanket for you!'

'Don't worry,' we shouted back. 'We don't need it.' The rays of the low winter sun were slanting through the glass door and landing on the bed. They warmed us perfectly well and besides, it was very romantic. We weren't even bothering with sheets.

'But I must give you a blanket!' Mrs Han insisted.

'And we do not need one, thank you very much indeed, Mrs Han.'

Mrs Han mumbled something unintelligible. We heard her clumping down the wooden stairs and then back up again, only this time she wasn't alone. We paid no attention.

The footsteps went into the room next door, the suite that opened on to the shared balcony. Then the voices became clearer, as if they were out in the open air. There were adult voices, and the sound of a child, too.

They were right outside our glass door. It sounded like the parents were in rhapsody at the view from the balcony. From the sudden silence of the child I guessed he was too. At a different view.

Too late I realized why Mrs Han had been so desperate to give us a blanket. What she had wanted to say was 'curtain'. I looked over my shoulder and into the eyes of a small boy's face. It was pressed to the glass, his two hands forming a visor against the reflection. I have no idea what he or his

14

parents did or said or what happened next because I yanked the discarded bedsheets over our heads and Crystal and I giggled until we slept the long sleep of the embarrassed. When we finally emerged for Mrs Han's home-cooked supper she grinned like a wise and indulgent aunt.

'Could we have that blanket now, Mrs Han?' we asked. She grinned some more, shook her head, and went to hang it up.

By the time we returned to Moganshan a month later Mr Han had become Lao Han, Old Han, and his wife Han Aiyi, Auntie Han. They charged us 150 yuan a night, including dinners. We were becoming friends.

Lao Han was born in Hangzhou in 1950. He was about to start high school in 1966 when the Cultural Revolution began and all education stopped. Schools were shut down or descended into anarchy as teenage Red Guards ran amok and humiliated their teachers.

'We spent our time walking from home to school and back again. There was nothing else to do,' Lao Han recalled. In 1969 he was sent down to the country to learn from the peasants, like millions of other youngsters. He ended up in Heilongjiang, the northernmost province of China up against the Russian border. It was there that he met his wife.

'They wanted me to work in the fields,' he told us, 'but I spent most of my time in the cookhouse. Then after three years they made me a teacher in the village school.'

I asked him what he taught.

'Everything,' he replied.

I sensed a missed ambition, a career wasted. 'Is that what you wanted to be? A teacher? Was that your ambition in Hangzhou, before they sent you away?'

Lao Han laughed. 'How could I know what my ambition

15

was back then? I was only nineteen! I had no idea what I wanted to do with my life.'

Now he and his wife were caretakers of this house in Moganshan. It belonged to a work unit in Hangzhou, a state-owned company that used it as a getaway, a place for meetings and leisure and the occasional office honeymoon. Lao Han insisted we kept the curtains drawn on the windows that faced the road in case passers-by noticed they were doing a little business on the side.

We had learnt our lesson about curtains and meekly obeyed. I was still reeling from the joy of discovering Moganshan, this tiny and forgotten piece of Europe hidden in the hills so close to Shanghai. It was the perfect antidote to the frantic life I had started in the city and I was determined to come back whenever I could. I did not want to spoil it.

Chapter Two

Exploration

Mokanshan is no place for those who wish to carry on through the summer the whirling gaieties of a Shanghai winter. But for health and tranquility, for long easy hours of reading and dreaming, for true rest and refreshment, for rambles through scenery to which every new turn and almost every hour of the day lends a special grace, a new suggestion, Mokanshan is surely unsurpassed.

North-China Daily News, 27 July 1919

Crystal and I adopted the Hans' house as our own. It was rare, if ever, that we had to share it with strangers, particularly during the late winter and early spring. We became jealously possessive of the bedroom with the fireplace.

By the late summer of 1999 there was a semblance of organization coming together in my Shanghai office, a system falling into place. Our business was still growing so fast that my partner and I were more like passengers than the captains of our ship, but we somehow found the time to create departments and appoint managers. We even treated ourselves to a personnel manager to go through the CVs and organize the daily interviews for all the staff we were recruiting. I was beginning to get my life back. Once a month I allowed myself the luxury of a full weekend off. I always went to Moganshan.

An American friend, Brent Beisher, and his Shanghainese girlfriend Leona, often joined me and Crystal. Brent had worked in an early Internet start-up, then as an editor at the *Shanghai Star*, a state-run English-language newspaper. Now he had set up a real estate company. Like me he was a merchant adventurer, an opportunist of the type that had drifted into Shanghai in their thousands in the old days and was now returning after a fifty-year hiatus. Yet while I liked to think I knew what I was aiming for and meant to see it through, Brent changed his company's direction every month. First it was a letting agency for newly arrived foreigners, then it was a sales agency. Then he was buying, restoring and selling old Shanghai houses. He was into anything that turned a buck.

Brent reminded me of Donald Sutherland in the movie *M*A*S*H*, both in looks and how he walked and talked. Over six feet tall, he was always half-shaven and had a hangdog and clumsily outspoken way of making friends with everybody. He seemed to shamble through life, never got stuck into anything, yet always got by. In many ways we were as different as chalk and cheese, yet we were becoming close friends. Also, like me, he was fascinated by Moganshan, particularly the houses, and had immediately fallen in love with the place.

Leona had a car, which meant our monthly commute no longer required crowded trains and expensive taxis either. It would be disingenuous to deny that Leona's battered Volkswagen Santana helped to cement my friendship with Brent, but the long road trips certainly built a bond. He and I sat in the front, the girls in the back. We went through his music collection on the car stereo, argued about how to run a business and took turns at the wheel. It was a good place to get to know each other. Neither of us had a Chinese driving license, but that was the least of our worries.

The old four-lane highway from Shanghai to Hangzhou was a dead straight, hundred-mile long high-speed dodgem course. The Shanghai toll-gate was not a toll-gate. It was a starting gate. Normally timid Shanghainese drivers were transformed into frenzied thrill-seekers as they left it. One wet and stormy night on the way back from Moganshan I counted thirty crumpled vehicles on the Shanghai-bound carriageway alone. The most dangerous vehicles by far were the coaches, whose drivers acted as if they owned the road, and the police, who did.

The regulation that the scene of an accident cannot be cleared until the police arrive created traffic jams so solid that they could never get through to do their detective job, which made the jams even worse. Further delays were caused by shameless Chinese *schadenfreude* and the invention of mobile phone cameras. Children posed with big grins beside burning wrecks, smiling mothers with arms around them.

We got lost every trip until we eventually pieced together a route by trial and error, reducing the journey from five hours to three.

The hellish car journeys made arrival in Moganshan all the more heavenly. When at last we turned on to the steep 'front' road that climbed in sharp switchbacks up the hillside, the only way was up. If darkness had fallen – often the case, thanks to the accidents and jams – the moon grew brighter and whiter and the stars appeared as we left the smog of the

19

plain, adding to the Peter Pan-like sensation of flying up into fairyland.

Each visit we called ahead to Mrs Han, gave her our estimated time of arrival and found supper waiting for us. She would bring up local dishes on a relay of trays which we ate at a long bamboo table by the French window. Brent and Leona said they preferred the suite to the room with the fireplace. I think they were being magnanimous. Han Aiyi was an excellent cook, if limited in repertoire. Local bamboo shoots were a prime ingredient, in a rich dark sauce if they were the root of the larger trees, the *maozhu* or hairy bamboo, lightly steamed if they were the smaller tender ones, *zhusun*, which had a texture like the nutty white stems of fresh asparagus. Many of the vegetables were *yecai*, wild. Some were broad-leafed, some thin and spindly, some like rocket leaves and others like nettles. We tried to establish their precise names in Chinese and English but Mrs Han kept repeating as if we were missing the point: 'They're *yecai*, that's all we call them.'

For meat she gave us the chickens that she kept in a coop outside the kitchen door. Head and feet attached, in a vat of water with fresh ginger and Swiss chard, she boiled them up into a delicious broth. Once we had drunk the soup we started on the meat: two courses in one bowl. Occasionally we tried a local wild boar. The meat was tough and almost impossible to pick from the small fragments of bone with chopsticks or teeth, but the hard-won morsels were rich and gamey.

To finish off we ordered a plate of Mrs Han's fries. How she created them is a mystery. They were perfect *frites*. Once we had stuffed ourselves with homegrown chicken, wild meat and vegetables and plates of the mystical *frites*, we moved next door to sit by the fire and play cards. Brent and I shared the bottles of whisky we took turns to bring with us. In the mornings we fried bacon from a supermarket in Shanghai, brewed fresh coffee in a percolator we left with the Hans, scrambled some fresh eggs from the surviving chickens and carried it all up to the balcony to breakfast in the morning sun. We made ourselves at home.

Sleep in Moganshan was like a coma. After the exhausting round of parties, the constant noise, the pneumatic drills, the hammering, the shouting neighbours, the brake-squealing horn-blaring traffic, the twenty-four-hour cacophony of Shanghai resurrecting itself, Moganshan was blissfully quiet. We slept long dreamless nights in the handmade cotton quilts which the Hans treasured like family heirlooms, hanging them to air on bamboo poles every time the sun came out and in damp weather tightly folding them away. They were heavy and stiff, yet when you climbed under one the thing somehow melted where it touched your body. Despite the thickness, they seemed cool in summer, in winter warm and cosy. Every first morning at the Hans' I woke up with no idea where I was. My head was as clear as if it had been rinsed in a mountain spring.

Getting out of bed was not easy. The quilts had cast their spell, trapped us in their magical web. Nor was the weather enticing during our earliest visits. In spring the mountaintop is more often than not wrapped in wet cloud and mist, a soggy blanket which the village seems reluctant to throw off, like one of the Hans' quilts, as if it dreads the coming of summer and the tourists. It would rather hide away and be left in peace with its memories and ghosts.

But it was those ghosts, of our predecessors in Shanghai,

21

and the urge to rediscover Moganshan as they would have remembered it, that coaxed us out on those damp mornings. After breakfast Brent and I went exploring while Crystal and Leona went back to bed.

We set off along the stone paths, slippery under wet leaves, that crisscrossed the hillsides through the bamboo. We branched off wherever we saw a tempting villa. Sometimes well-made steps led up or down to them, sometimes a muddy path.

All of the houses were big, square and solid. A few were very big, with three or four floors and small wings on one or both sides and broad terraces with balconies above. Each and every one was tucked into the hillside above a dry stone retaining wall that held it in place. Behind them and along their sides more stonework held the mountain from sliding down. Low front walls gave on to overgrown gardens and paved terraces cracked open by gradual subsidence. The massive walls swelled unevenly from the strain of fighting gravity for so many years.

The architecture was plainly western, late Victorian British crossed with early 1900s American homestead and a dash of Alpine lodge to allow for the slopes. It boiled down to a functional, easy-build symmetry. Here and there a token of chinoiserie appeared in the upturned corners of a pagoda-like porch or a stretch of square wooden latticework along a balcony. But those were the exceptions. The houses were simple stone boxes for summer living. Thick walls kept them cool and corrugated iron roofs kept out the rain and were cheap to replace after a storm.

The key distinguishing features, apart from the occasional turret or tower added like a folly, or a bay-windowed drawing room, were the terraces and balconies. Today, their inspiration

– the views they once commanded of endless hills – was blocked by grey green banks of bamboo and the knotted tops of untended trees.

Villas that had been converted into guesthouses and hotels were locked up tight through the long winter and early spring, waiting for the Moganshan season to begin in May. They were impregnable, so we skipped them. But when we came across an obviously abandoned house we lowered our voices, crept up close and pressed our faces to the grime-covered windows as if we were sneaking up on Boo Radley. In the dark interiors we made out hallway floors tiled in terracotta, red and yellow, bathtubs on ball and claw feet pushed up against crumbling plaster walls, and piles of cheap plain 1960s Chinese furniture – desks, tables and plastic upholstered armchairs – coated with dust and bat guano, rotting in the damp. Otherwise the houses were stripped clean.

We tested front and back doors and searched for a loose shutter or broken window. To satisfy our curiosity we were going to have to treat the derelicts the way foreigners once treated China. We would have to force our way in. With practice we perfected the art of breaking and entering. We heaved ourselves up on to window-sills that were caked with an odious mixture of dust and rat or bird shit, stuck our hands through broken or missing window panes and unlatched the frames. Then we wriggled through and tested our weight on the fragile floorboards.

Once we had explored the lower rooms we climbed rotten wooden staircases, keeping our feet against the sides which we guessed were more solid. Upstairs we ducked under sagging ceilings, stepped carefully around gaping holes in the floors, crossed to bedroom windows and peered out through dirty panes at the tops of the feathery bamboo and the grey mist.

If we could find a bathroom with its original floor tiles intact, perhaps an old fireplace in a drawing-room, we revelled in the faded history and tried to picture how the place might have been furnished. Those surviving original touches were rare however. The houses seemed to have been converted into dormitories, probably during the early Communist era, presumably for 'model workers' and Party officials. Every room was a bedroom or a bathroom. Windowless cubicles like rabbit hutches were crammed into large drawing-rooms. In some bedrooms we found wooden bed frames strung with rope matting and on the walls above them torn calendar pages from the 1970s with pictures of Mao waving from corn fields. A dusty brassiere was wedged between a ripped mosquito net and a broken window. Shards of glass from a broken thermos flask were scattered around a glazed brown jar that had contained homebrew, cracked and lying on its side.

One abandoned house below the ridge-top road had a concrete annexe stuck on one end like a lookout tower. This was no architectural embellishment designed by a long gone foreigner. The construction was recent, perhaps from the seventies. Once we had broken in we discovered it contained a stack of tiny bathrooms. The silver painted drains and pipes poked through the ceilings, floors and walls. The impression was of cheapness, history desecrated.

While Brent and I made our survey of Moganshan, the village that had first charmed me with its quaint other-worldliness revealed plenty of evidence of neglect as well as incongruous and ugly modernity. Garden ponds were full of weeds and litter and tennis-courts had been turned into vegetable patches or plantations of saplings, and then abandoned.

Piles of non-perishable multi-coloured refuse spread like avalanches below the gardens. Flimsy blue plastic bags hung from branches of pine trees, blown there by summer typhoons and stuck since like prayer flags. It would take years to rot them away.

Ugly concrete blockhouses and paint-flaked weatherboarded shacks had been built in gardens where pergolas had once stood. We assumed these were the cookhouses where work units had served up meals to cadres and model workers, who had sat at tables surrounded by the debris – chicken bones and prawn shells – playing *ma jiang* late into the night.

Decades-old cooking oil oozed like resin from holes in exterior stone walls that once held extractor fans. Wires and cables were strung through the trees in a tangled mess. Dirty white electric wiring was used for washing lines. In places the cables drooped below head height. There was no way of telling which were live, which dead.

One apparently abandoned house was actually inhabited by an old man and his wife. They looked as ancient and neglected as the building itself, which stood alone in a dense copse of pine trees at least a hundred steps up from the road below. The metal roof had rusted away in places, a first-floor window hung askew on one hinge and the eaves were either dangling in rotten shards or completely missing.

Under the lopsided porch at the front of the house the old man was hunched over a bench, picking through a pile of weeds: *yecai*. On a shelf by his grey head was a small transistor radio. He was listening to a popular show, *The Outlaws of the Marsh* – the Chinese version of *Robin Hood*, only with more hoods – narrated by a well-known radio actor with a rasping Beijing accent, who gave each character's voice such outraged rises and falls in pitch and tone that it sounded like he was recording on a roller-coaster. The voice followed you everywhere.

With a well-worn broad-bladed sickle the man's wife was chopping kindling. She was short and stooped, and wore a tattered, dirty white T-shirt. It was threadbare in the two patches where her sagging breasts had brushed against it a thousand times while she bent over her daily chores. Her upturned face was small, wrinkled and confused.

We asked if we could stick our heads inside their front door and the woman nodded. Along a dark hallway was a row of closed doors. We imagined we might have found some original furniture in them, but we were too embarrassed to ask if we could go further. The old couple seemed strangely unsurprised to see foreigners.

Our brief conversation was handicapped by their thick accents and our own Chinese. They were from Anhui, a province about fifty miles from Moganshan, and they spoke an outdated, old-fashioned Chinese of which we had trouble making sense. But we established that they were descended from the locals who had worked for the foreigners in the old days. They were not surprised to see us. They had seen plenty of foreigners before.

We mumbled our apologies for barging in and passed on. The man and wife bent back to their chores.

As we walked, Brent and I came up with categories for the buildings, or rather the state of the buildings.

There were modern, proper (as in licensed and official, meaning owned and managed by government officials) government hotels, generally set in the largest mansions. The exteriors of these were sometimes original but in most cases the wooden shutters and latticed windows had been replaced with functional aluminium frames. We knew what we would find inside because we had stayed in many similar hotels across China, in big cities and small towns: bedrooms with hard twin beds, plastic-coated furniture and *en suite* bathrooms in pale pink with loos that only flushed if you put your hand inside the cistern and pulled up the plug. And every floor tiled with big square white tiles. We had no interest in them. Besides, they were shut for the long off-season – according to the Hans, the busiest time of year was the school holiday period in July and August, when the mountain came alive and the big hotels brought in temporary staff from the local villages.

Then there were the work-unit guesthouses – unofficial hotels, in other words, because they had no licence to operate but all of them did and got away with it, which is quite normal in China. Like the official hotels, the guesthouses had usually had their guts ripped out and modern bedrooms and bathrooms installed, but there was a chance they had survived in something close to their original layout, not because of any desire to preserve their original charm but because the leaseholders could not afford or be bothered to change them. The Hans' place fell into this category. If we found a caretaker lurking about we asked to see the rooms, pretending to be scouting for our next visit. None of the guesthouses we saw were as appealing as the Hans' and we never found another bedroom with a fireplace.

The third category were the derelicts – our favourites. Finally we created the label 'inhabited derelicts', ruins with a roof and people living in them, such as the one in the woods. Unlike the true derelicts, they had soggy brown chickens pecking at the cracks in the lopsided stone paths, untidy piles of firewood and perhaps an old bath tub collecting rain water for a vegetable garden. The gap between the hillside and the backs of these rundown houses was invariably roofed over with a jigsaw of cast away corrugated iron and spare lengths of it leant up against the sides to protect useless junk from the rain.

We did not break into those. That would have been criminal. But if someone was home we asked if we could have a quick peek inside. To distract them from our nosiness, we engaged in what we believed was polite conversation.

These villas were divided up between as many as six couples, each of which occupied a few rooms originally granted as grace and favour apartments to their grandparents by the local government. The families had simply moved in when the original foreign owners, their former employers, left China in 1949. Now they paid a monthly rent of twenty yuan, approximately one pound twenty, to the local government, which was paid out of a monthly gratuity of two hundred yuan which they received – from the local government. They mostly worked in local hotels and restaurants, some of them in the village administration bureaux.

One dank afternoon Brent and I added one more category to our list: complete ruins.

Lao Han had told us about the remains of the first hotel on Moganshan, built in the 1920s on a spur on the mountain's southern flank. The place was known as Gun Emplacement Hill. It looked like one, standing out from the main mountain and with clear views on three sides, but it had never served a military purpose.

An overgrown path led down from the back road. The

only structure still standing was the hotel's impressive stone gateway. Behind the once grand entrance, amongst the roots of the giant sycamores and tall fir trees that had overrun the crest, we found a fetid water tank and an empty swimming-pool. Ankle-high remains of thick stone walls were laid through the undergrowth like a crossword. We tried to work out what had gone where but the rooms in the centre seemed too small, more like cells than hotel rooms. Perhaps they were store rooms in the cool heart of the building. The public rooms and bedrooms would have been on the outside edges to make the most of the views, but they had disappeared into thin air.

We took a detour on our way back, drawn along yet another overgrown path. At its end, at least a mile from the village, we came across a small shack in the woods. It was made of mud and brick and had a rusted tin roof. The doorway was open. An old man stirred from his wooden bed when we stuck our heads inside. He got to his feet and greeted us. His face was unshaven, the stubble a mottled white and grey.

'Do you live here?' we asked when he stepped outside to where we waited.

'Yes, most of the time,' he replied, yawning. 'I go down to my village when it snows.'

'What do you do?' There was no vegetable patch or any sign of daily life.

'I guard the bamboo, watch for fires.'

'Guard the bamboo from whom?'

'People coming to steal the shoots. They'll be out soon. This year it is forbidden to dig them up.'

Enormous cedar trees towered over his hut and the bamboo plantation began below them. I looked around the flat area under the trees. There were low piles of cut stone scattered between them.

'Was there a house here before?' I asked.

'Yes. A big one. Long time ago.'

Below me a large rectangular hole was sunk in the ground, the size of a twenty-foot container, surrounded by dense bamboo.

'And that was their swimming-pool?'

'That's right,' the old man said.

'But we're such a long way from the village ...' I tailed off, my question answering itself. People came here to get away from it all. And there was no bamboo on the top of the mountain then so this remote ruin, now lost in the dark woods, would have commanded stunning views. The ground fell away steeply beyond the empty hole. It had been an infinity pool, the type that you see in every advertisement for a spa resort. They knew what they were doing in those days.

We made our way back up to the Hans' via what had been the public swimming-pool, the only pool we found with water in it. The small concrete huts beside it, the old changing rooms, were locked with crusted padlocks. The disused pool, fifteen metres long by ten wide, was surrounded by a barrier of concrete railings topped with rusted brown barbed wire, the same colour as the stagnant water. Leaves had drifted into vague piles along the cracked edges.

We also found the old public tennis-courts. Once again Lao Han had told us where to look, otherwise we would never have guessed. Where five grass courts had once spread across a large flat area near the top of the hill a dense mass of wispy bamboo now formed an impenetrable chest-high jungle. At one end of the courts stood a building which

30

looked like a church. It rose almost as high as the bamboo above and behind it, which made it at least fifty feet tall, taking the slope into account. The building looked as impregnable as a medieval fortress, but we had to try.

We scrambled through a mess of rusting paint cans, broken cisterns, scraps of timber and a tap dripping into a cracked washbasin on the ground below it. Rotten window frames and wooden doors, salvaged from renovated villas, were stacked against the stonework. It was a junkyard. In the narrow space between the hillside and the back wall we found an arched opening in the masonry. It was blocked by old planks. We pulled a couple of them aside and squeezed in.

It was a cathedral, not a church. After the poky rooms we had been creeping around in the villas, the sense of space was enormous. We stood where the altar had been and looked up the nave, which sloped gently up and away from us. Above us massive concrete beams supported the wooden rafters and slats of the roof. Any evidence of worship and religion had disappeared. We searched for a trace of a cross, a sign of iconography, but there was nothing, not even a broken frame for the order of hymns hanging askew from a hook.

The floor was cluttered with work benches and carpentry tools. More timber was stacked in long piles against the walls. The workmen had made a corner office out of a thin partition about ten feet high and its makeshift door was padlocked. The more valuable tools must have been kept inside. The church was the village carpentry shop.

'Do you think the local bureau or whoever is in charge of this building knows the Bible?' asked Brent.

'Why?' I asked.

'Well, it seems ironic, Joseph of Nazareth being a carpenter an' all,' – Brent was from Georgia, 'and this church being what it is today, under the authority of official atheists.'

I caught his drift. 'It might make the people who built it smile,' I said, smiling myself.

We lifted the latch and let ourselves out through the foyer door. Before we shut it behind us we turned and stared at the vast space, both of us, without saying so, imagining we were members of a congregation arriving for a service on a Sunday morning in the 1920s.

Back at the Hans' place Brent and I described our adventures to Crystal and Leona. We stood in the main room. I wish I could call it a drawing-room, as it was meant to be. It stretched from front to back of the house and opened through two French windows on to the ground floor terrace, with its columns that supported the balcony upstairs. The Hans had placed a television and a karaoke machine on a low chest of drawers at one end of the room in front of a large window, and along the walls they had lined cheap chairs with plastic cushions still covered in their cellophane. A hearth and mantelpiece stood at the other end, directly below the fireplace in our bedroom. Two square *ma jiang* tables tried to fill the centre of the room and leaning behind the door were a couple of round table-tops that could be fitted on top of them for banquets. Otherwise the room was empty and bare, no rugs on the floor or pictures on the wall. The floorboards and doors had been painted a deep red ochre, layer upon layer applied over the years. Somewhere underneath was some decent timber.

'Just imagine,' I said from the hearth, as if warming the back of my legs in front of a roaring fire, 'just imagine what you could do to this place, or one of the houses we saw today. The locals don't get it, do they? They have no idea how these places were decorated and furnished in the old days. They use them for eating and sleeping, that's it. No idea of a sitting-room, a place to relax, sit by the fire, have a drink. It's so sad. Such a waste.'

'Then why don't we get one?' said Brent. 'We could all pitch in, share it. Do it up like it used to be.'

'Brent,' said Leona in her wise voice, 'you know we might move to America.' They were already talking about marriage. 'We would never use it.'

Crystal stayed neutral. Either she took it as a joke or she was not that interested. Somehow I could not see her as a country girl.

While I spoke as if I was describing a daydream, my mind was racing with the thought that it might actually be possible.

Looking around the Hans' place and thinking of the houses on Moganshan, it struck me that not a single villa in the village was rented out privately. They belonged to the state, or state-run businesses, or were derelict. No private summer homes remained. In the 1990s rural China was still flocking to the major cities in search of work and a better life. An affluent urban class who wanted to retreat the other way had yet to appear.

Moganshan was a backwater, a neglected and faded jewel. It could not be long before someone realized how precious it was and had the money to do something about it. To me it was obvious. And I was in love with the place.

With a jolt of conviction, I suddenly realized that I had to secure a quiet corner of Moganshan. Now. Before the rush that was sure to come.

I had no idea where to start, who to ask, or who was in charge. But I did know that in China there is always a way.

It would not be easy. Doing something for the first time in China never is, never was. There would be interfering bureaucrats and confusing rules to deal with, but the first and biggest obstacle would be the cultural gap that haunts every foreign-inspired project in China, no matter how run-of-the-mill it seems. In fact, the more normal it is for a foreigner, the more likely it is to meet with confusion and therefore obstruction from the Chinese.

Before we left that day I dropped a hint with the Hans. They were amused but promised to make some enquiries and introduce me to someone who might help. Lao Han worked part-time at the *Moganshan Guanli Ju*, the Administration Bureau which managed the mountain on behalf of the provincial government.

I could not help feeling he was only humouring me, as he had when he presented the twigs for our fire on that first visit. I pulled him aside, casting about for something to say that would make him realize I meant it. I couldn't come up with anything except the truth. It sounded rather pathetic.

'Lao Han,' I said, 'I'm serious. I need an escape from Shanghai.'

He nodded thoughtfully, looking away from me into the distance.

'Ma Ke,' he said, using the transliteration of my Christian name, and patting me on the shoulder, 'I understand. Don't worry. We'll find you a house.'

He was silent for a while, then looked at me, his face brightening. 'And we can be your housekeepers too. Now how about that? You'll need someone to look after the place when you are not there.'

'Of course, Lao Han.' How stupid of me not to have thought of it myself. It was the perfect way to get him on side. I wondered what he would charge for his services.

Chapter Three

Toehold

While the best building sites have as a rule already been taken, there are still many desirable lots for sale. Prices are higher, of course, but those who have time to search out the owners may still buy of natives. Those who buy of foreign owners get good measure as to area, while natives usually sell more than can be found within the stated boundaries. The trick is an old one and hard to avoid.

North-China Herald and Court Gazette,
28 October 1904

Four of us were crowded on to a small terrace amongst a collection of potted azaleas: Brent and another American, Mark Secchia, Mark's girlfriend Laurie and myself. We sat on tiny stools with our knees up to our chins. The azaleas belonged to Mr Ge, a middle-ranking official at the Administration Bureau. Tiny red buds were just about to become flowers. To break the ice I had asked Mr Ge how to say 'azalea' in Chinese.

'We call them cuckoo flowers, *du chuan hua*,' he said, and proceeded to tell us why. When King Du Yu of the ancient kingdom of Shu was assassinated, his spirit was transformed into a cuckoo. He was a good and popular king and to this day his spirit is still bitter and confused about being assassinated. Hence, every spring, when they are in full song, cuckoos weep tears of blood that fall on the azaleas and stain the flowers bright red. Azaleas thrive on Moganshan.

Mr Ge was not only a fount of horticultural folklore. He was also an estate agent of sorts for Moganshan, and that is why we had come to see him. He was sitting on a full-sized chair on the step into his kitchen, looking down on us. It was a fine Saturday. We had made a special weekend trip from Shanghai to hunt for a hideaway that three couples could share. We had been coming to Moganshan almost every month for nearly two years now. It was time to stop fantasizing about a house of our own and make it happen.

'I could show you number 160 or 161,' Mr Ge was saying, 'but I don't have the keys so you can't see inside.' Mr Ge did not seem particularly keen to do any business.

Brent and I grinned at each other. We knew both houses intimately. Number 160 had a broken basement window in its subterranean kitchen, while 161 involved a more challenging traverse across a narrow ledge of roof and then a window-sill to access an open shutter on the first floor. We had shown Mark and Laurie around them that morning. But both houses were massive, too big for us. They would have made good small hotels, which was a nice idea but we were too preoccupied with our businesses in Shanghai to consider it. We envisaged a modest three- or four-bedroom villa with garden and south-facing views, ideal for a stressed out Shanghai entrepreneurs' timeshare.

Mark Secchia and I had got to know each other when he had been my first sales manager in Shanghai. He had taken on the job for a challenge and had done it brilliantly, before he left to do an MBA at one of China's first ever business schools. In his mid-course work experience break, when his Chinese fellow students had applied for internships at McKinsey's and Anderson's and the other usual white-collar giants, Mark had set up a small business making home deliveries from local restaurants. This project had been such a success that he kept it running while he finished the MBA and now he was managing it full time. He called his company Sherpas, so it was appropriate he should have a mountain retreat.

Over the course of our recent visits we had made the rounds of the derelicts once again, Brent and I acting as guides. We were in earnest this time. We did not try to imagine how the houses had looked in the past but how they might look in the future, if we could get hold of one. We chose bedrooms, argued about where to put the dining- and sitting-rooms and the Americans confused me by calling the garden the yard.

In one house, number 140, we found a cellar dug out of the rock underneath. It would make a perfect den. The only access was through an outside door at the foot of some steps down the side of the house. There was enough room for a billiard-table between the stone pillars and a bar would fit perfectly along the back wall against the rockface.

The layout of the house above was also unusual for a Moganshan summer villa. It was roughly oval and centred on a vast drawing-room with west-facing windows. Upstairs every room had a balcony. From the empty glass cases that lined the walls of the main room we guessed it had been a museum. We liked it.

'Mr Ge, how about number 140?' asked Mark.

Mr Ge replied that it was due to be restored as a museum again.

'What of?'

'The secret police,' he said with a lopsided smirk.

Mr Ge was in his late fifties, and his whole face, not only his smile, was slightly lopsided, as if he had never quite recovered from a mild stroke.

'They used to have a local headquarters here in the old days,' he was explaining. 'Brought people up here, to that house.'

I suddenly realized what the cellar had been used for. Ge's 'old days' either meant early Communist China or the last days of the Nationalists under Chiang Kai Shek. Both Chiang's Blueshirts, his personal protection unit that doubled as his secret police, or Mao's State Security Bureau would have used similar methods on their prisoners, more than likely in that cellar.

'So it's not for rent?' Brent asked.

'No.'

It was a relief in a way.

We left Mr Ge and went back to our search, splitting up to save time. Once we had made a new list we would come back and ask Mr Ge about availability.

On the Sunday, when the weather had turned misty and a light drizzle was falling, Mark and I came across a flight of stone stairs behind a villa that Brent and I knew well. We had never paid attention to them before, assuming they led to a water tank or a vegetable patch. Mark and I started climbing, just in case.

After about two hundred steps the stairs disappeared into impenetrable bush. A path led off to the right. It was overgrown with weeds and bamboo but nonetheless it was a solid, well-made concrete walkway. We threaded our way along it, pushing the thin wet leaves out of our faces. After thirty metres we stumbled on an isolated house. It was a true derelict.

The stonework of the three-storey building was a damp dark grey, covered in lichen, the green shutters so flaked and rotten that the house was almost camouflaged against the dripping conifers that towered above it. Even for a derelict it looked neglected. It was surrounded by complete silence.

'What a place,' I said.

We did not hurry to make our usual search for an entry point. It was obvious. A window on the ground-floor terrace was wide open.

We looked at the dark hole.

'Want to go inside and check it out?' asked Mark.

'In a sec. No rush.'

I was admiring the masonry. I noticed a massive cornerstone at the outer edge of the terrace. It was the size a tea chest. How on earth had the builders got it up here? It must have weighed a couple of tons. As a token of modesty someone had painted a white line down the middle, faking a join, as if the workmen meant to say: 'It was nothing really. Think of it as two smaller stones we brought up one by one.'

The house was square, a typical Moganshan summer-house. The only 'feature', as such, was the recessed terrace on the right-hand side of the ground floor. It was about one and a half metres deep and the floor above was held up by two crumbling concrete columns, one in the middle, one at the far end. I looked up. The floor above the terrace was a solid row of windows and above that was a tiny dormer window in the rusting roof.

The sense of solitude was overwhelming. We had never found a house like it. Nor had we found a house where the windows had been left open so invitingly. Back down on the road there was one that had the single Chinese character *chai*, 'to be demolished', painted in white on its walls, and even that had been locked up tight. This one had the word 'Forgotten' written all over it. I liked it. I felt an empathy for it. Like us foreigners in China it seemed out of place, stuck out on a limb, occasionally remembered by someone who had a lingering memory of it, maybe.

'OK, let's go in and have a look,' I said to Mark.

Inside the open window the floorboards had rotted away. We stepped across on the beams and into the hallway. Apart from one gaping hole the floor here was solid. The stairs were intact too.

We peered into the main room. Treble windows ran down the south side, looking back along the path, and a large double one faced east, to the front of the house. It was a decent sized space, good for a sitting-room. Behind it was a kitchen and bathroom in one. A stone sink and work surface took up one short wall. Along either side were two pairs of dark cubicles, showers on one side and squat lavatories on the other. There were no doors on them. Across from this kitchen-bathroom there was another plain and bare room with its floor mostly intact.

Upstairs we found a balcony behind the row of windows. It must have been glassed in after 1949. Surely no summer-holidaying foreigner would have shut up a breezy balcony with the view that we could only imagine through the trees and the mist? We explored the rest of the first floor.

A small room tucked away at the back was panelled to waist height. The round holes in the floor gave away its original purpose. 'Panelled bathroom!' I shouted over my shoulder. 'Nice.'

I imagined a cast-iron bath standing against the back wall. It would be perfect.

Apart from the rotten and gaping floorboards and crumbling plaster on the walls, the house was well preserved. The roof seemed to have held off the worst of the weather and the patchy windows kept out the wet clouds. It was a solid building.

We went back downstairs and climbed out of the window from the floorless room which I had already bagged for my study.

More stone steps continued up the hill to the left of the house. We followed them and came to a small, squat cottage directly above the larger house. Metal bars blocked the ground-floor windows and the door, and right behind it two metal masts disappeared into the fog. It looked like a radio shack. There was no possible way to break in. We stuck our faces to the windows and made out some broken furniture and garden tools in the dusty gloom.

To the left of the small house a dense shambles of undergrowth covered what had been a large vegetable patch. Bamboo poles for runner beans had collapsed in a blackened heap, like scaffolding for a house that had never been built. Brambles had made a canopy over the mess and, scattered amongst the dense wild shrubbery that lined the bank above the vegetable patch, I made out hundreds of tiny red dots. Wild cuckoo flowers.

We were at the very top of the mountain. The trees and radio masts behind the small house stretched into the cloud. The wild ruin of the garden was open to the heavens. We poked around in it for a while then returned to the big house.

'This has got potential,' I said to Mark, looking up at it all.

'Nah, too far from the road,' he dismissed it. 'I liked 140 better. Good view, west-facing too. And much more fun design. Or one of those ones we passed on the road. You'd be too isolated here.'

'Precisely. That's the beauty of it.'

I had an inexplicable sense of certainty that this was going to be my house. I also knew with a sudden clarity that the others would drop out of the timeshare idea.

'This is the one,' I said to Mark.

In my mind's eye I removed the balcony's windows and installed sparkling white shutters around the ground floor. I replaced the roof and weeded the stone path. Then I turned around and chopped down the trees that blocked the view. The sun came out . . . in my day dream.

This was the one. The only disappointment was the lack of a fireplace and chimney.

We sat in mist-shrouded peace and quiet for a few minutes more, then set off down the hill back to the Hans, met up with the others and drove back to Shanghai in the Volkswagen.

My life in China's number one city had moved on since that first visit to Moganshan with Crystal in 1999. For one thing, she and I had split up. I had lost my nerve on the emotional rollercoaster of a relationship with a Shanghainese girl and jumped off at one of the low points.

The end had come during a late night argument about the

basis of love. We were at the Cotton Club, a popular live music bar. Crystal described a relationship as a battle you set out to win and only once you had won did real love enter into things. I argued that love was about surrender, mutual emotional surrender from the start. Crystal and I agreed to disagree. It was a friendly parting.

By then I had realized that my search for a girlfriend in Shanghai was doomed. The issue was a girl I had known in Guangzhou in south China, where I had spent a year as a China commodity trader before moving to Shanghai. Her English name was Joanna, her Chinese one Wu Ninghua, and I had never got over her, although we had never been partners in the modern sense. Crystal was not a patch on her once I had seen past the Shanghai glamour.

Joanna was twenty-six years old, a graduate of the Guangzhou music conservatory, a part-time model and very Cantonese: she spoke her mind. She had one too. During my first years in Shanghai we had stayed in touch. I called on her whenever I made a business trip back to Guangzhou, which is where I had met my business partner and my career as an entrepreneur had started. I had a lingering affection for the city, both professional and personal. After my work was done for the day I would meet up with Joanna and her friends for dinner and then drinks in the newest 'in' place. Sometimes Joanna and I slipped away to a quieter bar. Over warm pots of Shaoxing wine we talked late into the night. I made up excuses for frequent trips. Joanna and I both knew how strongly we felt about each other, but I was in Shanghai, she was in Guangzhou. Our paths had crossed once and now we lived separate lives. It seemed unlikely they would cross again.

Then, as often happens, especially in China, my life changed completely and almost overnight. Within the space of six months I bought my partner out of the business, reorganized the original Guangzhou operation in line with our prospering Shanghai one, and turned down a takeover bid from a major international player. Then I set up a properly licensed China foreign joint venture and launched a third office in Beijing.

I also fought off three high-level government investigations into my business, set up by well connected local competitors, which resulted in the payment of a couple of hefty fines. To prevent future attacks I was forced into partnerships on crippling terms with a couple of government agencies. Then my new Beijing office was raided by government friends of my new competitors in the capital. Meanwhile, just to keep me on my toes, another government-backed rival put out the word that I was a spy. It was a busy time.

Somewhere in the middle of the last paragraph Joanna and I got married. As I said, life is fast in China.

I needed a break. More than that, I had reached a stage in life and career where I desperately needed a place to escape with my new wife, where I could leave my battles, Internet and phone connections and do nothing except for some urgent gardening.

Joanna had already visited Moganshan and met the Hans, who chalked up another 'honeymoon' until I corrected them and they removed the quotation marks.

I had also introduced her to Mr Ge. As soon as we returned from our real honeymoon in Egypt, Joanna and I went back to Moganshan and asked him, in earnest, how we could lease the forgotten house. I was lucky to have married a woman who shared my desire to escape from Shanghai whenever possible, although that had more to do with her being Cantonese than a country girl. (The Shanghainese are not exactly popular with their fellow countrymen and the Cantonese are their polar opposites.) Having dragged her to Shanghai, it was only right that I should arrange that Joanna could leave it whenever she wanted.

'None of my business,' Mr Ge replied in response to our enquiry, looking happy.

He explained that the army had a permanent lease on thirty houses along the ridge, from below the Hans' place up to and including the one we were interested in. The properties were supposed to be used by senior officers as rest and recuperation villas but, seeing the potential for profit, the army had rented out half their houses to local companies like the one the Hans worked for, and allowed the other half to fall into disrepair.

This time, the cultural difference worked in our favour. The army landlords, when we eventually tracked them down to their ramshackle office, were so surprised at someone wanting the abandoned house two hundred steps from the nearest road that they readily agreed a price, produced a contract and took our money. They threw in the upper shack as well for a nominal addition to the rent.

It happened so suddenly and apparently effortlessly. After a couple of almost perfunctory meetings over several months, my new wife and I had a large summer house for ourselves, a guesthouse for friends and a space to make a garden. All for one thousand pounds per annum, on a ten-year lease. I was over the moon.

Of course it was not that easy.

The rental contract was so one-sided it was almost pointless.

It ran to a mere page and a half and the terms included the clause: 'If the tenant does not fulfil his obligations such as payment of electricity and water bills in a timely manner, the landlord may cancel this agreement and is not obliged to return any rent that has been paid in advance.'

'So how do we pay those bills?' I asked Major Ma, the officer in charge of the Chinese People's Liberation Army Nanjing Military District Hangzhou Sub District Rest and Retirement Unit Moganshan Sub Unit, or 'Hangliao' for short.

We were sitting in Ma's office on the first floor of a dilapidated house across from the Hans'. This was the headquarters of the Hangliao. The room was furnished with a desk and chair, a round table with a couple of cheap plastic chairs and a bed in one corner. The floorboards rose in the middle of the room like the deck of an old sailing ship.

Major Ma was wearing a khaki tunic with brass buttons and red collar tabs. His top button was undone. He sat beside me at the round table, the contract slanted between us. It was a warm spring day.

Ma was a short man with a bean-like face that reminded me of pictures of Deng Xiao Ping, the architect of modern China. He was full of good humour and enthusiasm. I imagined him in front of a platoon of soldiers, laughing at himself as he gave their orders. When he spoke he grabbed my elbow, then my knee if he was close enough. If we were standing he liked to poke me in the stomach. His answers to most questions began with: 'Mr Mark, you listen to me now . . .' delivered in an irresistibly imitable squeaky voice.

'You pay us,' he replied.

'By which day each month, Major Ma?' I persisted.

'Mr Mark, you listen to me now, you don't need to worry about that!' he laughed at me. 'We'll come and find you whenever we want you to pay.'

Trying not to explain it in black and white in case I gave him an idea, I insisted on clarification. 'But Major Ma, it says here that we must pay the bills on time or else you can take the houses back.'

'Yes, I know it does but don't you worry about that. You listen to me, Mr Mark, we'd never do that. I am telling you, you don't need to worry about that at all.' He was so excited his voice had reached a squeal like nails on a blackboard. I recoiled from his jabbing finger.

When I leant back in to the table my eye fastened on the reciprocal clause about the landlord's obligations. 'If the landlord fails to supply water and electricity to the tenant, the landlord shall compensate the tenant. Such compensation shall be agreed according to the facts and after friendly negotiation between the two parties.'

So if we did not pay a bill for water because they did not ask for it, we were thrown out. If the water supply was cut off for however long, we talked about it. Standard old-style Communist China contract terms.

There were more.

Soon after the clause stating: 'the tenant shall be responsible for the administration and thought-education of any members of staff and guests on the premises,' came the Chinese version of *force majeur*.

'If the army or the local government by reason of a major change in policy require to repossess the property, the tenant shall immediately vacate the property. Compensation shall be mutually agreed thereafter.'

The clause was perfectly straightforward. Like many an agreement in China this one was going to depend on mutual goodwill. I did not bother questioning it.

But there was something else that was nagging my hard-earned China business sense: the contract made no mention of the Hangliao's right to sublet the houses. And there was no mention whatsoever of the garden for the upper house. I had established by now that the Administration Bureau effectively owned the entire mountain as well as administering it.

'Major Ma,' I asked. 'Please forgive me for raising such a petty problem, but the contract makes no mention of you, the Hangliao, having the right to sublet the houses. You told me yourself that they belong ultimately to the Administration Bureau. Surely you need to state here that you can rent them out. It must be standard for a contract like this. In fact it certainly would be in England, or Shanghai for that matter.'

'Mr Mark, you listen to me, no problem at all, quite out of the question.' He laughed long and loud. 'To even think such a thing is ridiculous,' he went on, his voice still unnaturally high. 'Of course we can rent you the property. It has nothing to do with the Administration Bureau whatsoever!'

I persisted. 'Then it should be no problem for you to slip in a clause to that effect. And it would be a comfort to have the garden mentioned in there too, while you are at it. Please.'

Suddenly his face grew stern and his voice dropped a couple of octaves. 'Mr Mark, now you listen to me.' He looked me straight in the eye. 'All our contracts are the same. None of them have that clause you are talking about. You want to see one?'

His face brightened. He stood up and went over to a filing cabinet, then turned with a smile and a sheaf of papers in one hand. He slapped them on the table.

'Look!' he was giggling again. 'And we never put in anything about the outside areas either, as you can see for yourself. Never been an issue.'

Out of courtesy I glanced at the top sheet. I scanned the characters without reading them.

'So you see!' Ma was back in good humour. 'There will be no problem about that.'

Something else I had learnt from bitter experience was this: when someone in China says there will be a 'small problem' he means there is a big problem, but he does not know exactly how big. When someone says 'no problem' he means he has no idea what he is talking about.

As if sent by fate, at that very moment an unlikely saviour walked into Ma's office. It was Mr Ge. Here was a perfect opportunity to get my concerns out into the open.

'Mr Ge.' I stood and shook his hand. 'How good to see you. You've come at exactly the right time.' He smiled his crooked smile.

I repeated what I had said to Major Ma and then asked Ge outright: 'Now you, Mr Ge, as a representative of the Administration Bureau, can surely answer this silly question of mine . . .'

He smiled again, pointing the upturned corner of his mouth to me and then Major Ma.

'Major Ma is absolutely correct,' he said, turning back to me. 'Don't worry, Mark, the Hangliao can do whatever they want with those houses. We wouldn't interfere, don't worry,' he repeated for good measure.

I thanked Mr Ge and was happy to be proven wrong. Ma was grinning broadly.

'You see! I told you to listen to me,' he said.

I signed the contract and handed over the first three years' rent, six thousand US dollars in cash.

I was euphoric. My dream had come true. I was the first foreigner to move back into a house on Moganshan for fifty years. I had secured my secret hideaway, my retreat, a terrace where I could drink a Scotch as the sun went down, where I could forget about business and invite friends for weekend parties, a place where I could pretend I was not in China.

I used to scorn the true 'expatriate' foreigners in China. In my book 'expat' was a four-letter word. I thought the standard foreign businessman on a posting to China with his family and villa, car and driver and month-long summer and Christmas holidays was missing the point.

China was not built of brand new office blocks and villas complexes. It was a teaming, noisy, cut-throat market like Hua Ting Lu, the famous knock-off street in Shanghai that the foreign manager's wife thought was a quaint source of fake designer goods for cheap Christmas presents and an amusing place to take visiting friends and family. Those markets stood for all China, desperate to make a buck any which way and damn the next man in line. If you wanted to get into real China you had to get in there and fight on your own, one to one. You guys can't take it, or so I thought.

It was people like me who lived and worked in the thick of it, who had studied and spoke the language, who uncovered and tackled the problems head on; we were the people getting the most out of China and putting something into it too. We were living it. We could hack it.

Well, I couldn't hack it. Not now, after six long years. I had only cracked once. It had been a hell of a shock to be walking along a busy Shanghai street one sunny day and suddenly burst into tears. I had quietly taken myself back to the UK for a break soon afterwards. Whisky-fuelled chats with my long-suffering wheelchair-bound father, and a visit to my mother, an ex-teacher, helped me pull myself back together.

It was on my return that I bought out my business partner and lost myself once more in work, but for my own company now. I had a clear long-term goal and a good plan for getting there. But the stress still built up, as stress does. Alcohol and cigarettes and wild parties made it seem easier to cope, but they were actually making things worse.

Of course, what saved me was getting married. Joanna is wise in the way only women can be. During those long conversations over dinner and drinks in Guangzhou she had explained more about China and the Chinese than experience could ever have taught me, and soon after our married life began I discovered that Chinese housewives like to be involved in their husband's working lives as well. That took a while to get used to. At first I was frustrated to be hearing about staff issues via my wife, and to be told her opinion of my partners with whom I had worked for years. But then I came to see the benefits.

As a foreigner in China you will never ever overcome the natives' deep-rooted preconception that 'You do not understand China.' Having a Chinese wife who could promise those people that she would get the message through to me, and also make a case on my behalf, at the very least earned me some grace.

Our first child was due soon, too. That had not relieved the relentless pressures of Shanghai business, but it had stopped me partying so hard.

Now in Moganshan I had somewhere to unwind and recharge. Somewhere healthy, too. And I was going to eat my words about expats. I still did not like the term but I was happy to accept that I needed an escape. The only difference was; mine would be in China, on a mountain covered in azaleas, a place where I could quietly go cuckoo on my own terms.

As I left Major Ma I called Joanna back in Shanghai. I gave her the good news about the contract and went down the hill to book a start date with the contractors who were going to restore the houses. They were on standby.

The office of General Manager Li of the Moganshan Administration Bureau Construction Unit looked like an real office compared to Major Ma's, and General Manager Li looked like he did some real work. There were architects' drawings unfurled across a large sloping table and his desk was cluttered with pens and pencils, notebooks, sketch pads, a bashed up calculator and a couple of phones, along with the standard clutter of a Chinese office desk: a large glass ashtray overflowing with cigarette butts, a couple of packets of opened cigarettes, another in its cellophane, a Nescafé jar half full of seaweed-like tea-leaves at low tide, and a toppling pile of name cards.

The first time Joanna and I had met General Manager Li his attitude had been straightforward and businesslike.

'Of course you have the option to go to another contractor, for example from the local town, to do your houses,' he had explained early in the meeting. 'But they will have to pay a fee to work on the mountain, which will end up on your bill.'

We smiled. He went on.

'My teams, the official contractors for Moganshan, don't have to pay the fee, naturally. And don't worry . . .' (we were making a determined effort not to look worried) '. . . we'll give you a good price, one you couldn't get from someone else, if you could get a quote from them anyway.'

We smiled some more to show how thankful we were that he was not going to rip us off completely. But there was more to come.

'There is however one major expense which you must prepare for,' Manager Li was explaining. 'I am afraid it is quite unavoidable too.' We steeled ourselves.

'It's the rubbish removal fee.'

Manager Li smiled like a man explaining table-manners to a small child. 'The rules are very strict. We have to take the rubbish from the demolition, the old fittings like the old baths and lavatories etcetera, down the mountain to a proper tip. We need to hire trucks to do this. Normally the rubbish removal fee is at least five thousand kuai.' He used the colloquial word for yuan. 'So for your two houses you can expect a fee of ten thousand, maybe something in the teens.'

'There is no alternative or cheaper method?' we asked. We had no idea what the total bill was going to be but ten thousand yuan for throwing stuff out seemed disproportionately high.

'Absolutely not.' General Manager Li sat back in his chair and tried to look sympathetic.

The day I signed the contract with Major Ma, General Manager Li had the quotations ready on his desk, four pages of close-typed characters and numbers to the third decimal point for each house. The details went down to the weight and price of nails and the measurements of every length of timber. As we had been warned, the largest number on each list was the rubbish removal: eight thousand yuan for the big house and 6,500 for the smaller one. Just over a thousand pounds – almost one year's rent. Since we were having two fireplaces and chimneys installed for a quarter of that it was indeed out of proportion.

The fireplaces had been a pleasant surprise. I had been planning to search out and buy imported and doubtless expensive wood-burning stoves so we could use the houses in winter as well as summer.

Mr Pan Guang Lin, our foreman, had listened patiently while I mused out loud where to put them in the houses. Then he dropped his bombshell.

'Why wood-burning stoves?' he asked. 'I could make you a couple of fireplaces and build chimneys. Probably cheaper too.'

He stepped back in surprise when I spun on him as if he had just told me we were distantly related.

'You're serious?' I exclaimed. 'You can make fireplaces, just like that?'

'Sure. What's so difficult?'

'But, Mr Pan, you don't understand, I mean, you, um, my God, that would be fantastic, er, I mean . . .' I tried to calm down.

'Could you put them on the list, please?' I asked.

I approved the quotation and handed over a small up-front payment, shook hands with General Manager Li and set off for Shanghai. Pan and his team would be starting in a matter of days. The work would take about two months, which meant the houses would be ready in time for July and August, the hottest months of the summer. I started thinking of the housewarming party, the barbecue we were going to have in front of the large house. If it rained we could use the ground-floor terrace. And perhaps I could persuade my friends to help me start clearing the garden. I imagined us sitting around a bonfire of the rubbish, drinking whisky in camp chairs late into the night. It was going to be an excellent summer.

Two days later General Manager Li called to announce that work had begun. Or that's what I expected him to say.

'There is a small problem,' were his first words.

Here we go. 'What is it, General Manager Li?' I asked, pretending to believe him.

'Apparently the Administration Bureau does not approve of the Hangliao renting the houses to you.' I took a deep breath as he went on. 'Since my unit comes under the authority of the Administration Bureau, I have been told I cannot start until the problem is worked out.'

You are used to this, I told myself. When has anything been easy in China? Keep calm. But still I felt as if I had been smacked in the solar plexus with a sledgehammer.

'And will it be worked out?' I could not help asking despite the fact that Li should, officially, have no idea.

'Oh, I am sure it will be. Don't you worry,' said Li, with a tone of knowing more than he was letting on. 'They just have to *tiaozheng* a bit.'

In my largest Chinese–English dictionary the translation of *tiaozheng* is 'adjust, regulate, revise'. For example, cadres 'revised the work unit production plan' back in the 1950s. In modern-day China the much-used word has come to mean: 'reach a mutually satisfactory temporary solution to a tricky problem for which there is no black and white answer, because the whole system is set up to create such problems and allow for their temporary solutions.' In other words, Major Ma would have to give a little something, not necessarily money, perhaps just a concession, to the Administration Bureau. It was parish council politics.

Immediately after I had spoken with Li I called Major Ma.

'What has happened?' I asked.

'Just a small problem,' he repeated Li's words but did not sound as cheerful as usual. 'We can work it out. Mr Mark, just listen to me: don't you worry.'

After a few minutes of prevarication, I wheedled the truth out of Ma.

'The Administration Bureau say we don't have the right to sublet the houses,' he said. 'They belong ultimately to the Administration Bureau and our agreement with them does not state clearly that we can rent them out, like a standard contract would.' I waited for him to finish quoting my words back to me with 'like in England, or Shanghai'.

Ma had repeated exactly what I had said to him in his office a few days ago. The Administration Bureau was interfering, precisely as Mr Ge had said they would not. I asked who it was at the Bureau who had raised the issue.

'Why, Mr Ge of course,' said Ma as if I was stupid.

I kicked myself. I had been stupid.

'Can I come to Moganshan and talk to the Bureau?' I asked Ma.

'No need, no need,' he replied.

'But Major Ma,' I pleaded, 'surely it might help if I was to, say, come and invite someone to dinner perhaps?'

'Mr Mark, you listen to me now. I can sort this out. Don't you worry,' he insisted, sounding annoyed at my idea.

I did worry, very much. I called Lao Han. He gave me words

of reassurance too, more convincing than Ma's. And he explained that there really was nothing we could do. We had to wait for the Hangliao and the Bureau to work things out.

'They're jealous,' said Lao Han. 'The Hangliao have rented a few of their buildings out recently and the Administration Bureau thinks they are making money. But the Hangliao, strictly speaking, can do what they like.'

In my business life I had bounced between party departments and government bureaux like a ping-pong ball for years, always in trouble with one or the other. I was lucky to have a middle man who dealt with the details and kept track of who I was supposed to be apologizing to, what for, and when.

Lao Han had taken on the role of our middle man in Moganshan. I trusted him although I knew what he would expect as a reward. He would secure for himself a position as our housekeeper or as the locals in Moganshan described it 'house-watcher'. The benefits were not limited to a monthly salary. He would have another couple of villas under his control and a garden for growing vegetables.

'Give me a call when you have some news please, Lao Han,' I said.

We hung up and I turned back to my desk. I tried hard to ignore an almost imperceptible loss of enthusiasm for my work, and for China. But I still felt it.

Chapter Four

Foothold

Those who have built good comfortable cottages and have learned the local conditions can thoroughly enjoy themselves. Visitors who want rest and quiet will find it an almost ideal retreat ... If you are open to conviction, each man has the best location, the most convenient house, and the most superior tenant, excepting his auditor, of course.

North-China Daily News, 31 July 1901

Two months had passed since I signed the contract and handed over three years' rent to Major Ma. The temperature in Shanghai had been rising relentlessly since the seasonal 'plum' rains had finished. Now July was almost upon us. Our cool summer weekends at our mountain retreat, if we had one, were slipping away.

There was plenty to keep me distracted. SARS (Severe Acute Respiratory Syndrome) had struck China in March that year, 2003. My new Beijing office was hit hard, not by the disease but by its repercussions on daily life, which most people even at the time agreed were almost as traumatic as catching the potentially lethal infection itself. The capital and the majority of the country were in a state of centrally coordinated panic.

In a break with traditional Chinese secrecy about national disasters the Beijing municipal government admitted to the World Health Organization how many cases of the disease there were in the city. Events we were sponsoring were cancelled, and foreigners, our clients, fled the city, women and children first. Everyone on the streets wore a face mask. They became fashion items, in different colours and patterns. The knock-off markets started selling them in Burberry check.

I was going through a commercial crisis and flew up and down from Shanghai to Beijing and on to Guangzhou. Travel within China was strongly discouraged. Quarantine regulations were in force across the country and airlines ordered to seat people as far apart as possible. Coughing or sneezing in a check-in queue was like dropping a hand grenade.

Only in Shanghai, where the local government flatly denied there were any cases of the disease, did business continue as something like usual, although the Rolling Stones cancelled their China debut in the city. In our Shanghai apartment we were kept busy by our new-born daughter, Isabel.

Not until 24 June did the World Health Organization declare China SARS free. On 1 July, the date when old Shanghai's merchant adventurers and their families traditionally began their annual migration to Moganshan, I called Major Ma.

'It's taken care of, Mark,' he screamed. I held the phone away from my ear. 'Everything is sorted out. You can start restoration! Didn't I tell you to listen to me?'

He refused point blank to explain how he had done it.

I called General Manager Li with the echo of Ma's high-pitched voice still ringing in my ears and the surprise still sinking in.

'I know,' Li said calmly. 'Pan will begin tomorrow.' And he hung up.

Everything started moving. I rushed out to Moganshan by train and taxi to go over the plans once again.

Pan Guang Lin dressed smartly for a builder, a dark jacket over his collared brown T-shirt, scuffed shoes the only clue to his profession. He had a dense mop of black hair that almost curled, a podgy nose and small round eyes. His face always looked ready to take offence, as if he had been bullied at school and no longer even tried to stand up for himself, but those small round eyes also displayed a kindly forbearance of the demands he knew he was about to hear.

Pan's standard greeting was to thrust a local Liqun cigarette at me. My standard response was to refuse politely and insist on my own Malboro, which I offered him in return. He said my Malboro were too strong. I replied that I thought them weaker than Liqun.

The ritual offer and refusal of alien cigarettes and our disagreement about their strength reminded us that we saw things differently, and set the tone for the debate that always followed, about what Joanna and I wanted doing to the houses and what he was capable of doing to them.

The whine in Pan's voice rose in proportion to the difficulty – as he saw it – of whatever we were requesting. As it did so he looked away from me as if shy of showing how much pain I was giving him.

The day I asked him to leave the interior stonework of the upper house uncovered he squealed in agony like a crescendo in a Beijing Opera. I had arrived on my first progress check immediately after his men had stripped the walls. The old stones, dusted with a fine yellow powder from the straw and clay which had covered them for decades, looked beautifully rustic, how I imagined the walls of Silas Marner's cottage.

'But then we'll have to fill the cracks in,' he wailed out of the corner of his mouth. His teeth were clamped around a cigarette. 'It would be so much simpler to plaster over them.'

It perplexed me how Pan could so readily and apparently easily build a couple of fireplaces and chimneys, yet he complained about a little stone wall restoration. I insisted and he gave in with a hopeless shrug.

Other than the fireplaces, the removal of a wall to make a bigger sitting-room in the small house and the complete overhaul of the kitchen and open-plan lavatory cubicles in the big house, there were no major or technically challenging alterations to be made. We were not working on an ancient castle or a centuries-old farm building that had been chopped and changed over the years or gone to ruin. Nor was there any need to alter or update the structures to make them habitable by modern-day standards. We did not even have any recent and ugly additions to demolish, like that concrete turret of tiny bathrooms in the villa below us.

We were dealing with two stone boxes, one with two floors and one with three, with boxes for rooms and square roofs. They were simple and symmetrical, like a five-year-old's drawing. The houses had been designed as private summer homes, they had survived basically intact as such, and that is exactly what we wanted them to be again.

We also had the benefit of a Chinese team of builders, fast and cheap – even after General Manager Li's closed bidding process. For the price of a loft conversion in a London semi we were getting two stone shells rebuilt from the ground up.

One important detail, not difficult, was the opening up of the first-floor balcony in the main house.

'So,' asked Pan, looking straight at me for a change. 'You want the windows out?'

'Yes please. Open up the balcony.'

'Got it,' he replied. And I set off back to Shanghai.

On my second visit I stood with Pan outside the main house. We waved packets of cigarettes at each other and looked up. Through the mesh of bamboo scaffolding I was disappointed to see the balcony was still hidden behind a solid wall of windows. Mr Pan invited me inside.

'Be careful,' he said.

The house had been gutted of floors, walls and stairs. It was an empty shell. The new beams and rafters were held up by rust-stained stanchions, one remaining internal wall and the exterior stonework. Plastic sheeting had been spread over the timber frame for the roof.

I climbed a ladder on to the raft that was the first floor – it seemed to float in mid-air – and stepped towards the bedroom that gave on to the balcony. The room was to be our showpiece, the guest bedroom. It was slightly smaller than the one we had selected for ourselves across the corridor but it would be bright and airy thanks to the windows on to the balcony. The morning sun was going to flood through them when I pulled the curtains back and announced fresh coffee outside to surprised friends from Shanghai. I had it all planned out. I walked through the door frame.

The room was as dark as a prison cell. A black wall of raw wet concrete had replaced the windows that divided it from

63

the balcony. I choked with horror. When I found the air to speak, I screamed.

'Mr Pan!'

He stepped up beside me. 'What's up?'

My mind was shouting, 'What the hell ... ?' but the Chinese equivalent wouldn't come with it. Instead I whimpered. 'Where are the windows?'

'You told me to take them out,' he replied.

'Not these ones.'

'Yes, you did.'

'Mr Pan, I said the windows on the balcony. Not the windows in the room.' It was so dark I couldn't see his face. He did not reply. 'Put them back,' I forced myself to be calm, 'please. And remove the outside ones.'

Now Pan spoke up. 'But that will be extra work.' His voice started moving up the scale. 'We have finished this room now.' And finally came the catch-all: *'Mei banfa.'*

Mei banfa means everything from the literal translation: 'There is no way', to 'I can't be bothered' via 'You'll just have to live with it.' Mr Pan was using it in this instance to say, 'OK so we mucked up but can we forget about it please and get on with the rest of the work?'

'Mr Pan,' I said, looking severely into the blackness where he was standing and letting the anger into my voice. 'Yes, there is a *banfa*. You find the bloody windows and you put them back in the bloody wall.' I heard Pan sigh.

Outside the upper house the carpenters had set up a workshop under a sheet of corrugated iron fastened between three pine trees. The circular saw stood in a knee-high sand dune of woodchips and sawdust. Piles of timber were stacked nearby and covered with broad red, white and blue strips of plastic sheeting. We had asked for shutters to be put on to every ground floor window of both houses. The carpenters were making them by hand, knocking them out as if they had done little else all their lives.

This surprised me. The houses being restored in the village had aluminium sliding windows, made to measure by a local factory. I assumed that shutters were a dying art or would likewise be mass-produced somewhere locally and then slotted into the frames.

I pulled General Manager Li's quotation out of my briefcase and looked down the list of numbers. Fifteen pairs of handmade shutters for seven hundred US dollars. Not bad. The slats tilted to let light in too.

They say you can only have two out of three with construction: speed and/or cheap price and/or high quality. Speed and cheap are standard in China. It is assumed price is the most important factor in any deal and the whole country is in a rush. Quality will arrive in due course.

The houses were completed in under three months, by the end of September. Thanks to frequent trips to Hangzhou's new B&Q superstore for some decent materials, the quality was not bad either.

Our guest cottage looked cool and inviting with its Spanish stone floor and original stone walls. It would be cosy in winter too. A brand new fireplace dominated the expanded sitting-room. It had been made with composite stone, which did not match the beautiful old walls if you looked too closely, but it was a handsome piece of masonry nonetheless. A broad mantelpiece ran along its top. I lit a bunch of crumpled newspaper in the grate. The flames flew upwards as if desperate to escape. The chimney worked.

Upstairs in the small house the floors had been replaced with pine that Pan had stained to look like hardwood. He had also taken out the ceilings to show off the rafters. The cottage looked exactly like a holiday home in the West Country or the Welsh hills.

The bigger house wasn't as cosy but it already felt like a second home. My study, the first room I had stepped into with Mark, was lined with fitted bookshelves, the walls painted a pale green. Across the hall the sitting-room's main feature was another fireplace, smaller than the upper house's one but just as good-looking. I did the newspaper test and it sucked up the flames with a barely audible swoosh. Mr Pan seemed to know how to build fireplaces and chimneys.

The kitchen had been equipped with a gas range and oven, a luxury for China. They stood where the showers had been. The lavatory cubicles had become a self-contained downstairs shower-room. Upstairs, my dream bathroom had been re-panelled exactly as Mark and I had found it – much to Pan's chagrin, who thought tiling would be more practical. The new wood had been stained a rich brown. At one end was a cast iron bath that Lao Han had begged from a neighbour who was using it to store charcoal briquets on his balcony. He had given it to us for free. Only three of the ball and claw feet were intact and we had switched them so it was impossible to see the wooden chocks holding up one of the inside corners. It looked perfect. That was a dream come true. The only incongruity was the bath taps, which were ugly and functional. It would have been impossible to find an original pair in China. When I turned them on, no water came out.

I went to the head of the stairs. 'Mr Pan!'

He had been accompanying us on our final tour and was downstairs with Joanna.

'Mr Pan!' I shouted again.

Joanna had his undivided attention. I heard her raised voice but couldn't make out what she was saying. She has a quick temper, my Cantonese wife, something to do with being a southerner. I had cruelly threatened Pan with it over the past few months. My standard threat if he gave me one too many *'mei banfas'* had been: 'Mr Pan, if you can't find a *banfa* then I'll ask my wife to come and find one for you.'

It had proved remarkably effective. One time when Joanna had come with me to check on the work in progress I had sneaked a photograph from the upstairs balcony – it had been opened out by then – and on my next solo trip showed it to Pan. Joanna was standing over him as he sat on the low wall outside the main house, her pointing finger inches from his nose. I laughed when I showed it to him, hoping he would find it as amusing as I did.

'Can I have that?' he had asked with his bashful smile, reaching for the photograph.

'Of course, Mr Pan.' I handed it over.

'Thanks.' He had taken it between his thumb and forefinger, pulled his cigarette lighter out of his jacket pocket and set fire to it. The glossy print curled and gave off a puff of black smoke. Then he dropped it and we both laughed, me rather more than him. I had found it funny. He was recovering face.

When I emerged through the front door, the pair of them were sitting on the same wall outside the house. Joanna's finger was stabbing the air in front of Pan's face again.

Rather than step into the crossfire I decided the best solution was to distract them both, for Pan's benefit as well.

'Mr Pan, there's no water upstairs.'

Joanna fell silent.

'I know,' he replied honestly. 'There isn't enough pressure to get it up there. I think you should put a pump in.'

'Mr Pan, couldn't you have told us sooner?' Despite my good intentions my own voice was getting louder.

'Maybe.' Again that honesty. 'But I thought it would be better to wait until you got here. Then you could decide if you wanted a water pump or not.'

I smiled. It was impossible not to imagine he was having a joke at our expense. He had earned it.

'Yes please, Mr Pan. Could you arrange it?'

'Of course.'

It took another month for the houses to be fit for living. Not because of the lack of water upstairs. Pan had that fixed that afternoon. We needed furniture, a lot of it. The idea was to furnish both houses in something like the style they had once been cluttered with – *huigu* as the Chinese call it, 'back to the old'.

Lao Han suggested Nanxun, a town on the far side of Huzhou, to the north of Moganshan. He described enormous markets full of furniture there. Joanna and I decided to make a detour on our way back to Shanghai. We had borrowed Brent and Leona's car to bring a load of bedding and other basics with us.

Nanxun sits in the middle of the old Hu Qing Ping highway, a worn out toll road between Huzhou and Shanghai. The town itself was not difficult to find but its suburbs sprawled for so many miles along the main road that we could only take a wild guess at where to turn off. After half an hour driving up and down dusty streets bounded by building sites we stumbled on a furniture market. It was big, as Lao Han had said.

A massive and ugly circular hall like a Soviet sports stadium housed the furniture dealers under two roofs. One covered the outer ring, the other the centre. Dividing the two and open to the sky was a mini ring road for delivery trucks. Tunnels led off through the outer section and into the vast wasteland that surrounded the place. Three-wheeled bicycle carts were jammed inside them. The drivers squatted beside them under bright wet ponchos. A light rain had begun to fall.

The dealers were huddled around tables, smoking and playing cards or *ma jiang*. They looked up and stared at us but made no move to attract us into their cavernous stalls. I overheard one or two mutters of '*laowai*', the possibly polite, possibly derogatory, name for foreigners: 'old outsider'.

The furniture – beds, dining tables and chairs, oversized desks and cabinets – was brand new, mass-produced and made from cheap timber. It had been lacquered with a dark brown fake grain and then painted with a thick coat of varnish that shone like suntan oil. The thin cushions on the chairs were shrink-wrapped in a protective plastic film that could be left on for years, as it had been in the Hans' place. The designs were solid and square. If you left it in its wrapping and did not knock it about too much the furniture would last for years looking brand new. It was horrible.

In vain we searched for something vaguely stylish, a little unique, but it seemed as if the entire stock had been made to the same template from the same cuts of timber, sanded and glued and dipped in plastic. Disappointed, we made our way out through one of the tunnels past an open-bed truck overloaded with hundreds of identical chairs.

As I turned the car back on to the highway I asked my cost-conscious wife a question. 'Why don't we go to one of those antiques warehouses in Shanghai?'

She did not reply. She did not have to. I knew perfectly well what she was thinking: 'Too expensive.'

'You never know, we might get a decent price if we buy enough,' I said to her right ear.

Still no response, which was: 'Still too expensive. The houses are only going to be for weekends.'

'Well, we could just go and look,' I carried on. 'Surely there is no harm in that.'

I knew perfectly well that furniture from such a place was going to be expensive but my heart was set on doing our houses justice. There was no way I could explain that to Joanna. I certainly couldn't justify the cost. So I didn't try to.

I was thinking of the vast aircraft hangar-like stores that sold original and reproduction antique furniture on the outskirts of Shanghai, where suburban streets had once been lined by mock-Tudor houses like London's stockbroker belt. The furniture would be ten times the price of what we had seen in Nanxun, but it had a hundred times more style.

The vast antique emporiums smelt of dust and history and wood glue. Under their high ceilings concession-era art deco met drab Communist junk in a forest of fake Qing. As with modern Shanghai, past and present, West and East were chucked in on top of each other like the glass towers that overlooked the surviving alleys and grander houses of the old foreign concession areas.

The good stuff, the genuine articles, had been built by master craftsmen to foreign designs during the early twentieth century. It had furnished the mansions of British and

American property and shipping tycoons, the company flats of young men starting careers with trading companies, and added a touch of international sophistication to the homes of the wealthy and the gangsters. There were low hardwood armchairs whose sides swept back with the curves of a 1930s Lagonda. Their painstakingly re-upholstered leather cushions invited you to unbutton your dinner jacket and sink into them with a cigar. Square and solid side tables with grooved legs like Doric columns only lacked a pile of *New Yorker* magazines, an oversized onyx cigarette lighter and a silver monogrammed box holding eighty Dunhills. There were drinks cabinets with wings that swung out each side for hanging stemmed glasses, whose tops had once been cluttered with cocktail shakers, bottles of bitters and cut crystal decanters of sherry and whisky, and beds whose art deco bas-relief headboards brought to mind the skyline of downtown Manhattan.

The pieces had survived in the same mansions and grand houses which, since 1949, had been divided and partitioned into the cramped apartments of Shanghainese families. Now, as the old lane houses of downtown Shanghai were demolished to make way for the new city's skyscrapers, the mansions converted into slick bars, restaurants and offices, and the ageing residents moved out to the brand new suburbs and dormitory towns to live with their children, canny local dealers and foreigners who knew their business were collecting the battered, torn and overlooked remnants of a long gone era, restoring them and selling them at prices that wouldn't have looked out of place in London.

They were reproducing them to order, too. The replicas were so well made it was often safer and better value to buy brand new antiques rather than real ones. That was definitely the case for the intricate Chinese furniture, which might be Qing Dynasty but had more than likely been knocked up by the dozen in a workshop out the back. The places were lined with rows and rows of the stuff, organized by type.

Some of the outlets were sophisticated operations with English-speaking staff. Their preferred customers were the dealers who shipped container-loads to Europe and America. Next were the 'expat *taitais*', the foreign wives, sent over by the new friends they had made at their first expat wives' coffee-morning at one of the city's Irish pubs. While her husband was struggling to work out the office politics of the Shanghai branch of his international corporation, the wife got stuck into the complicated calculation of what furniture would look good back home, or in the summer house they could afford once this posting had been completed, and what in the meantime she needed for the vast and empty mock-Spanish villa she was rattling around in, shadowed by a maid who barely spoke a word of English but was desperate to clean something. The Shanghai antique industry was thriving.

Joanna and I had contributed when we restored our Shanghai flat and we had a favourite dealer, Mr Yang. Mr Yang was a shady character from out of town and employed a unique business model. He was rarely to be found in the same place for more than a couple of months. He moved between soon-to-be demolished factories and vast temporary lean-tos on new wasteland, wherever he could find space for his pile of scavenged junk. Nor did he restore it and display it. He left it as junk, outside in all weathers. If you could find something in the mess and had the imagination or the confidence to picture it in your sitting-room, Yang would take a small deposit off you and one day, according to his mood, the piece would be delivered to your home, beautifully restored. Yang's prices were unbeatable and the quality of the end product was faultless, but you paid in uncertainty as to whether it would ever turn up.

The reason was simple. Yang was an alcoholic and a gambler. He had to keep moving address because he defaulted on his rent and needed to stay ahead of his creditors. The deposit you paid for your furniture did not go to his workmen or his outside contractors. It went on drink and cards. If he stayed sober and won, your delivery date moved forward. If he got drunk and lost, you waited.

It had been a couple of months since we had seen Mr Yang. We were still waiting for a couple of chairs for our Shanghai apartment but he had moved on again and his mobile phone was out of service. That was unusual, even for him. I wanted the chairs and I also wanted to see what he had that would fit in Moganshan.

I asked around at some of the more respectable and expensive dealers, the ones with actual shops. They all knew Yang and his reputation.

'He's really gone and done it this time,' one of them told me. 'Had to leave town for a while.'

Eventually I was given a vague address. Yang was back in Shanghai, somewhere near a cross street on Wuzhong Road, a long arterial avenue that runs out of town through a suburb known as Korean Town.

At lunchtime on a hot summer's day I slipped away from the office and went out there by taxi. The journey took almost an hour. The directions were so imprecise I could only drop myself off at a guess. I started sweeping the area on foot.

Stretched between the major roads into Shanghai was a maze of long streets lined by the blank walls of factories and warehouses, broken here and there by short strips of grubby noodle and barber shops. There was little traffic. My frustration built up as I came up to a possible hideout of Yang's only to find it wasn't and that I had another couple of hundred metres to go before the next likely spot.

I covered blocks that went on for a couple of kilometres each way. I was hot, tired and angry by the time I caught sight of one of Yang's workmen. He was loitering in a gateway on a road I had already searched. It was three o'clock in the afternoon. I walked up to him.

'Is Boss Yang in?' I asked.

'No. He's not here,' the worker replied loyally.

'You're sure?'

'Definitely.'

I pushed past him. Yang's new place looked like a disused garage. It was smaller but more solid than one of his usual hideouts. The concrete floor was covered in oil stains. There was not as much stock as usual either. Yang must have had a run of bad luck. An indoor shed was tucked up against the back wall. The door was open so I put my head through it.

There was Yang out cold on a metal framed bed, his face as red as a beetroot, a dirty pink bed sheet patterned with roses scrunched up underneath him. I kicked the underside of the bed, hard. There were no springs, only a wooden board. It hurt but the noise and thump woke him up.

'Where are my chairs, you lazy bugger?' I shouted at him. I could not help a smile, half of triumph at finding him, half with the satisfaction of kicking him out of bed. 'And where the hell have you been?'

74

Yang looked up at me with the pained red eyes of a terrible hangover. 'Uh? Hello, Mr Mark.'

He sat up slowly and explained in a slurred voice that he owed money to his upholsterer, who was holding our chairs hostage. Because they were originals they were possibly valuable. I got the address out of him and the amount he was in debt, a little more than we were due to pay for the chairs. On my way out I had a quick look over Yang's junk heap. It was definitely not up to his usual standard. We would have to go elsewhere for Moganshan.

A few days later I paid his debts, got the chairs, and Yang disappeared forever. I missed him.

All we needed for Moganshan was some semi-respectable junk, something that looked as if it had been in the houses forever. Yang's usual selection would have been ideal.

During our search for Yang we had got to know a Mr Zheng, one of the dealers who delighted in telling us what a rogue Yang was.

Mr Zheng seemed exceptionally reliable by comparison. He also had a suite of bedroom furniture that I had been keeping my eye on whenever we dropped by on our hunts for Yang. I had asked him once if he would sell me a few pieces of it. The complete set was far too much for our Shanghai flat. But Zheng would not break it up. Now we had more than enough room for the lot in Moganshan.

The set was a classic example of 'Chinese foreign' furniture commissioned by a wealthy Chinese or more likely his wife to emulate the foreign neighbours, probably in the late 1930s: a solid double bed with matching bedside tables, large dressing table, linen chest, enormous three-door closet, and a breakfast table and four chairs, all veneered in the same dark walnut and in good condition. The simple design was restrained, not as ostentatious as many such imitations. Mr Zheng had almost given up trying to sell it as one lot and dropped hints that he might give me the bits I had asked about before. It had been hanging around his store for over a year. He was ecstatic when I told him we could take it all. We agreed on five thousand yuan, about four hundred pounds and half the price he had mentioned the first time I asked. I imagined that in London it would fetch ten times as much, properly restored and with a 'made in Shanghai in circa 1930' label on it. The trouble would be getting it to Moganshan. Mr Zheng promised to arrange everything. He also agreed to store, at his warehouse, a couple of sofas we had ordered from Ikea. We ordered some more bits and pieces from him, drawers and cabinets and bookshelves, and a replica desk for my study, made to measure. When the desk was finished he would have everything delivered by container truck. He didn't even ask for a deposit.

Chapter Five

Official Reception

Yesterday was a remarkable day in the history of Mokanshan, as this place was visited by no less personage than the prefect of Hoochou, attended by the magistrate of Wookong... All partook freely of the tea and light refreshments offered... We were not told the object of their coming, but presume it was to give an official recognition to the residence of foreigners upon these mountains.

North-China Daily News, 19 June 1900

The day the furniture was to be sent from Shanghai, Joanna and I had an important engagement in Moganshan. We had invited to dinner every local official who'd had anything to do with the renting and restoration of the houses so far.

No occasion or event in China, big or small, is considered suitably commenced or complete without a banquet. A formal dinner takes the place and significance we give in the West to champagne toasts, signing ceremonies, casual meetings, important meetings, and thank you letters. Neglecting to throw a banquet at a time like this would be like refusing to shake hands on a deal in London.

We were about to take up weekend residence in our newly

restored villas. It was necessary to show our gratitude to the people who had helped us, worked for us, and even those who had obstructed us like Mr Ge. We were to give them face and thanks and the opportunity to try to drink me under the table.

The junior officers from the Hangliao in charge of water and electricity were specifically invited. I was keen to start off on the right foot with them since they apparently held the power of life and death over our tenancy. Major Ma would of course be there and Mr Ge had graciously accepted too. General Manager Li and Pan Guang Lin were being softened up before we finalized their bill. Lao Han was to be the master of ceremonies and would no doubt join in the drinking.

The venue was the Hans' house. Han Aiyi was preparing a spread of her finest dishes: wild boar and hare, home-raised chicken soup and fish steamed in garlic and ginger, as well as several plates of standards such as fish flavoured meat, red cooked pork and a small hillside's worth of bamboo shoots, wild herbs and vegetables. By my special request there would also be a large bowl of her Moganshan fries.

We had ordered as many bottles of good quality *bai jiu*, the Chinese sorghum-based liquor, as we were likely to drink, plus a few more in reserve. Moganshan locals knocked back the fiery grain alcohol like iced water after a hot day's work on the bamboo plantation.

I was also bringing to our banquet a case of Johnny Walker Red Label to supplement the *bai jiu*. Over the years I had presented the occasional bottle of spirits, usually brandy, to government officials at the appropriate opportunities, such as Chinese New Year or National Day, but never had I followed the custom on a scale like this. Now was the time to splash out. Everyone at the dinner would be getting a bottle of whisky and a little speech I had prepared. I wanted to make an impression.

The truck with the furniture had left Shanghai at nine o'clock that morning. The twenty-foot container had been a devil of a job to load and was packed to bursting according to Mr Zheng. Even the spare seat in the cab had been taken up with an old television set. It should be with us by midday.

Pan had his men standing by to help with the unloading. Instead of lugging everything up the two hundred steep steps from the road to the houses we had decided to carry the furniture along a narrow dirt path through the woods behind the houses, a shorter and more level route Pan had used for the heavier building materials. It would be an obstacle course but it was still an easier route. Daylight was an important factor.

Joanna and I relaxed when we heard the truck was on its way and concentrated on the banquet. Lao Han talked us through it one more time, how to treat Major Ma as the guest of honour but give due deference to Mr Ge, where to sit them, the order of the dishes and so on. We re-counted the bottles of *bai jiu* and I stashed the whisky in a corner. Lao Han had put a large round banquet tabletop on to one of the *ma jiang* tables at the fireplace end of the long drawing room where Brent and I had first fantasized about renting a house in Moganshan.

The room still looked bare. The thought that in a few hours our truckload of furniture would be arriving and at last we could put the finishing touches to our houses, recreating what a house in Moganshan should look like, gave me a surge of satisfaction.

After lunch Joanna called Mr Zheng in Shanghai. Had he heard from the driver? How was he getting on?

Zheng said yes he had, all was well and the driver should be with us any moment.

That sounded about right. It was five hours since he had left Shanghai, plenty of time for a slow truck to get here. We hurried back up the hill.

It was a dry autumn day. The leaves on the sycamore trees were turning pale gold. We sat on the low wall in the sunshine opposite the Hans' house to wait for the furniture truck.

As a child I used to spend hours on the high granite wall at the front of our house in North Wales, waiting for guests and school friends to arrive from England most weeks of the summer. From my perch I had a view over the Dee River valley and could glimpse stretches of the road that ran along it from Corwen, the road the new arrivals would drive up. That day in Moganshan I enjoyed the same childish thrill of patient anticipation. Any moment now the truck should appear on the road below us. It had to come this way.

Joanna and I chatted about the houses, how to arrange the rooms and where to put each piece of furniture. We wondered how often we would come up from Shanghai and counted up the excuses for parties. There were birthdays, national holidays, Christmas and New Year. But first we must have a housewarming party. We went through the guest list. And we couldn't wait to see Isabel running around on the lawn we had mapped out beside the upper house, replacing the tangle of weeds. Where could we hang a swing for her, and build a tree house? We discussed what flowers to plant, what vegetables. Lao Han would help with that. He and his wife were now firmly established as our house-watchers.

Major Ma passed by and greeted us with his usual cheerfulness. I stood up and he poked me lightly in the chest with one finger. Thanks to the wall behind my knees there was no retreat.

'I told you not to worry, didn't I?' he shouted in his sharp voice.

Then he expressed his regret that he could not attend the dinner at Lao Han's because he had been summoned to Hangzhou. His number two, Captain Yang, would stand in for him. We thanked him for his concern that the electricity and water were connected and he walked on.

I was sorry he would not be joining the party. Despite my complaints about his patronizing tirades and the impression I did of his shrill voice, which made Lao Han laugh, I liked Major Ma.

I looked at my watch. It was three o'clock, almost an hour since the last call to Mr Zheng. The truck had still not arrived. We called again.

Zheng assured us that everything was fine. He had no reason to doubt the truck was not already on the top of the mountain. Applying the double advantage of a language with no clear tenses and the Chinese logic that if you say something convincingly enough then it must be true, he declared: 'It has already arrived.'

'Well, then where is it?' we asked back.

'Hang on, I'll just double-check,' he replied.

Two minutes later he called again. 'You did say your address was Moganshan Road didn't you?'

He had called Joanna's phone and she was repeating for my benefit.

The dread hit me like a missing twenty-foot container

truck. There were two Moganshan Roads we knew, one in Hangzhou and one in Shanghai. Mr Zheng was carrying on. 'I know it's not the Shanghai one, because you would have said if it was, and you wouldn't have expected us to take so long to get there, so it must be the Hangzhou one, right?'

Joanna and I were both speechless. Joanna's face began to change colour. I gently took the phone from her and spoke to Mr Zheng.

'We are on Moganshan Mountain, the actual village, in Zhejiang, one hour north of Hangzhou. We're not on Moganshan Road. Not the one in Shanghai, and not the one in Hangzhou.' It was difficult to keep my voice steady. 'Mr Zheng,' I added, 'we did explain this on the detailed instructions we wrote out for you and asked you to give to the driver.'

'Well he's on Moganshan Road in Hangzhou,' Zheng replied, as if he had not heard a word. 'Where are you?'

'Mr Zheng, you did give the instructions to the driver, didn't you?' I repeated.

'I explained them to him, yes,' he replied. 'He can't read much, actually.'

'Bloody hell,' I muttered. 'Mr Zheng, please give us the number of the driver and we'll speak to him ourselves.'

A minute later I was on the phone to a man who sounded so incompetent he should not have been allowed to drive a hula-hoop let alone a truck. Somewhere in the garbled panic I distinctly heard 'Moganshan Road, Shanghai', 'not allowed on highway', 'lost in downtown Hangzhou', 'stopped and fined by police' and finally 'What number Moganshan Road?' I handed the phone to Joanna before I screamed.

Determined to do better, she listened calmly and then spoke. Then she hung up.

'He says he couldn't drive on the highway because the tolls are too expensive. Then he got lost in Hangzhou and the police fined him because his truck isn't allowed downtown during the day. Now he is on Moganshan Road. I told him to follow it north out of the city towards Huzhou and turn off at Deqing. I think he understood.' She paused to check she had everything correct and then remembered the last bit. 'Oh, and he wants us to pay his fine.'

She had just finished speaking when the phone rang again. Joanna answered.

'Yes. North.' I heard her say. 'Towards Huzhou.' Pause. 'No, we are not in Huzhou, we are in Moganshan. It's on the way to Huzhou.' Another pause. 'The signs say Huzhou. Look for the signs.' She listened intently. 'Yes, I know we are not on Moganshan Road. We already told you that. But Moganshan Road becomes the road that leads north to Huzhou, the G104. Moganshan village is just off of that.' She pulled the phone down from her ear, let it hang by her side for a moment, looked up at the sky, then lifted the phone again. 'Tell you what, why don't you get on to the G104, head for Huzhou and call us when you get to Deqing?' She hung up, apparently without waiting for his answer.

'Christ, he's stupid,' she said to the top of the wall.

I looked at my watch again. It was a quarter past three. I guessed that, allowing an hour for the driver to get lost on a dead-straight intercity highway, we would see him about five o'clock. That was before the dinner and definitely before dark. It normally took one hour from Hangzhou to Moganshan.

By five o'clock Pan Guang Lin was calling my mobile every few minutes. He was getting impatient and with good reason. The men he had ready for the unloading were eager to go home for their supper, a meal they normally took soon after five. The driver had still not appeared and our calls only seemed to confuse him. I went in search of Pan.

I pressed the recall button on my mobile and handed it to him while it rang. 'Pan Guang Lin, please could you help me find out where the driver is and when he is going to get here? Maybe I am missing something because of my bad Chinese,' I pleaded, my face a picture of innocence. 'I'd appreciate your help.' He took the phone and I looked across at the sun that was getting lower in the sky, over to the west.

'Where are you?' I heard Pan ask, then: 'What? Say that again?' He looked at me blankly, the phone to his ear. 'You are on a main road? Which one?' Another blank look. 'You don't know? But you think you are near Deqing.'

I was enjoying watching Pan's face as it tried to relay to me what the driver was saying. Suddenly he exploded.

'What do you mean you don't think you can find Moganshan? It's a bloody mountain. Look up and you'll see the damn thing!' I couldn't help smiling but caught myself and in an instant altered my expression to exasperated sympathy. 'You see what I mean?' I shrugged at Pan.

He turned away from me and suddenly burst out with: 'If you don't know where you are then how the hell can I tell you how to get here from there, you idiot!' I was amazed at the transformation in the normally placid Pan. It got better.

'Wind down the window then and stick your stupid head out of it and ask someone!' Pan was fuming by now. 'And while you're at it, ask them how to get to Moganshan too!' He thrust the phone back at me. Then in his normal voice he whined with theatrical cadence, 'That man is a motherfucking idiot.'

I used to think it was only foreigners who could not contain their frustrations in China.

Neither of us had any idea when the truck might turn up, but at least Pan understood how impossible it had been for me to tell him earlier. It was almost time for our banquet.

'Send your men home and let's go and eat too,' I said to Pan. 'We'll deal with the truck when it comes. Somehow.'

We crossed the road to the Hans' house. Mr Ge was already there drinking tea. He gave me his trademark crooked smile. I couldn't tell if he was congratulating me on getting through his obstacles and at last finishing the restoration of the houses or warning me to watch out for another trick he had up his sleeve.

I phoned Joanna. Lao Han called up the army. Within twenty minutes we were seated, Joanna and I, Mr Ge, General Manager Li, the water and electricity officers from the Hangliao, Pan Guang Lin and Captain Yang, Ma's deputy. There was another man whom I had never met before. He was introduced as Mr Zhang from the Administration Bureau. When I asked what he did there, I was told he was in the administration department. I left it at that. Lao Han joined us and took up his role as master of ceremonies. Joanna was the only woman at the table.

The banquet started quietly. I forced myself to smile as I listened to the foreigner friendly clichés for the thousandth time, addressed to me with patronizing grins. 'Do you miss Western food?' 'Do you like Chinese food?' 'Can you cook it?' 'You use chopsticks well.' 'Your Chinese is very good.'

And so on and on. I replied exactly as I had a thousand times at hundreds of other banquets, summoning as genuine a smile as possible from somewhere deep within my patience. 'No, yes, no, thank you, thank you.'

Once we'd run out of platitudes, no one quite knew what to say next, or who to, so we talked about the food – standard small talk at any Chinese banquet.

Pride of place on the table, before the expensive fish arrived, went to the wild boar, hacked as usual into gristly knots of meat and bone and stewed in a thick dark sauce. I had never seen a boar in the wild in Moganshan, or anywhere else in China for that matter. From the frequency of its appearance on local menus and tables we should have been tripping over the things every time we went for a walk. Perhaps they were bred in secret by local farmers.

'Oh, they're everywhere,' said Mr Ge. 'But they only come out at night.'

Our guests insisted I took the choicest pieces of the local delicacy. I made a determined effort with the awkward lumps, smiling through my locked teeth and greasy fingers as I did so.

'Delicious,' I declared as a tiny morsel of meat slipped down my throat. Everyone looked on with approval. I was careful to hide the meat I could not detach by placing the soggy lumps with their bone side uppermost on my plate, once I had finished pretending to savour them.

The chicken soup was Han Aiyi's *pièce de résistance* – for everyone else that is. I was waiting for the fries. Once we had drunk the broth we attacked the carcass with our chopsticks. It was a team effort, pulling, prodding and tugging until a piece of breast or brown meat came free.

The chicken helped break down some barriers, as did the

bai jiu, which was being poured out non-stop by Lao Han. Captain Yang proposed a toast. He began with a question.

'So Mark, how does it feel to be the first foreigner to be back in Moganshan after fifty years?'

I smiled. Yang couldn't know how closely his words echoed those of a senior Shanghainese official I'd met at the rocky start of my business career in the city: 'How does it feel to be the first foreigner publisher in Shanghai for fifty years, Mark?' And just as that official had ignored my Chinese business partner, so Yang ignored Joanna, my Chinese wife.

The Shanghainese official had engineered the shut down of my business just three months after he had uttered those warm words of welcome. It been a hell of a job to get going again after that. How long would our luck hold in Moganshan?

I glanced with carefully composed naivety at Mr Ge and then thanked Yang. 'I am very happy Captain Yang, and I look forward to being a good and long-term tenant. Cheers!'

I sensed it was time for my little speech. Once I had drained my tiny glass of *bai jiu* and held it upturned over the table I began. 'Gentlemen, speaking as a foreigner returning to Moganshan, I have small presentation to make.' They looked interested.

'As you know, we have different tastes in alcohol, foreigners and Chinese.' They smiled. 'You like *bai jiu*,' my hand swept over the glasses that were being refilled by Lao Han, 'and we like *yang jiu*.' I used the generic term for 'foreign liquor'.

'In particular,' I went on, 'in Moganshan in the old days foreigners would have enjoyed a glass of whisky – one of our favourite *yang jiu* – on the terrace while they watched the sun go down. Now I hope, just as I am sitting here with you drinking Chinese *bai jiu* tonight – and enjoying it too,

I must say,' smiles all round, 'you will come and join me for a foreign-style glass of whisky on our terrace one evening and we can watch the sun go down just like they did in the old days.' Our terrace faced east, but that was a minor detail.

I reached behind me and pulled the first bottle of Johnnie Walker from the box. 'And knowing that it takes time to acquire a taste for whisky, I would like to present each of you with a bottle.' I held it up. 'So you can practise at home.' There was some laughter. 'Once you have got to like it, do please come up and have some more with me.'

I handed out the bottles, one each, including Lao Han. The gift and the speech seemed to go down well. The Red Labels were studied closely. I wondered if they would ever drink the contents. Lao Han would for sure. He had enjoyed the occasional shot with me and Brent over the years.

My presentation over, we got back to drinking *bai jiu* and everyone forgot about whisky. Joanna was joining in, which was making a good impression on our new neighbours. We were not yet drunk but the atmosphere was becoming much warmer.

Suddenly I remembered the furniture van and, as if by magic, my phone rang. It was the driver. He had finally arrived, at the worst possible moment. I looked out through the window. Dusk was turning to full darkness. I cursed and nodded at Pan. He stood up. I whispered a word in Joanna's ear and stood up too.

'My apologies, gentlemen, but I must go and see to this furniture delivery. I shall be as quick as I can. My wife will be your host.' Pan and I left.

The truck was up the road at the turn off for Queer Stone Corner, a scenic viewpoint at the back of the mountain.

Before I could say a word the driver leant out of his window and started spluttering at me. 'Where do you want this unloaded? I have to get back to Shanghai. It's dark already you see, and that makes the driving harder. No one told me it was such a long way ...' I wanted to punch him. He seemed to be deliberately taunting me from the safety of his cab. But all I could do was stare at him in wonder. Pan had gone to get his men.

I told him to drive up the back road, turn around at the top and come back down to where I would be waiting. The third explanation, he got it. By now Pan's men were emerging out of the gloom. Their habitual cheerfulness made me feel better. We walked up to the path and met the truck as it came back down the hill.

'Stop here!' I shouted up at the cab.

The driver pulled on the handbrake. Stopping in the middle of a one track road did not concern him in the slightest. His main worry was the brakes.

'Get some stones!' he shouted. 'And put them under the wheels. Quick!'

He leapt down from the cab and came round to the back where he unlocked the doors and swung them open, ignoring us as if we were a bunch of workmen at his beck and call.

'Can you get this lot off fast?' he asked. 'I got to be going. Oh, and here's the bill from Mr Zheng. And what about the fine I had to pay in Hangzhou?' he waved some scraps of paper at me.

I rounded on him and spoke firmly. 'You will stay here until everything is carried to my house. You will not be paid until it is. If anything is damaged because it is dark and we cannot see the trees we have to carry it through, I will deduct what I think appropriate from the bill and deal with Mr Zheng myself later.' I had already called Zheng and told him what to expect.

'But . . .' he started and I snapped.

'Shut up.'

'. . . don't forget there's a TV in the cab too,' he snivelled.

Pan's men were heroes that night. We had one torch which we hung from a tree halfway along the path. The woods were as black as pitch otherwise. In the darkness four men carried two houses' worth of furniture up a steep slope, along a narrow precipice, through fifty metres of trees, over a water pipe and down the broken stone steps to the front of the upper house. It was a dry night with no sign of rain, so we left the furniture out in the open. By the time we had finished my whole body was pulsing with pain.

The driver had not lifted a finger.

'Here's the money for Mr Zheng,' I said. 'I am keeping back ten per cent,' which happened to be his delivery fee. 'When I can see the furniture in daylight tomorrow and find out what damage has been done by the trees, I'll call Zheng.'

He opened his mouth to complain.

'And as for your fines in Hangzhou,' I pre-empted him. 'That's your fault and you pay. If you had taken the highway like you were supposed to I would have paid you back the tolls, like I said I would on the instructions which you never read. Now get lost.' The driver started muttering.

Pan stepped forward. I had never seen him look so angry and determined. He was holding his arms slightly out from his sides, fists clenched.

'But I haven't got a torch to get back through the woods,' the driver was whimpering.

90

Pan took one more step and looked hard into his face. 'You heard what the foreigner said. Fuck off.'

The driver turned and disappeared into the night.

Now I knew why Pan had burned that photo.

I thanked the workmen, Pan and I put our arms over each other's shoulders as we went down the steps back to the banquet. We had been away for an hour and had missed the serious drinking, the main fun. We could hear the noise from a hundred metres up the road.

The party was loud and messy. Piles of bones and scraps covered the flimsy plastic sheet that protected the tablecloth. The ashtrays were overflowing with cigarette butts and more were stuck upright in the piles of debris. Flecks of ash were scattered across dishes and utensils. A bowl of Mrs Han's fries, overlooked and soggy, sat in the middle of the table. I looked at them sadly. Everyone was shouting, particularly Joanna and Captain Yang. Lao Han was interrupting now and again with a wave of his hand, his forelock drooping over his forehead, drunk in its own way. Mr Ge's cheeks were red. The other two men, Li the water officer and Mr Zhang from the Administration Bureau, were happy but silent, content to watch and listen and enjoy their own quiet drunkenness. The electricity officer had already left.

'Your wife issan exc'llent drinker!' shouted Captain Yang as I stepped back into the room with Pan. 'Very good drinker!' He stood up and took my hand, dragging me towards the table. 'I'm telling you. Sh'really knows how to drink!'

I let him push me down into a chair and hand me a glass of *bai jiu*. I was looking forward to it. A stiff drink was exactly what I needed.

'Let's have'nother toast!' It was Joanna, thrusting her arm

91

past me. Her face was bright red too. She tipped the glass up without waiting for any response.

I smiled and drank.

'So . . . Mark,' Yang asked again. 'Howd'sit feel to be th' first f'reigner in Moogun'shan?'

Lao Han answered for me. 'Cap'n Yang! Les drink with th' first f'reigner back on Mog'shan!'

'Yuh,' contributed Joanna.

I stood and drank again. The others half rose then sank back into their chairs.

'Now if you'll excuse me,' it was Li, the water officer, 'I'll be leaving first.' He gave the standard turn of phrase which excused him from making an excuse. Zhang got up too.

'And me,' said Yang.

The party was over. It was only eight o'clock. But that is the way: hard and fast, then early to bed to sleep it off. The men rose and held their bottles of whisky. 'Thank you,' they said one by one and on buckling legs walked on to the terrace and turned towards the road. I held Pan back for a quiet toast of thanks for his help with the furniture and then bade him goodnight.

Joanna walked out with Mr Ge, clutching his arm. I watched apprehensively. Was she going to say something embarrassing about the trouble he had given us? I followed closely behind.

'Mr Ge,' she said. 'Y'know we're very happy to be here. M'usband likes this place very much. Thank you . . . thank you . . . for all your help.'

Mr Ge made dismissive noises.

'No, seriously . . .' Joanna was swaying on her feet. 'We realize how much you did for us, and we'd just like thank you . . .'

Was she being sarcastic or was she genuinely trying to patch things up with Ge while he was in a good mood? Joanna kept on gushing.

At last, after many protestations of goodwill from Ge, she let him go and turned to come back into the house.

'Well done, honey,' I said, walking beside her and prepared to catch her if she stumbled. 'Looks like you did an amazing job with those guys.'

I meant it. The evening seemed to have been a tremendous success, largely thanks to her. I would not go so far as to say that our influential local friends had taken us to their hearts but they seemed happy, if only for the novelty value, to have us in the village. The banquet had made the right impression. The *bai jiu* had worked its magic. Our residence had been blessed with alcohol and official sanction.

Joanna walked straight on without looking up. I followed her back to the table where we sat down and reached for a packet of cigarettes. Lao Han started clearing up.

'You don't know ...' Joanna slurred at me. 'You don't know ...'

And then she fell off her chair.

Chapter Six
Weekend Life

As the big world below has optimist and pessimist, so the little world up at Mokanshan has enthusiast and dismalist. It reminds one of the story, two guests at a table looking at the same jug, one said 'pass that milk' the other said 'thank you for the cream.'

North-China Daily News, 13 September 1919

The weekend we threw our long awaited Moganshan house-warming party, one of the houses caught fire.

The pair of them were furnished, and spotless. Inside and out they looked like life-sized doll's houses. Every bedroom had a bed, bedside tables, table lamps and a chest of drawers. The sitting-rooms were stuffed with sofas and Mr Zheng's cheap antiques and we had laid rugs across the wooden floors. Curtains, made from leftovers at a local textile factory, hung in every window. The kitchens gleamed.

The vision I'd dreamt of in the Hans' empty drawing-room three years ago had at last become reality. We had restored two Moganshan villas to something like their former glory. The final step was to make them feel like homes.

It was late October and the leaves had fallen from the

trees. The days were warm under clear skies and autumn sunshine but in the evenings the temperature dropped sharply. It was perfect weather for trying out the fireplaces.

Brent and Mark came for the party. So did Kirk, an Australian who had helped me get started in Shanghai, and his girlfriend and daughter. Kirk's business partner Jules, an Australian–Chinese, had also come with him.

As well as Leona and their young son, Brent brought his new business partner. His real estate company was concentrating – for the moment at least – on finding old concession era apartments for foreigners. The partner's name was Scott Barrack, another American, and he was with his girlfriend, Jennifer. Finally there was Jozef, a Belgian entrepreneur.

The guest cottage had been designated the party den. When darkness fell after the inaugural barbecue outside the main house and we had put the children to bed, the boys crept up to the cottage for a game of cards and whiskies by the fire. The girls stayed with Joanna in the main house, curled up in big armchairs and sofas with blankets over their knees.

I had asked Pan Guang Lin not to throw away the timber harvested from the gutting of the houses. He had left neat piles of rafters, collar beams and scantling, along with a tangle of dusty lath, the latticework that had held the plaster on the walls. Protected by sheets of twisted corrugated iron, the wood was as dry as the dust that coated it. I had already cut some of the rafters into log lengths. We had a good supply of perfect tinder.

We laid a fire in the cottage and lit it. Within minutes the brand new fireplace was an inferno. Flames licked the white paint at the back of the hearth and blackened it into broad strips that swiftly merged into one. We threw on more logs

95

and the seven of us sat back, spellbound by the other-worldliness of the scene.

I have made my friends at the usual stages in life: school, university, army, and during my brief stint in a proper job as a commodity trader. I guess the closest ones are from my army days. I was only a straightforward infantry officer on a short service commission of four years and I never went to war, but sitting in a puddle at 3 a.m. in the bottom of a trench on a winter exercise, sharing a last soggy cigarette, creates bonds you do not often find at the next door desk in a classroom or an office.

In China however, I had also made friends that I felt I had really been to war with. It is tough doing business in China. Not only for foreigners. Chinese entrepreneurs go through the same hell by a different route. But if you are a foreigner you are at a disadvantage from the start, not only because of who you are but also because you think like a foreigner and always will, no matter how hard you try to adapt.

There is fierce competition of course, as there is anywhere in the world. But that is not a problem in itself. The problem is that China is a one-party totalitarian state, which makes the laws to suit itself, and since the state is also the biggest commercial operator in the country – *ergo* everyone's competitor – the competition can seem rather unfair. It also makes business battles particularly vicious.

Of course my friends and I knew the risks and how tough it would be to overcome them. That is one of the reasons we came here. But like anyone who bites off more than he can chew, thinking he can cope – and every single foreign businessman in China has bitten off more than he can chew, no matter what he tells you – we were constantly surprised, and often horrified, by what we had got ourselves into.

In the cottage that evening was a group of young foreigners who were building businesses in China if not for the first time ever, then at least for the first time since 1949, and under the capricious control of a Communist system that desperately wanted to be capitalist in everything except name. We were pioneers of a sort, and we were successful too. The brands each of us created are well known today in Shanghai, Beijing and some cities further afield. One of us had already been illegally copied in Mongolia. Another was soon going to take his company international on his own terms. Yet another of us was going to lose everything in a couple of years.

Above all, our common experience was of the fights, mainly with Chinese officials. Every one of us had been raided by government bureaux who did not know quite what to do with us, before being summarily fined, threatened, intimidated and bullied. But somehow we had survived. We were battle-hardened.

That made us a tight gang. We needed each other, not for favours but moral support. Three of the people in the room had worked with me, Mark, Kirk and Scott – you do not ask men like them to work *for* you, although I had technically been the boss. They had seen me and stood by me in situations so gut-wrenchingly stressful that I would have been crying on my mother's bosom if she had been there. But she wasn't and they were.

Now here we were in Moganshan, sitting in front of my very own fireplace and holding a glass of whisky topped up with spring-fed tap water. The worries and battles of business life were a thousand miles away, and fifty odd years too. No foreigner in China had sat where we were, like we were, for at least that long. It was a special moment.

We turned off the main lights and let the fire spread its warm orange glow across the stone walls of the cottage. I felt a surge of contentment verging on pure bliss. We raised our glasses and toasted our hideaway. My friends knew this place was for them as much as for me and Joanna. Then we started a card game.

Before we got stuck in, Scott and Jennifer went to bed in the room above us. It was unlike Scott to leave a party early but apparently it was too soon in his relationship for him to try, or to want, perhaps, to spend all night with the boys.

The remaining six of us settled into the game. It was poker, seven card stud. Mark tutored those who needed help. We used the pieces from a game of Risk as betting chips. Gradually we got the hang of it and the stakes started rising. There were a couple of bottles of whisky, a bottle of vodka, and some yellow cans of tonic on the low table in front of the fireplace. Mark was drinking out of a small flower vase. When the ashtray filled up we threw its contents into the blazing hearth. Now and again a change in the wind sent a back draught down the chimney and smoke puffed into the room. We ignored it and played on.

At midnight Joanna came up and told us she was going to bed. Kirk's girlfriend and Leona had already crashed out. She commented on the smoke, but we were too absorbed by the game to pay any attention.

'We'll open a window in a minute,' Mark said, his back hunched over the table.

I had drunk enough and could see that the others were going to play late into the night. It was a good opportunity to slip away. I was about even too. So I stood up.

'Goodnight everybody,' Joanna and I said in unison.

'Fantastic place, you guys,' Mark replied, lifting his head from his hand for a second. 'Amazing.'

To a chorus of 'night' and 'see you tomorrow', Joanna and I let ourselves out into the fresh air, sucked in some deep breaths and stumbled down the steps to our house and bedroom. No sound came from the children. Kirk's daughter was in the guest room, Brent's little boy in with Isabel. The alcohol, the pure joy, the mountain air and a hug from Joanna had me asleep in seconds. I was very happy.

Then Scott woke up. He said later that it was the noise of a *ma jiang* game that had done it. Between rounds the tiles are shuffled with a sharp clack that sounds like prawns being tossed into a wok of scalding oil. It is certainly loud enough to spoil a good night's sleep, as I remembered from the small alley where I had first lived in Shanghai.

But no one was playing *ma jiang*.

Scott rubbed his eyes and reached for a towel. He wrapped it round his waist and, leaving the light off so as not to wake Jennifer, tiptoed downstairs. At the bottom he stage-whispered, 'Guys! Can you keep the noise down a bit! And be good if you could let the fire go down too. It's pretty smoky up here.'

And then someone turned on a light.

A dense cloud of smoke was floating against the ceiling of the sitting-room. Smoke was pouring down from the first floor too. It was seeping out in thick streams from the staircase and the landing.

Jules bounded up the stairs and pushed past the half-awake Scott into his bedroom. He flicked on the light, startling Jennifer, who sat up with the bed clothes against her chest. The room was thick with smoke.

'Guys!' Jules shouted at the top of his voice. 'The house is on fire. I'll go get Mark.'

The crackling *ma jiang* sound that had woken Scott was the floorboards of his bedroom readying to burst into flames. As he and Jennifer grabbed their clothes and threw them on, Scott stepped too close to the chimney where it passed up the inside wall. He leapt back with a howl. The wood had scorched his bare feet.

Jules ran out of the front door and thumped down the steps, two at a time. They took him right past our bedroom window.

'Mark! Your house is on fire! Get up, mate! Fast! Mark, for Christ's sake get up!' he shouted in his strong Australian accent.

My first reaction was perfectly natural.

I raised my head, turned to Joanna and said, 'Don't worry, they're just mucking about. Secchia's trying to get me back for a prank I played on him. Go back to sleep.' And I laid my head back down on the pillow.

As I shut my eyes I heard Jules crashing through the front door and up the stairs. Then he hammered so hard on the bedroom door I thought he was going to punch right through it.

'Mate, this is serious. No joke. I mean it. You better come up.' He disappeared. I heard him in the kitchen, crashing through the cupboard under the sink.

I sat up. I could hear shouts coming from the cottage. If this was a joke they were doing a damn good job of it.

Still cynical, I got dressed, found a torch and dozily walked up the steps.

Until that day I had never been in a house that was on fire. Like all disasters, natural and man-made, you never think it will happen to you, particularly not your own house. I was more surprised than worried.

I stepped though the door into complete chaos. The guys were running up and down the stairs with anything that could hold water: saucepans, buckets, kettles, plastic soda bottles with the tops cut off. It was splashing on the walls, down the steps, on to their legs. Water was pouring through the ceiling of the sitting-room. In the fireplace a soggy mess of blackened logs and ash was steaming in the grate.

I went up to Scott and Jennifer's room. The furthest wall was hidden by the smoke. They had kept the windows shut, as you should when a house is on fire. Jules had a wet handkerchief wrapped around his face and was kneeling on a wet towel on the floor, hacking at the boards with a pair of garden shears. His white singlet was streaked with soot. Scott and Mark were stepping round him and pouring water down the side of the chimney-breast where Jules had cut a small opening in the floor boards. Smoke was pouring out of it.

Jules is built like an athlete, not an ounce of fat on his body. His brown biceps did not quiver as he drove the twin blades into the floor and wrenched at the planks. But the new floor was holding firm. He raised the blades high above his head and brought them down with all his strength. They bent at a right angle to their handles.

'Mate, you got an axe? This ain't good enough.' He looked up, hot but calm, holding the broken shears.

'Fraid not' I replied.

'How about rocks from outside?' It was Jozef, who had been watching and thinking.

'Bloody good idea, mate!' And Jules shouted downstairs, 'Somebody get some rocks. Big ones!'

101

Scott appeared with a small boulder from the broken down wall that ran alongside the garden. 'How about this one?' he asked.

'Great,' said Jules. He stood up and heaved it over his head. 'Stand back!' he shouted and dropped it at his feet. The stone bounced. We leapt out of its way. But it had smashed a hole in the floor.

'Water!' Jules screamed and Secchia appeared on cue with the biggest saucepan. The contents disappeared into the hole and a cloud of steam came straight back.

'Shit, that's hot,' Jules said.

Taking turns with the rock and the mangled shears we dug up the floor, starting by the chimney-piece and working back towards the door on the opposite side of the room. The rafters underneath were black and cracked. The fire had followed the channels between them towards the landing outside the room. If it had made it, or enough air had met it halfway, the floor would have gone up in a flash. The traces of burning stopped just inside the bedroom door.

Jules looked at Scott. 'Mate, you don't know how close you were to being kebabbed.' We laughed at the joke. Scott had Lebanese ancestors.

Brent pointed out that if Scott hadn't gone to bed early then the fire would probably have been beyond control before we found it. It had been a damn close thing, not least for Scott and Jennifer.

Once the splintered and stoved in floor was soaked and the smoke had turned to steam we slowed down. Then someone pointed at the stone wall to the right-hand side of the chimney-piece.

'Guys, it ain't over yet. Look. The wall is on fire.'

We stared at it. How can a stone wall burn?

A steady stream of smoke was pulsing out from the cracks in the mortar. Someone ran downstairs to double-check there was no trace of fire below in the sitting-room. It was fine.

'Here we go then,' said Jules, and he stuck the bent shears into the wall between two large stones. We wrenched and heaved and pulled one of them out. It crashed to the floor. Then we pulled out another, and another. Every time a stone came out we poured water into the widening hole. But the wall kept smoking.

'Must be some wood in there somewhere,' I thought aloud. 'Maybe when they built the house sixty years ago. Must have used small bits of timber to prop up the masonry.'

The hole was getting so big I began to worry we were going to bring the wall down. 'That's enough!' I shouted, and we kept pouring water into the rubble.

A sleepy Pan Guang Lin turned up, roused from his bed by my irate phone call and desperate appeals to bring an axe. He had brought two crowbars, too late.

Joanna was with him and once she'd had her say we took turns to tell him what we thought of his chimney-building skills. He sat on the dishevelled bed and looked at the matchsticks we had made of the brand new floor that he had so cleverly stained to look old and authentic. He was silent while we shouted at him.

'But some sparks must have gone up the chimney and set fire to it,' he protested eventually. 'You were having too big a fire. That's what did it!'

As far as I knew only old chimneys that have not been cleaned catch fire. Brand new chimneys do not catch fire unless there is a major fault in their construction, like a hole, or several holes, in this case right next to a wooden floor. I explained my theory to Pan, with liberal use of the Chinese word for 'bloody'.

As the smoke died away and we were certain the danger had passed, we relented. I was beginning to feel guilty. I liked Pan.

While we had been upstairs, Joanna and some of the boys had moved the furniture from the sitting-room out into the garden. The ceiling was dripping with water.

I patted Pan on the shoulder. 'Come on, Mr Pan. Let's have a beer.'

Everyone grabbed a can, stepped outside and slumped on to a chair or the sofa. Pan stood in the doorway looking around the soaked sitting-room. I stared at our smoldering dream.

Mark Secchia spoke first. 'If anyone says that was the hottest housewarming they ever went to . . .'

Jules flicked his beer at Mark's head and got up to punch him. They tangled on the sofa and all of us laughed with relief.

Pan Guang Lin was back at work the next day. The bench saw and lathes were set up again underneath the trees, piles of cement and sand reappeared beside the garden wall and his men squared off our crude demolition job on the bedroom floor.

Two weeks later Joanna and I returned to find the house looking exactly as it had before the fire. I was impressed. Pan explained that he had sealed up the inside of the chimney. There was no chance of another spark escaping through a crack, which he now agreed was how the fire had started.

I had already laid a fire in the hearth. Not a big one, but I picked out some damp wood to go on top of the kindling.

It would smoke nicely. Pan watched me, his face confident. I lit the newspaper and stood back.

'Let's see, shall we?' I asked Pan. We waited for the smoke to rise up the chimney, then walked upstairs.

The late afternoon sun was shining through the back window of the bedroom, its rays slanted at a perfect angle to pick out the fine dust that stirred from the floor under our feet. It also cut beautiful beams through the wisps of smoke, growing thicker as we watched, that started to stream out of a crack in the new plastering on the chimney breast. The hole was high up, right beside a wooden rafter, an ideal place for another fire to start.

Pan did not say a thing. He didn't have to.

We walked back down the stairs. Smoke was coming out of them and rolling downwards like a carpet. I guided Mr Pan outside to sit on the garden wall. He offered me a cigarette. I took out my own.

'You'll have to do it again I'm afraid, Mr Pan.'

'I don't understand,' he replied. 'We fixed it.'

We sat in silence for a few moments. Then he perked up. 'I guess we could put a metal tube down the chimney. But that will cost you. It wasn't in the original estimate.'

I remembered I had not paid his final bill. I remembered something else too.

'Would you come with me, Mr Pan?'

I stood up and walked towards the far side of some scrub between the house and the woods. Pan followed.

Just inside the pine trees I stopped and waited for Pan to stand beside me.

'See that?' I asked, keeping my voice cheerful. 'Wasn't that in the estimate too?' I pointed to the slope below.

It was a landslide of smashed toilet bowls, white kitchen tiles, carpeting, underlay, a bathroom sink, metal piping, electric wires, empty cement bags, paint cans . . . the entire previous contents of the two houses apart from the timber, plus builders' rubbish. It had been hidden just out of sight.

'Now if I remember rightly, Mr Pan, I am due to pay a large amount of money for the removal of this rubbish.' I knew it would never be taken away, but it gave me some ammunition for my argument about the chimney.

'So you will fix the chimney properly and you will take away this rubbish.' I had to make a pretence of insisting. 'And then we will add it all up and settle your bill. OK?'

Pan gripped his chin and looked at the debris. His hand dropped and he made as if to say something, then thought better of it. 'OK.'

He walked down the steps to the front of the house.

I went back into the big house and told Joanna how I had confronted Pan with the evidence of the rubbish. I had avoided mentioning it until then, for Pan's sake. She fumed for a while, then relaxed. It would be a useful bargaining tool.

Isabel was playing with some wooden toys on the low table in front of us. She had reached the 'cruising' stage and was pushing herself around the edge of the table, approaching the toys from different angles. The new-found mobility was clearly delighting her.

I lit a small fire in the grate. At least we still had a good fireplace in this house, and a chimney that did not leak. After the fire in the cottage we had checked it thoroughly, right up into the attic. It was sound.

I sat back on the sofa as the kindling caught and bloomed. We kept a close eye on Isabel. By evening we would have a solid fire to sit beside while we watched a DVD, once we had put our daughter to bed. Perhaps a bottle of wine...

And then the smoke started billowing into the room. It was pouring out of the fireplace in a solid rush. Joanna picked up Isabel and ran outside. I dropped to the floor and crawled up to the grate, as close as I could without scorching my hair, and looked up the chimney.

'The stupid bastard!' I coughed. 'He's blocked the chimney!' I lunged for the windows and yanked them open. Thank God I had not put any logs on top of the kindling. The fire went out as quickly as it had flared up.

I called Pan immediately. He was turning into my mountain nemesis.

'Mr Pan, what have you done with the fireplace in our other house?'

'I fixed it too. I put a baffle across the bottom so no sparks could go up the chimney and start a fire like in the cottage,' he explained as if it was the obvious thing to have done.

'But Mr Pan, there was nothing wrong with it! It was working just fine. And blocking it won't stop sparks going up anyway! It's holes in the chimney that are your problem, as you just agreed. And unbelievable as it might sound, judging from your workmanship, there are no holes in this chimney.' The words were out of my mouth before I could stop myself.

'Well what do you want me to do?' he asked, as if I was the one trying his patience, not the other way round.

'Come and unblock it, please, as soon as you can!' I hung up.

Back in Shanghai the next day, I did what I should have done months before. I Googled 'how to build a chimney'.

What I found was a revelation. I learnt about fireproof bricks, heat-resistant mortar, flues, draught-excluders, smoke boxes, dampers and the physics of airflow through a house.

But my new knowledge was too little too late. Pan's idea of chimney construction was to build a brick tube up through a house and stick a concrete slab on the top to keep the rain out. We had two straight-sided vertical tunnels. We were lucky they drew any smoke up at all.

We resigned ourselves to having small fires in our big house – the baffle had been taken out but the jagged edges that remained made the chimney temperamental at best – and opening the windows when we did, or else we invaded the peace and solitude we promised our friends when they came to stay in the cottage. Pan had inserted the metal tube so that chimney now worked a treat.

It did not take long for word about our Moganshan retreat to spread. Over the months of the following summer a stream of friends trooped out to see us. They brought parents on trips from home, children, maids and drivers, and more friends, who went back to Shanghai to tell all their friends. We squeezed them all in and put up the overflow in one of the guest houses nearby. Lao Han was happy to take in the extras.

He and his wife kept the houses clean and tidy, pottered in the garden, grew their own vegetables in the flower beds, and once or twice accommodated their own overflow in our houses. We were not happy when we found out about it but there was no point creating a fuss.

Whenever Joanna, Isabel and I arrived in Moganshan, often after dark and tired from the four-hour trip by train and taxi, Han Aiyi got out of bed and came to meet us at the bottom of the two hundred steps. She insisted on carrying her own weight in bags up to the houses. I argued fiercely with her, more because I enjoyed the physical exercise of lugging stuff up myself than out of kindness. The work made arriving at the house more of an adventure and shocked my body awake from its city sloth. We brought the supplies we needed for the weekend and usually yet another load of clothes or superfluous clutter from our apartment in Shanghai. The kitsch I had received over the years from business acquaintances included brass sailing ships, miniature terracotta warriors, statuettes of fishermen poets, scrolls of poetry with fish swimming up the edges and more miniature teapots than you could shake a kettle at. They all went to Moganshan; the worst, or best, depending how you looked at them, into the guest cottage.

Once we had turned on the electricity, the water, the water pump and Han Aiyi had told us what she had done for us over the past fortnight, she would sit and play with Isabel for a few minutes and then slip away into the darkness, walking down the pitch black steps without a torch.

The next morning we would find a small pile of fresh vegetables on the doorstep, left by Han Aiyi at dawn.

Our visits grew less frequent as winter closed in. The houses, which had been cool in the summer, were turning into fridges. We bought a couple of electric radiators and shipped boxes of spare winter clothes up the mountain.

I tried to chisel flat the rough edges of the chimney in the main house where Pan had removed his baffle. My research on the Internet had told me that chimneys worked best with smooth sides. Then I experimented at making a smoke box by jamming bricks up the flue. I raised the grate and put large stones beside it, anything I could think of to make the fireplace draw better. We needed it now.

Nothing worked. Occasionally the wind blew in our favour and sucked the smoke up. Then it might change direction or die away and suddenly the cosy sitting-room filled from the top down. We could only open the windows and huddle closer to the fire, our backs cold, our feet warm, as if we were camping.

Joanna had the brilliant idea to buy electric blankets, a comfort I had always associated with grandparents' bedrooms. I soon changed my mind about them. Jumping into a hot bed was a new and pleasant experience. It was also the most economic form of heating available in Moganshan. The heat was going nowhere but to us. The warm air produced by every other device we had so far – electric radiators, fan-heaters and fireplaces – soon disappeared through our un-insulated roof or was blown away by the winter wind that whistled through the ill-fitting windows and doors. Summer houses are definitely best for summer living.

In January the water froze in the pipes, which were mostly above ground, and the houses became uninhabitable for a family. No hot water, no running water at all.

Pretending to Joanna that I needed to check up on things, I made a couple of solo trips during the depths of winter. For me Moganshan was not just a summer weekend retreat. It was a desperately necessary escape from Shanghai.

If they knew I was coming, the Hans filled buckets with water from the spring in our garden – which never froze – and left them in the kitchen. By the time I arrived there was usually a sheet of ice on them. On one occasion it had formed slabs so thick I could stack one bucket on top of the other.

110

But domestic life was possible for a couple of days. I relished splashing my face with the icy water in the mornings and enjoyed the logistical challenges. When I reappeared in Shanghai Joanna told me I looked and smelt as if I had been living in a tent.

In winter the mountain was almost deserted. Only the few permanent local residents, not even a couple of hundred people, lived there year round and most of the very old went down to the local town to stay with friends or relatives as soon as the annual freeze set in. Moganshan became a ghost town again.

One moonlit night in February I arrived in the village at about midnight. I had spent the day in a town called Yangzhou near Nanjing, not far to the north, where I had sat through a frustrating meeting from nine in the morning to three in the afternoon without a break. Six hours of repeating myself to a Chinese official who played a vital role in the survival of my business. Six hours of listening to him repeat himself.

He called me stubborn. I called him stupid, politely. He called me stupid, rudely. I called him stubborn. Round and round we went. But there was nothing else for it.

We were sitting in the lobby of a hotel beside a floor to ceiling glass wall overlooking a green lawn that was big enough for a cricket pitch. The official wanted shares in my company and I was happy to offer them to him. He deserved them for the support he had given me over the years. But as I was trying to explain that day, there was no hope of shares unless he came good on his promise to hook us up with a proper government partner under a proper agreement. Only then would my company and business have any value in the corporate sense. He wanted the non-existent shares

111

first. It was a classic China business situation: horse and cart, chicken and thousand-year-old egg. We were both right and we were both wrong.

I had known what I was letting myself in for that day. I had also known that the perfect antidote to the frustration would be a night on my own up in Moganshan. I had slipped a packet of bacon into my laptop case, hoping Joanna wouldn't notice.

Late that afternoon, faced with the choice of a bus back to Shanghai or on to Hangzhou, I made a timid call to Joanna on my mobile. I felt like a child making up an excuse for his parents so he could stay at his best friend's house.

'Honey, it really has been a horrible day, very difficult meeting, and I have just noticed there is a bus to Hangzhou from here. I am going to try and get to Moganshan for the night. I could use the peace and quiet.' The excuses tumbled out.

'I knew it,' she replied. 'I saw the bacon. I'm not stupid.'

That made me feel better. It was impossible to tell if she was angry or showing off.

The coach was almost empty. A man sitting beside the driver gossiped like they were old friends. Behind me three other men stretched themselves out and fell asleep. I read a book in the dim overhead light.

As the bus passed Huzhou on the highway, half an hour north of Moganshan, I made my request. I knew it was against the rules but would the driver mind dropping me at the exit for Moganshan?

He frowned and did not take his eyes off the road. I put in a few more words of persuasion.

After a long and awkward silence he said, 'Against the rules.'

I started pleading.

'OK,' he replied, looking at me at last. 'I might be able to make an exception. But you must ask all the passengers if they agree.' I smiled.

The passengers were asleep and it seemed unfair to wake them. I considered bluffing it but the driver was watching me in the mirror. I gently nudged the first man. He stirred and eyed me with curiosity.

'Do you mind awfully . . . ?' I started.

'No problem.' He cut me short. He had heard my conversation with the driver.

So had the other three. I walked back up the aisle in triumph. The driver was good as his word. He pulled on to the slip road and spoke to the toll gate attendant. Then he drove through, did a quick U-turn and the doors hissed open. I tried to tip him the price of a bowl of noodles but he would not hear of it. I was so grateful I forgot to pick up my book. I had reached the last chapter.

I stepped down and set off along the overpass to the main road. The first taxi stopped for me.

Half an hour later I was walking along the road on the ridge below our house. I was wearing a three-piece tweed suit, trilby and overcoat. I had wanted to show the Yangzhou official that he was dealing with a gentleman who was as good as his word. On my feet was a pair of old army drill shoes whose steel heel caps cracked on the hollow concrete road like a drill sergeant's on parade. The moon bathed the concrete road in a pale white glow. Other than the sound of my heavy heels there was complete silence. I felt like a ghost. If a local had seen me, I was sure and secretly hoped that they would leap out of their skin with fright. Here was a foreigner, dressed down to his button flies the way we used to sixty years ago, in Moganshan at midnight, walking along a deserted road under a full moon.

I desperately wanted someone to bump into me. I slowed my pace to increase the chances. I walked on past the two hundred steps to our house and up to the edge of the old tennis-courts. No one was about. I was alone. My freak show would be missed.

But by now my imagination had got the better of me. I stood stock still in the silence beside the tennis-courts and gave up trying to be the ghost of a China resident Englishman from the 1930s. I imagined I was one, alive and kicking.

In my fantasy the undergrowth that covered the old tennis-courts vanished in a blur of moonlight. The courts were flat as a pancake again, the chalk lines glowing faintly. To my left and above me on the hillside, in all the weeds and bamboo, the spectators' pagoda rebuilt itself. The thicker bamboo became the columns that supported it.

Of course there was no one playing tennis. It was the middle of the night after all. I had left a party at that large house with the broad terrace behind me. I could hear the strains of a Noel Coward song on the gramophone. I was a bachelor and I thought I had caught the eye of the daughter of a certain Colonel Hayley-Bell, who was there on her own. The rest of the crowd I was quite familiar with. We saw each other regularly in Shanghai.

We had talked politics; what would Japan's next move in North China be, did they plan to interfere in Shanghai, would the new Chinese Nationalist government last for long? The chap from the British Consulate had gone on for

114

so long about the official position that a few of us had slipped out on to the terrace to gossip about new arrivals in Shanghai, including, quietly, the pretty young girl who was in the room behind us, Mary Hayley-Bell.

She almost caught us at it when she stepped outside herself for a breath of fresh air. That could have been embarrassing, but we neatly switched the conversation on to the upcoming party season. I do not think Mary noticed. She sat with us for a while and, like preening cockatoos, we had tried to amuse her with our witty remarks about Shanghai society.

I was a little drunk but I had been well behaved and all was good with the world. I was pleased with the impression I thought I'd made on Miss Hayley-Bell. How was I to know that a touring English actor called John Mills would turn up one day and play tennis with her on these very same tennis courts and then, one later day, marry her?

The house of my friend was around the corner, below the path. We were going deer hunting tomorrow . . .

I snapped out of it. It was getting cold. But for a brief moment I had been a young Englishman, walking to my bedroom in a villa across a bamboo-covered hillside on a chill Moganshan night in the 1930s, my path illuminated by the moon.

I let myself into the house and lit the fire, relieved that for once I did not have to worry about asphyxiating my family. I sat in front of it with a glass of whisky. The awful day of Chinese officialdom was completely forgotten. The questions of life were reduced to which leg to cross over the other. It was pure heaven, the innocent joy of life on Moganshan. The only thing missing was a jug of cream for my coffee in the morning. Milk would serve in its place.

Chapter Seven

Village Politics

The military officials seem friendly and determined to fulfil
their obligations. The people seem good natured and to
desire that their traffic with us may increasingly continue.
The glorious mountains with their attending exhilarating
climate and sparkling unboiled water ever abide.

North-China Daily News, 6 July 1900

China is a bureaucratic country. It has been throughout its
long history. Ancient China created civil servants – hence
our term mandarins – and Communist China has refined
bureaucracy into a black art, one reason why communism
has endured so long here. Chinese Communist bureaucracy
is in fact about as perfect, by which I mean confusing, as
bureaucracy can get. The catches run from 22 to infinity.

Bureaucracy extends even to a backwater like Moganshan,
and up to the top of the hill and our two isolated houses on
it. Official meddling is one side of life in China from which
there is no escape. Furthermore, Joanna and I are a unique
case and anything unique or different attracts official interest
like a city construction site pulls in peasant workers from
the countryside.

We are unique because we were the first individuals to rent a house in the village exclusively for our own use, and one of us is a foreigner. To complicate matters even further, we had three, possibly four, authorities to answer to, none of whom had clear precedence over the others. Our landlords were the People's Liberation Army, tenants in perpetuity of the Zhejiang Provincial Government, who in turn were represented by the Moganshan Administration Bureau. That's three of them. Yet everyone knows the mountain is actually run by the police, who do not get along with the Administration Bureau and have nothing to do with the army.

I have had plenty of experience dealing with Chinese bureaucrats. More than is healthy. Thanks to their regular visits to my Shanghai office I developed a paranoid fear of men and women in uniform – for they all wear uniforms. In taxis I had to stop myself from ducking if we passed a traffic cop. If I stood beside a uniform in the lift to my office when we were in a tower block in the early days, I would break into a cold sweat. The brown-suited Shanghai street sweepers gave me the jitters.

But experience has helped. I have conquered my fears and learnt how to deal with Chinese officials, and developed a straightforward procedure for keeping them happy in Moganshan.

Once we had settled into the houses, a weekend rarely went by without a visit from someone in uniform. They always came at an awkward moment: we would be sitting down to a meal with a group of guests, or I was busy cooking it, or we were enjoying a lie in or, most annoying of all, I could be sitting on the loo in our panelled bathroom, admiring the prospect down the long path – my favourite loo view –

when a couple of men in green uniforms and yellow epaulettes would appear at the end of the path. I would grab the curtain, yank it across the window, swear to myself, pull my trousers up and dash downstairs.

The police and the army in Moganshan are polite, no question, but on their house calls they do not exactly ring the bell and call you 'sir'. An obvious difference between them and police officers I have met elsewhere is the shouting. I am used to shouting from the army – I was in the Guards where we spent most of the time shouting at each other – but I was now very much a civilian and spending my weekends on the quietest mountaintop in China. So it did seem unnecessary.

They also expect your immediate attention. Excuses such as: 'I am just in the middle of cooking dinner/sleeping/having a bath' are useless. They will stand outside and shout some more until you open the door.

Whenever they appeared, there was a standard procedure to follow. Step number one was to invite them to sit at the table on the terrace and have a cup of tea. If they declined then I knew we were in for an easy time. If they accepted I prepared for step two, which was simple: shut up and listen. The policeman, army officer or Administration Bureau representative would then begin to talk, loudly.

During the ensuing lecture I took pains to show that I was hanging on every word. I laughed when they smiled, looked sombre when they turned serious. The most important thing was not to let my attention wander, or be seen to. It was also a good idea to interject whenever possible with contrite expressions such as 'I see,' 'Absolutely,' and 'Of course, I quite agree and understand.' One or two reasonably well-spaced, 'I am sorry but as a foreigner I never realized. Thank you so much for explaining this to me,' worked wonders if delivered with sincerity.

At step three the flow chart splits. Either I would have to read and then sign a piece of paper, or else hand over some cash. Sometimes both. This can be a major issue when you run a large business in Shanghai, but at the Moganshan level it was always best to sign and pay on the spot. What harm was there in promising to buy a fire extinguisher sometime in the next twelve months, or committing yourself to never knowingly invite spies and drug dealers into your house? Or set up a brothel for that matter? They were perfectly reasonable requests.

The pay offs were generally small too. After the hundreds of thousands I had paid out in Shanghai, who was I to quibble over a non-existent neighbourhood watch scheme at eighty US dollars a year?

In some cases the fees could be deferred indefinitely. It took practice to work out which ones. We still owe our landlords a couple of thousand yuan for the compulsory lightning conductors which they were going to install two years ago. That was a simple case of agreeing to pay *when* they were installed.

My preferred solution for getting through the bureaucratic maze was the signing method. It lets you get away with almost anything and it's the cheapest option too.

It was early on in my China career, as a student in mid-eighties Beijing, that I first picked up the trick. I had been formally thrown out of the Beijing Language Institute for not attending the mandatory number of lectures, fifty per cent of the total, during my first term there. 'Sign this promise to attend more lectures and we'll let you back in,' they said. So I signed. I was allowed back in.

The following term a student prank resulted in a summons to the Beijing Police Office Responsible for Foreigner Residents.

'Did you do it?' I was asked.

'No.'

'Sign here.'

I scrawled my signature. The policeman sighed with relief and put the piece of paper in his desk. I got away scot-free.

Another trick that foreigners take a while to get used to in China is this: you never, ever, volunteer to follow the rules. You wait for the rules to catch up with you. This works for a good reason: no one knows what the rules are.

I am showing my China age, because things have changed for the better over the eleven years that I have been living and doing business here, but the rule about no rules still applies if you are engaged in an activity that is remotely out of the ordinary, or you are the first to try something, which we were with Moganshan.

There were a lot of rules to do with safety, especially fire precautions. Considering the near burning down of the cottage they had a point, but they did labour it.

Captain Yang was the man in charge of fire safety for the Hangliao. Sitting across from me in a bamboo chair on our terrace, he would pat me on the knee as if to reassure me that the process would be painless, then thrust a couple of sheets of paper into my hands and ask me to sign them, immediately.

It is the first directive that I remember the most fondly.

After a general introduction along the lines of: 'The tenant agrees to voluntarily abide by the regulations of China and the People's Liberation Army and submit to the inspection and supervision of the relevant local departments governing hostelries,' which suddenly became specific with: 'and is forbidden to store in or near the property inflammable materials or chemicals,' I came to a major problem in paragraph 2.

'It is strictly forbidden, inside the property, to light fires or use fireplaces.'

'But Captain Yang, how are we going to heat the houses in winter if we can't have any fires? You know we installed fireplaces at great expense. They are our main source of heating.'

'Yes, but fires are dangerous. You know yourself how dangerous. Look what happened to House 25.'

'Captain Yang, we've had it fixed, three times no less. We have tested it. There is no risk any more.'

'Ah, that was indeed a one-off accident. But,' he came back with, 'do you know how fires start in chimneys?'

'No, Captain Yang, please tell me.' I had to give him some face.

'Rats,' he said. 'Rats get into the chimney and make nests, and then the nests dry out and catch fire.' I looked surprised. 'Birds too,' he added as an afterthought.

I had an idea. 'But surely, Captain Yang, the best way to stop rats and birds building nests in chimneys is to light fires regularly. Then they never get the chance to settle in.'

'Hm, well yes, you have a point there.' He looked rather disappointed. 'But whatever, you still can't have fires.'

I read aloud, slowly and deliberately, through the other restrictions. '"No smoking in bed and signs saying No

Smoking to be placed at the head of each bed." Captain Yang,'
I said, 'you know we are not a guesthouse.'

'Standard!' he snapped back.

Next. 'It is strictly forbidden to burn piles of leaves. They
must be disposed of in a rubbish bin.' Mrs Han broke that
rule on our behalf almost every week.

After the rules about the number and specifications of fire
extinguishers and lightning conductors required for each
house, and a strict reminder to unplug electrical appliances
when absent, came a more serious exhortation: 'No un-
authorized change to the use of the building as leased, no
yellow, gambling or drug-related activity, or smuggling,
counterfeiting, sale of fake goods or similar activity.' Yellow
is the Chinese for blue, as in pornography, sex for sale, etc.

There was more: 'If religious studies or other illegal
activities, especially Falun Gong-organized activity, is
discovered on the premises, the tenant must immediately
telephone the People's Liberation Army Hangzhou Rest and
Retirement Unit Moganshan Sub Unit.' The telephone
number was given in bold.

So no saying prayers before bedtime for Isabel then.

Captain Yang was getting impatient. I was tired from
deciphering the repetitive prose. I signed. He smiled and
patted me on the leg one last time.

'And no other illegal activities,' he said as he stood to leave.

I struggled to think of one not listed in the piece of paper
I had put my name to. I had renounced religion, registered
as a Chinese citizen and volunteered for the People's Liberation
Army. That pretty much covered it.

Signing meant I could enjoy the peace and quiet until the
next directive came down from on high, via the army chain

of command and finally to us, their tenants, which required a redrafting of the original with a minor alteration or addition. One month the fire safety instructions returned with a clause inserted about birth control, forbidding guests to have babies in our house unless they had permission and it was their first child. Then there was the strict reminder that we were responsible for the 'thought-education and right thinking' of our staff. I gave Mrs Han a lecture. But still she burnt the leaves.

Joanna's reaction to Moganshan bureaucracy surprised me. Once Captain Yang, or whoever had upset our weekend, had left she would fly in a rant about how she was Chinese and had her rights and how dare they push her around and ask for 'fees' for services that they would never provide.

Then I realized that it was precisely because she was Chinese that she took it so badly. For the first time in her life she was being treated like an outsider, in her own country. As a foreigner I was more than used to it. For me the bureaucracy in Moganshan was nothing compared to the nightmare of business life in Shanghai.

Besides, Moganshan was my refuge, my escape from all that. I had made a conscious and determined decision not to let the hassle get me down. I paid the fees, signed the regulations, and then I sat on the terrace with a glass of whisky to watch the mountain's evening shadow creep away from me across the Zhejiang Plain, back towards Shanghai, where my troubles could stay for the weekend.

We didn't let the edicts get in our way. Captain Yang interrupted me when I was chopping firewood. I signed and then went back to my pile of logs. He came to find me in the garden, walked past the blackened patch of last weekend's

123

bonfire, shook my hand and asked me to sign another round. He admired my new chainsaw on a shelf in my study.

But he never caught me smoking in bed.

My blatant disobedience of the rules and Captain Yang's polite blindness to it were given a sobering pause for thought in the mid-winter of our second year in Moganshan.

The Hans' house burnt down. Completely.

A young couple from Nanjing had been staying in my favourite room and lit a fire in the fireplace. Just as with our housewarming in the cottage, sparks had somehow escaped from the chimney, except there was no one in the attic room up above to notice the smoke. Lao Han was away in Hangzhou. Mrs Han was asleep at home a few hundred metres away. The honeymooners were alone in the house.

By the time they realized what was happening the roof was ablaze. It was too late. They had grabbed their possessions and ran for it. The house was burnt to the ground. When we next came up the mountain we found a blackened shell, the walls standing only a couple of feet high. It was a sad sight. In place of the house that reminded me of my family home in North Wales, the ruins brought to mind the castles there that I used to explore with my friends. The tops of the pine tress that surrounded the house had been burnt away, leaving tall black spikes.

The Hans were devastated. They had just renewed the lease, under their own name this time, and meant to turn the house into a proper guesthouse. They had already put down the first three years' rent with the Hangliao and were planning the renovations. I had spent some time giving Lao Han what I hoped were good ideas, with the foreign market foremost in mind.

When we bumped into Han Aiyi at the foot of the steps to our house, she burst into tears. She was a shadow of her tough little five foot self. Her shoulders slumped, her face was set in sadness and her eyes looked desperate, pitiful. They had lost everything. There is no such thing as fire insurance in Moganshan, nor house insurance.

Between sobs she told us the story. She was too heart-broken to be angry but it was obvious she wished the guests had tried to do something instead of just upping and running. We were careful not to remind her what a close call we'd had ourselves. Lao Han, when he dropped by later that day, was more outspoken. We sat outside on the terrace smoking cigarettes. He squarely blamed his guests for starting the fire and then doing nothing to stop it. He punched his legs as he described how frustrated he had been, stuck in Hangzhou. The fire was a full-scale calamity.

I asked him what would happen to the house now.

'Who knows?' he replied. 'We haven't got the money to rebuild it, and we can't use it. The Hangliao might ask us to pay for the damage even. But we have nothing left. All our money went on the rent. It's a big problem. The Administration Bureau is getting involved too. Maybe they'll try to take house back from the Hangliao. Who knows . . .' His voice trailed off.

I wondered if we could do anything to help.

I was just beginning to replenish the savings that had gone into our own houses. Maybe we could invest in the Hans' house. On an even playing field it would have made sense, a ripe opportunity to help build a guesthouse with style from the ground up. But there would be endless squabbles between the opposing factions who already had an interest in the

125

house, and the blame game for the fire was only just starting, so I'd only get caught in the crossfire. Rich and stupid foreigners are fair game in China, especially ones who try to be 'nice'.

Besides, we had our own problems. Soon after the Hans' fire I went up on my own again. Major Ma's replacement, a Major Wang, came up to the house for an introductory visit. He was alone and in uniform. I poured him a whisky and we sat on the terrace. He seemed quite the officer and gentleman. He also looked rather dour. We talked about whisky, which he was patently not enjoying, and we chatted vaguely about the army, Chinese and British. When the opportunity presented itself I dropped in my platitudes about enjoying life on the mountain, loving the houses and the care we were taking with them.

'Yes, there is a small matter we would like to discuss with you,' said Major Wang. 'Is your wife at home?'

'No, she is in Shanghai, I am afraid.' I replied. 'Anything I can help with?'

'No . . . No, just a small thing. But it would be better to talk to your wife about it. Nothing really.' And he rose to leave. 'Perhaps you could ask her to come down and see us, next time she is here,' he said over his shoulder.

A fortnight later Joanna reported to the Hangliao while I waited nervously at home and played with Isabel. She returned looking grim.

She came straight out with it. 'They want the houses back.'

I could not believe my ears. I knew this sort of thing happened in China. You heard stories of it everyday. And I knew we had taken a big risk, pouring every cent we had into our dream. Maybe later, in a few years perhaps or when we had to pay the next tranche of rent we could expect some problems, but now, before we had finished the first year of the contract? That was unfair.

A hard knot twisted in my stomach. 'What reason did they give?' I asked as calmly as I could.

My mind was desperately running through the possibilities. Was it something to do with the Hans' place burning down? The new Hangliao chief, Wang, was he sweeping out the Hangliao, stamping it with his authority? What about the other houses? A couple more just below has recently been restored from derelicts by local companies.

'Major Wang said there was a change of policy.' Joanna explained. She was doing a good job of keeping her voice matter-of-fact. 'So I asked what policy? And he said, economic policy.'

I had to laugh, bitterly. Joanna was still talking. 'They want them for their own use. Something about a senior officer who likes them.'

The Hangliao had recently brought some men up who had more stars on their collars than I was used to. 'Just looking around,' one of them had said cheerfully. My dread of Chinese uniforms was still with me. Who knew how many times they had been here when we weren't.

'There were nine of them, all in uniform,' she said. 'It was intimidating. I wish you had been there, but they insisted on just me. One or two of them were senior people from Hangzhou. I think they actually wanted to frighten me.'

I gave her a hug. 'And what did you say to them?'

'I got angry. Those bullies. I told them they had to do three things. One: show us a formal document which explained the 'change of policy'. Two: we had to agree the amount of money they must repay us and set a date for us to leave. Three: they pay us. Then we leave.'

'How much?'

'I told them we spent a million.' She brightened. 'That worried them. You should have seen their faces. And I made it clear that we wanted it back from them.'

My wife often made me nervous with her bold statements. This was one of them. Then I thought again. If this was the west, we probably could have claimed a significant sum for breach of contract, as well as a refund for our outlay, which was probably just over half a million. I let Joanna's exaggeration pass. Now was not the time to nit-pick.

'How did it end?'

'I screamed at them. Told them that there are laws in China now, that they can't do things like this, that we have a lawyer – you do have one don't you? – and that we weren't going to leave. Or if we did agree to leave they have to pay us a million renminbi, cash. And I made it clear that they can forget any bullshit about you being a foreigner.' Her face was colouring, her voice rising. 'I am Chinese and the houses are in my name and they can't do what they bloody well please. I have my rights!'

'Well done,' I said gently, praying that her temper had exhausted itself.

'Bastards,' she muttered. 'How dare they?'

We sat for a while, each of us lost in our own thoughts. Joanna was fuming about how insulting it all was. I sadly prepared myself for a premature end to our mountain idyll. I had been through enough ups and downs in my business life in China. The feeling of dread and bitter disappointment was familiar. You get over it.

But it was a damn shame. We were beginning to feel at home. We had enjoyed many good times and had plans for the houses, the garden, trips to make from the mountain, parties. The trees were turning green. It was mid-spring. In a few weeks the houses would again be the heat retreat they were designed as. Our first full season, and it was going to stop before it started.

Lao Han came by that evening. He had heard. He always heard. We asked his opinion.

'Don't worry,' he said once he had heard Joanna's story. 'They won't dare to actually kick you out. Too much trouble for them. Just take it easy with them, be patient,' I looked across at Joanna, 'and it'll all blow over.'

We tried to take it easy. Joanna cheered herself up with the idea that we might get back more money than we had put in. I resigned myself to another bad China day, if it was coming.

It didn't. A month later we had heard that we were to be allowed to stay in the houses after all. There was no second interview for Joanna, no formal announcement, and no hint of apology or regret for putting us on edge. Word was passed via Lao Han that they had changed their minds. Why they did we will never know. I like to think that it was Joanna's ferocity that put them off.

It took us many months to relax again. Whenever we arrived after a tiring journey from Shanghai and walked up the two hundred steps, I could not help worrying that we would find the locks changed or the lights on and a bunch of army officers and their girlfriends smoking foul-smelling cigarettes and playing *ma jiang* in our sitting-room. When the big house came into view from the end of the path, the relief on finding it was still ours almost hurt.

But our army landlords had not finished with us.

Major Wang took his responsibilities seriously. He didn't smile much and he didn't shout at all. And he certainly never poked me in the ribs like Major Ma. He wore a pained expression up and down the stairs to our house, which added yet more severity to our meetings. I later discovered he was suffering from cancer.

During his short tenure on Moganshan, before he was given a medical discharge, Major Wang developed an obsession with spies.

One weekend he summoned me for a chat. I asked if he would not prefer Joanna to go in my place, but Wang wanted me. I wondered if he was going to announce another change of heart about the houses, a new order from above. I went through my usual attack of nerves as I walked down the steps that hot summer morning. I felt like a schoolboy on his way to the headmaster's study. I couldn't help thinking how there is nothing like life in a country ruled with random strictness by temperamental officials to keep you young.

Major Wang was upstairs in the bare office. I almost put my feet together and saluted as I walked in. He invited me to sit at the table. Captain Yang appeared behind me and made some tea.

I muttered some small talk about how happy we were to continue to be tenants of the Hangliao. Wang stared at me with a blank look in his eyes. His mind was obviously more concerned with whatever important things he had to say in this meeting.

130

'Yes, we are happy that you should remain in the houses,' he said. 'But there is something we need to talk about. Just a small matter.'

I braced myself for a big one.

'Your friends,' he said, looking even more serious than usual. 'We do not like it that you have so many friends coming to see you.' He paused to let the weight of his words sink in. I spent the time wondering if he could possibly mean this.

'Please explain, Major Wang.'

'Your friends are foreigners. It is not good that so many foreigners come here.' My evident confusion – I was utterly amazed, and trying hard not to look it – made him jump a few lines in his carefully prepared speech.

'Spies,' he spat the word out. Now I really did look dumbstruck, so he went into more detail. 'So many foreigners, some of them are likely to be spies.'

Spying on what? This was a holiday resort.

'It would be better if you did not have so many friends. People coming to stay. Of course,' he smiled, to reassure me, 'we don't think you are a spy. You are welcome to use the houses. But we really would prefer that you do not have your friends to stay.'

'Major Wang, I can assure you that none of the people, my friends, who come to my house are spies.' I was dying to tell him how when I was in the army the Intelligence Corps had serious concerns that I might have been a Chinese spy, and more recently how my Chinese government-backed rivals had spread the rumour that I was British spy. Even my business partner had once expressed doubts. If I had not got so bored with the stories I would have found them

131

amusing. But being asked to cut back on my social life because of an army officer's paranoia was going too far. I got serious myself.

There had recently been a well-publicized case of some senior PLA officers passing information to Taiwan, China's 'renegade province'. A state of all but undeclared war exists between the two 'territories', despite the massive investment of Taiwanese companies in mainland China. It is too long and complicated a problem to go into here. But in response to the shocking discovery of PLA officers spying for Taiwan, it was easy to imagine the orders and warnings flying down the chain of command, political commissars giving lectures on patriotism and the overreaction that can only happen in a politically motivated army. It was obvious that Major Wang had received such an order and it was his duty to pass on its import to me, the most likely provider of a safe house for spies in Moganshan.

'Major Wang, as you know yourself from the newspapers, the spies whom I think you are worried about were Chinese nationals, or at least ethnic Chinese, like Taiwanese, and as you have just said yourself, my guests are foreigners,' I used the term that clearly implied Caucasian. 'None of my guests are Chinese.' Not strictly true, but Major Wang seemed to think otherwise.

'Well,' he replied. 'I want all your foreigners to register at the police station and with us. Just to be sure. And keep the numbers down. If the same people come on a regular basis and we get to know them, that would be better.'

'What about if I have Chinese friends?' I had to ask.

'They do not need to register. They are Chinese.'

I did not think much of Major Wang's counter-espionage.

I thought the whole point of being a spy was to be as inconspicuous as possible – not, I hasten to add, that I knew anything about spying.

Suddenly an idea came into my head. Wang might be thinking about the radar station on the hilltop across from our house. It stood on the site of what was once the foreigners' favourite pagoda. The views must have been stunning. It was called Tashan, Pagoda Hill. At the highest point on the mountain, the radar was visible for miles around. You can't hide radar stations. I didn't know what it was there to track and I had never asked. I assume it had something to do with the military airfields near Hangzhou. (And they were hardly secret since they were next door to the old Hangzhou airport. The first time I flew into the city we descended over long lines of fighter jets.)

'Ah, Major Wang, I understand,' I said with an innocent smile. 'You are concerned about the radar station.'

I half-expected him to come out with: 'What radar station?'

He nodded, though it looked like he was trying not to.

'Please relax about that.' I thought I would try to cheer him up. 'When I walk past there with my 'friends', I always tell them to look the other way.' I laughed. He smiled, reluctantly.

At least I had got him off the subject for a moment. Our talk switched to the usual topics of open fires and smoking in bed. But Wang seemed distracted, keen to pass on his superiors' message. Somewhere in his desk there must have been a text he was referring to, a list of points which he was obliged to tell me. Once he'd done so, his duty would be done and I could go home and forget them and so could he. There was no paper to sign this time. There never is when it comes to spying.

After a couple of minutes of small talk he changed the subject again, abruptly. 'Actually, Mark,' he said, recovering his severity in a flash. 'Going back to what you said a minute ago, it is quite appropriate. I would appreciate it if you could indeed tell your friends not to look at the radar station.' He had been thinking about it the whole time we had been talking about something else.

I almost choked. The idea was ridiculous. I imagined myself briefing friends not to look up before we went on a walk.

Communism has a remarkable capacity for self-delusion. Making radar stations disappear by power of suggestion was beyond me. But what the hell.

Radar station? What radar station?

Chapter Eight

History Repeats Itself

A NEW SUMMER RESORT

In the Huchou prefecture, North Chekiang, is the Mohkönsan,
a range or cluster of mountains which will no doubt attract
an increasing number of seekers for summer houses.

The first ever mention of Moganshan in the *North-*
China Daily News, 20 July 1898

Sir John Mills, British film and stage icon of the 1940s and
50s, really did meet his wife in Moganshan. As a young
jobbing actor in 1930 he toured the Far East with a theatre
company called 'The Quaints'. Colonel Francis Hayley-Bell
of the Macao Commission of Chinese Maritime Customs –
Mills's second father-in-law to be precise – owned a large
summer house on the mountain.

John and Mary might of course have met in Shanghai, or
somewhere else in China, and then got to know each other
at her father's holiday house. But I prefer to think of their
first meeting taking place fifty metres below my study, on
those weed-infested tennis-courts, and that's the story I tell
any British visitor of the right age, and film buffs.

I am a poor historian. But I am trying to be a better one.

I am asked so many questions by so many visitors that I can't help sounding like one.

My main source is the Shanghai Library archives, a collection of every newspaper, magazine and directory printed in Shanghai from 1850 to 1950. The newspaper of record is the *North-China Daily News* and its weekly summary, the *North-China Herald*. They were founded in 1850 by a Mr Henry Shearman, auctioneer, and covered every aspect of life in the foreign concessions of the city from shipping and passenger lists, share prices and court gazettes, to women's fashion, sport, and where to go for the summer holidays. The archives contain an almost complete collection of the *Daily News*, in priceless leather-bound, battered volumes.

Despite its improvised *pinyin*, the romanization system for Chinese characters which was not standardized for another sixty years – hence Mohkönshan and Mokanshan – its ponderous prose and patronizing attitude to 'the Chinese', all typical for its day, the *Daily News* is a reliable and comprehensive source. I concentrated my search on the summer issues of the paper, where there were plenty of mentions.

My main disappointment was that Moganshan received far less coverage in the *Daily News* than Kuling, a much grander hill station established only a year earlier, in 1897. In one example where the two places appeared on the same page of the *News*, Kuling was given thirty column inches, Moganshan a mere five. Perhaps that's why the first mention of Moganshan highlighted the place from the start as 'a suitable resort for persons of moderate means'.

I followed up on my research in Moganshan itself, asking persistent questions of people like Lao Han, Mr Ge and our neighbours, but the communal memory was dim and one-sided. The locals who witnessed the old days are the aged children of the carpenters, masons, housemaids and chair porters who worked for the foreigners before 1949. That means they had to be at least seventy-five years old, preferably older, to have been aware of what was going on. When I asked them who lived where and when and how and in what kind of style, I always heard the same disarmingly frank answer: 'Oh yes, lots of foreigners in those days. Very lively, it was.' Pause for eyes to look into middle distance. Then: 'All gone now.'

I did have one remarkable stroke of luck however. On a Saturday morning I was in the estate management department of the Administration Bureau. It was a courtesy call. I was dropping by for a cup of tea and to give some face, as you do in China to officials who have a vague influence over your life. Mr Shen, the man I was giving it to, had recently hiked up to our house to show me a faded photocopy of an old photograph of some Chinese servants with long Manchu pigtails outside a Moganshan villa. He thought I might be interested and I was. The hairstyles clearly date the shot as pre-1911, the first year of the Republican period, when everyone cut their hair as a sign of progress. He had told me the original photograph was in his office. The real reason I was there drinking tea and being polite was to ask if I could see it.

Mr Shen pulled a buff-coloured file out of a cupboard and handed it over.

'It's in there somewhere,' he said, and laid it on the desk.

I opened the file, and immediately forgot about the photograph. At the top were recently dated – within the last fifty years – photocopies of property deeds and exchange contracts, handwritten in beautiful Chinese calligraphy. What I came across underneath them made my heart skip a beat. Here were documents in English, and they were all original: letters, deeds, architects' notes, sketches of gardens, pencilled memos from lawyers to purchasers. Every single word was perfectly legible, written in a beautifully cursive and pain-stakingly measured hand that flowed across the page like a careful chain of thought.

The photograph was paper-clipped to one of the letters. It was a snapshot, two inches by three and a bit, and was badly creased as if it had been kept in a wallet. I studied it briefly but other than an everyday image of servants pottering outside a house there was nothing of historical interest.

Besides, I was far more interested in the documents by now. I was looking at undiscovered primary source material, every historian's dream.

The house where the photograph had been taken and whose file I was reading is stuck on its own in the woods round the back of the mountain. It is unusually isolated, even for Moganshan, and one of my favourite places. A hidden path leads to it from behind the boiler house of the White Cloud Hotel. You have to duck under a thick pipe that runs to another outhouse and then climb through the hotel's rubbish tip before the stone walkway appears. The building is a ruin, hemmed in by untended trees and surrounded by chest-high weeds. I have heard talk of poisonous snakes and also how a young boy, who would have grown up to be brother-in-law to Mr Ge, had died there in the fifties. He was playing in the woods, fell off a wall and broke his neck. It is a beautiful place. It is also easy to imagine it being haunted.

I unfolded the blueprints of the house and its grounds. The drawings were more of a rough sketch, but still clear. They showed a terraced garden above the house, a swimming pool below and to the right, and a small guest annexe. I made a note to look for ruins of the annexe and the hole where the swimming-pool had been next time I went round there. The small estate had belonged to a Victor Grosse, the only Russian to own a villa in Moganshan.

This prompted a memory from the Shanghai archives. I looked up the jottings I had made in my notebook.

In 1922, on 27 August, Miss Elizabeth Grosse, eldest daughter of Mr and Mrs Victor Grosse, at the 'old church' in Moganshan married a Mr Trautschold, Russian Consul General in Harbin. Victor Grosse, it was noted, had previously served as Russian Consul General in Shanghai and was now the assistant commissioner for Russian affairs.

After the wedding ceremony: 'bride and groom were carried away on mountain chairs gaily decorated for the occasion, followed by the wedding party along the narrow paths on the ridge towards the northern slope of Mokanshan, where surrounded by a lofty bamboo grove stands Villa Victorella, the property of the bride's parents. There on a terrace overlooking a magnificent panorama of the northern valley and the surrounding bamboo clad hills a reception was held. At this beautiful spot the newly married couple intend to spend part of their honeymoon.'

So it really had been a beautiful spot.

I asked Mr Shen if he had any more files like this one.

By now some other people had come into the small office and were lingering with no apparent purpose. General Manager Li had dropped by to drink tea and smoke. He was sunk low in a well worn armchair against the wall. Mr Shen's deputy, Mr Fang, was slouched behind his desk, also drinking tea. General Manager Li tossed cigarettes like sweets up on to Fang's desk every few minutes. Mr Shen seemed not to have heard my question, so I repeated it.

'Department Chief Shen, do you have more of these?' I held up the folder. 'I would love to see them if you do.'

Mr Shen remained silent. Fang however spoke up. 'Yes,' he said, and waved his hand at the cupboard behind his back. 'They are in here.'

My pulse quickened again. 'Um, is there any chance that I could have a look, please Mr Fang? I'd love to find out about the original foreigners who came up here. My friends are always asking me questions about them.'

Mr Shen spoke. He was, after all, the man in charge. I deferred my attention to him.

'I hear you were in the army, Mark,' he said.

'Er, yes I was.'

'Which one?'

'The British one.'

'Ah, not the American one?'

'No.' I wondered where the conversation was leading.

'I was in the forces too,' Mr Shen said.

He went into detail about his service career. He was in the navy at a base in Zhejiang, on coastal patrol vessels. For several minutes we swapped stories of pay and conditions, uniforms, food, insignificant and meaningless ex-serviceman chit-chat. At last there was a pause and I again asked about the files.

'And how old is your daughter?' Mr Shen yet again seemed not to have heard my question.

So we talked children. Where did Isabel go to school, what language did she speak at home, what did she eat and so on. Mr Shen had a nephew who was studying in the United Kingdom at a college in Birmingham that I had never heard of. I praised it to the skies. Then we came back to children in general.

'The trouble with our children,' Mr Shen said, 'is that they have six parents.' He held up one hand with the thumb and little finger extended, the Chinese signal for six. He was referring to the one child policy, and an unintended result of it, two parents and four grandparents looking after and spoiling every single child. Off we went on the one child policy.

I was not going to get a look at the files. By now everyone in the room was joining in the conversation. I threw a last look at the closed cupboard door, waited for an appropriate opportunity, and stood to leave.

'Come by and drink tea any time,' said Mr Shen as he showed me to the door, his hand on my arm. 'See you soon. Bye.'

I walked slowly up the hill to our house, wondering what I had done wrong in Shen's office. As I stepped through my front door, I was surprised to find him waiting for me. He must have sprinted up by another route.

'Mark,' he pulled me in by the arm. 'I am sorry about that.' I looked perplexed. 'But you see,' he was talking rapidly, only a little out of breath, 'I have to be careful with those files and there were too many people in the office. I cannot show them to anyone willy-nilly.'

'Why not, Mr Shen?' I had to ask.

'It's like this,' Shen explained. 'You see, every year we get at least one person coming to the Administration Bureau asking for their family's old house back. It is very difficult. You know the whole village is owned by the provincial government. These people give us no end of trouble.'

'Surely not foreigners?' I asked.

'No. Chinese,' he replied.

Not a few Chinese, politically-incorrectly referred to back in the day by the *Daily News* as 'a better class of Chinese', had bought property and built houses on the mountain in the late 1920s and 30s. I guessed it was their 'better class' descendants to whom Shen was referring. They would more than likely be Taiwanese or Hong Kong Chinese today, possibly American, and from old time Chinese Nationalist families.

'I see,' I said. 'But Mr Shen, I am only trying to clear up a few questions of my own. And besides, I am more interested in the foreigners who were here. I doubt they would turn up and demand their property back.'

Shen did look doubtful.

'Tell you what,' he said. 'I'll give you a call when no one is in the office, and you can come down then. I'll get out the files that have English correspondence in them. You can go through them, take notes, find the answers to your questions. Just keep quiet about it.' And then he left.

So, based on the Shanghai archives, the letters and papers from Mr Shen's cupboard that I was allowed to glance over, some rusty local memories, and a generous helping of hypothesis, I pieced together a working history of Moganshan – or one that works for the majority of our curious visitors at least.

The first foreigners to come to China in any significant

142

numbers, from around 1850 onwards, can roughly be divided into two categories: missionaries and drug dealers. The former spread the word of God, inviting the Chinese to believe it and thereby find salvation from their worldly cares. The latter sold them the more direct route.

They were both here thanks to China's defeat in the Opium Wars, so-called because Britain and the other great powers of the day had run out of hard cash to pay for all the tea we were importing from China, so we traded Indian opium for it instead. When the Qing Imperial government protested, the British Navy blew some Chinese coastal defences to smithereens and then invited the Emperor to sign away control of a selection of ports under what have been known to the Chinese ever since, quite rightly, as the 'Unfair Treaties'. And the prime commodity we shipped into them thereafter was, of course, opium. The treaties also stipulated that we could import the Christian faith.

The foreigners' key bridgehead into China was Shanghai, at the mouth of the Yangzi River. The word they used for their status was 'extraterritoriality', shortened for convenience to 'extrality'.

With profits from the drug trade the uninvited foreign guests built the majestic Bund, Shanghai's picturesque waterfront, a race course, greyhound stadium and suburbs with tree-lined avenues. They turned farmland into parkland, dredged the city's Huangpu River for their cargo ships and navies and lived lives completely removed from the swarming 'Chinese' city of Shanghai that their own eclipsed and encircled. In other words, they did as they pleased.

Meanwhile, the missionaries disappeared in the hinterland to remote villages, major cities and small townships in between. The American Presbyterians (South) raced the American Baptists (North) like Klondike gold prospectors to bring the word of God to Chinese peasants who could not read any words at all. As one Nathaniel Peffer, wrote in the *Daily News* in 1924: 'young men and women went out to redeem the heathen. Their faith was simple, their beliefs were untroubled by doubt, their minds virgin of anything resembling an awareness of comparative religion, their experience in life and their knowledge of the world even more limited . . . They 'brought the Word' unto 'them that sit in darkness' and on the brink of damnation.' They also fed them. Chinese converts were commonly known as 'Rice Christians'.

Shanghai had one major drawback however, one it shared with the Yangzi River valley, mid-China's main artery for trade and God's highway to the heathen masses. (The missionaries ran up and down it like it was Jacob's Ladder.) The drawback was the climate. It was abominable, and still is. Winters are bone-chillingly damp, springs permanently soggy and summers unbearably hot. The only tolerable season is autumn.

In those days before air conditioning, summers were lethal, potentially life-threatening. The crowded city of Shanghai and the mud bowl of the Yangzi valley acted like a Petri dish for tropical and contagious diseases. Malaria, typhoid, cholera and dysentery were the main killers. Mere heat stroke could knock off a grown man within a day. Less life-threatening but most unpleasant were heat rash, scrofula and common or garden eczema. Missionaries seemed particularly susceptible to 'nervous exhaustion'.

The late summer issues of the *North-China Daily News*

published lists of the season's infection and death rates like football results. On 30 August 1899 for example, for Shanghai: Small Pox 1, Cholera nil. Typhoid Fever 6, Typhus Fever nil. Dysentery 20, Diphtheria nil. Measles 25, Scarlet Fever nil. Whooping Cough 27, Influenza nil. Tuberculosis 5, Malaria 32. Lobar Pneumonia nil, Infantile Diarrhoea 13. Total deaths in foreign community, 10. Not a bad month, for the foreigners at least. The disease and death rates for the Chinese population were not given.

Like Google pop-ups, scattered through the summer pages of the newspaper were advertisements for 'Chapoteaut's Posphoglycerate of Lime, for nervous exhaustion' and 'Clark's Blood Mixture, for scrofula, scurvy, eczema', and etcetera. Maintaining one's health was a major preoccupation, and the health of one's vulnerable children was of tantamount importance.

Writing to the editor of the *Daily News* from Hankou on the Yangzi in 1896, a missionary complained for a long paragraph of the insufferable heat. He ends on a plaintive note: 'Both our children were stricken with fever; they could neither eat nor sleep in such an atmosphere, but wailed on incessantly, getting feebler and thinner day by day; till, looking on their shrinking and pinched faces, the Doctor said: "If you do not take these children away they will die."'

And die they did, not those ones as it turns out, but many like them.

When Shanghai approached boiling point in July the readers of the *North-China Daily News* took the only option open. They left. Women and children went first, packing up household equipment and servants and decamping to Yantai in northern China, then known as Chefoo, or making a short voyage across the Sea of Japan to the seaside towns of Kobe, Osaka and Yokohama. The husbands stuck it out a while longer until they too reached the point where 'the burden laid upon us has often been heavier than we could comfortably bear . . . The Shanghailander is determined to get away from the Settlement if he can and longs for Chefoo sands or the hills of Japan as eagerly as the cockney craves the shrimps and the Ethiopian serenaders of Margate.'

Day-to-day business was left in the hands of the newly arrived junior clerks and Chinese compradors.

The annual exodus became such a regular event that the *North-China Daily News* could run the same content year after year, like that quote about Ethiopians and Margate. It was reprinted as a spoof in August 1898, word for word, from an edition thirty years earlier.

Decamping every July to northern China and Japan was a major and expensive undertaking, not only for Shanghailanders but also and especially for the isolated missionaries. First they had to get their families to the coast, a journey involving long trips by barge and houseboat down the Yangzi River and canals to Shanghai. Only then could they board a coastal steamer for the resorts. What they needed was a cool hill station, something like Simla in India.

In 1895 they found one at Lushan, in Jiangxi Province. They renamed it Kuling, a deliberate and clumsy pun.

While it was ideal in many respects – high altitude broad plateau, unoccupied except for a few monks who were easily moved on, convenient for Yangzi River travel – Kuling still had two disadvantages. It was a hot and uncomfortable three-day river journey from Shanghai, the main source of summer vacationers and potential paying guests for the missionary house owners, and secondly, which only goes to show how desperately such a heat retreat was needed, it was quickly overcrowded. Every single building lot was sold within its first few months of existence.

There was one more problem that reared its ugly head right from the start of Kuling's development. That was the awkward relationship between the missionaries and the drug dealers. For obvious reasons, they did not get on very well, despite valiant and polite attempts. As the *Daily News* reported: 'The delightful quiet of the off season has set in. The spiritual peers who sit during the summer season have contrived to get a leg into the winter community's affairs by appointing a moiety of the membership of the newly instituted Church Interim Committee. It has been meekly suggested that they have no right to take any interest in off season affairs at all.'

As well as having more time on their hands and being based closer to the potential hill stations, the missionaries benefited from another unbeatable advantage over the laity. A clause in the terms of the Unfair Treaties stipulated that the only foreigners who could own land outside of the concessions and treaty ports were the missionary societies. So every foreign businessman had to go through them. That not only gave the men of God first choice, it also allowed them to indulge in a little property speculation of their own to supplement their meagre stipends. Hence the adage: 'The missionaries came to China to do good. And they did very well.'

Immediately Kuling had been overrun and 'spoilt', like modern-day backpackers the China-based foreign community set off on the hunt for the next undiscovered hideaway. They also hoped to find it closer to Shanghai.

It is probable that the very first foreign visitors to Moganshan's lower slopes came from Hangzhou, half a day's journey to the south. Or maybe they dropped down from Huzhou, equidistant to the north. Both cities, one big, one medium, were bases for the 'young men and women [who] went out to redeem the heathen'. Perhaps they noticed the mountain from the canal that connected the two cities. Cross-country travel was always by boat and Moganshan would have been clearly visible from the waterway. I imagine a small group of commuting clergyman gazing into the distance from the deck of a houseboat, tugging at their dog collars on a hot clear day and chancing to see the green-coated hill, so near yet so far and so high that its summit must surely be cooled by a fresh breeze.

The first appearance of Mokanshan in the *Daily News* also mentions how 'missionaries of the hardier type have rented rooms in Chinese houses about halfway up the south eastern slopes, at intervals, during the past eleven years.'

That would be them I guess.

The report goes on to describe the local houses, however, as: 'in no sense desirable for long residence, as they are smoky, dirty, poorly ventilated upstairs, and below', the Chinese 'crowd all day and gossip all night'.

So the missionaries explored the deserted mountaintop above them and decided to build their own village. The attractions included fresh spring water, easy access from Shanghai – compared to Kuling – and, as the *Daily News* pompously put it: 'arrangements now being made for minimizing expenses'. In other words: a poor man's Kuling.

When word of Moganshan reached the wider community

in Shanghai, reconnaissance trips were made in late summer of 1897 and the spring of '98, and the rush for the 'New Kuling' began. God raced Mammon for the heights, and God won again. He always did in those days. But this time the commercial classes came a close second.

Within a year the entire upper slopes of the mountain were under foreign ownership. Some foreigners came only to speculate, bidding fiercely against each other. They made a quick profit from other speculators and the genuine seekers of peace and quiet.

So far as I can work out by matching up the *Daily News* and local lore, the first purchase in Moganshan was made by the Revd J.W. Farnham, Shanghai-based director of the Chinese Religious Tract Society and board member of the Foreign Missions of the Presbyterian Church, USA, Central China Mission. Directly below his name on the first ever list of the first foreigners to build houses on the mountain, are the Revd Joseph Bailie and a Mr Edward Evans, both with their wives and children.

For fifty Mexican dollars, the standard medium of exchange, Farnham bought approximately thirty hectares of a tea plantation on the top of the ridge. It was divided into three lots and two of them promptly sold on. If the sales price was anything like the plots at Kuling, Farnham would have made something close to a profit of 1,200 per cent.

Once the frenzy had calmed down and the speculators left the mountain with their takings, the first thing the new residents did was set up an official body, the Moganshan Summer Resort Association. Every inaugural member apart from the treasurer was a reverend. Next came the committees, each chaired by a divine chairman.

The Sanitation Committee took the lead. Everyone was here for their health after all. Next in approximate order of importance were the Road Committee, Transport Committee, Supplies Committee, Judicial Committee, Resthouse Committee and, exercising God-given precedence over the lot, the Church Committee. By 1914 there were so many committees – a Swimming Pool and Tennis Court Committee had been added to the list, and one solely concerned with the supply of fresh milk – that the Association set up a Nominating Committee to keep track of the myriad committee members.

Edicts flew across the slopes, delivered by hand to lot and house owners. The content and pronouncements were finally resolved upon, seconded and approved at the Annual Meeting of the Association, the full minutes of which appeared in the *North-China Daily News* every first week in August.

The minutes offer a sample of the important issues of the day.

1899, Sanitation: 'Parties building shall insist on having the native contractors remove the night soil for their own workmen.' The native contractors would have been keeping it for the vegetable patches beside their straw huts. Night soil, better known as piss and shit, was a valuable commodity in China. It still is in the countryside. When I was clearing undergrowth I found a barrel of it sunk into the earth at the edge of our garden. It smelt like it had been there since 1899.

Same year, Post: 'Subscribers to the mail service when posting letters, papers, etc, shall furnish the name of the sender for the convenience of the postmaster.'

1903, Transport: 'Owners to be present as far as possible while their baggage is being weighed' by the coolies who will be lugging it up the hill.

1911, Sanitation: 'There is a tendency on the part of some cottage occupants to allow servants to deposit egg shells, tin cans, etc., in places which can be seen from the public roads. These, while not a menace to the community, are unsightly.'

1913, Swimming Pool wades in with its own governing body: 'The committee feels no hesitation in endorsing the Mokanshan swimming pool as perfectly safe. Parents, however, should not allow their children to remain in the pool until they become too chilled.'

1915, Church Committee pipes up: 'There must be no violation of the Sabbath on the estate, such as building, repairing, outdoor or noisy games, and all are respectfully requested to avoid as far as possible unnecessary arriving or leaving.' That one definitely did not survive into the modern-day.

And if you stepped out of line from 1921 on: 'Those who refuse to abide by the rules and regulations of the Association [shall] be deprived of all privileges, such as tennis, the library, sanitation, etc., and ... this rule shall apply to all guests as well as owners of the property concerned.' Harsh.

Moganshan became a mini European metropolis, micro-managed along the same lines and principles as the foreign concessions in Shanghai – which everyone on the mountain had come to escape.

There was still fun to be had however. The new resort was especially attractive to families with children. Not only were the little ones the most vulnerable to life-threatening diseases in pestilent Shanghai, they also needed to be kept amused for the long summer holidays. They flocked to the mountain.

Rena Krasno, a Russian Jewish exile, used to come here with her family in the 1930s. She is alive and well and living in California, a sprightly eighty-four-year-old, or so she sounds in her emails. I got in touch through the doyenne of the modern-day American community in Shanghai, Tess Johnston, once a consular official and now the self-appointed chronicler and guardian of Shanghai's concession era architecture.

I sent Rena a list of questions about the old days in Moganshan. It was exciting to be in contact with someone who had lived and partied on the mountain in the old days. I particularly wanted to know the answers to some puzzles that had been bugging me

'How did the Chinese villa owners who came up later get along with the foreigners?' was one of them. And: 'What was the annual children's stunt night?' I had come across references to it in several *Daily News* reports but there was never any detail as to what it entailed. I imagined kids bungee jumping out of pine trees.

Last of all, I wanted to know how it ended for the foreigners during and straight after the Second World War. I was hoping for graphic descriptions of them being evicted by the People's Liberation Army, Communist Party cadres seething with rage as they chased the foreign oppressors and illegal land grabbers down the mountainside, hurling their capitalist trinkets after them. The *North-China Daily News* had understandably not gone to print from the date of the attack on Pearl Harbor to the end of the war and then again fallen silent as the Communists completed their liberation of China in '49. And I was not going to get any juicy accounts of repossession from the locals, least of all Mr Shen.

Rena wrote back at length, about eating cakes and playing

games, the dominant images of her teenage summers on Moganshan. She did not answer any of my questions.

'The villa had a big crowd of guests,' she wrote, 'who had to be fed daily. It was crowded with mothers and kids (most of whom were friends from school), our cook was from Shanghai, my grandmother supervised the cooking and the food was superb. All the youngsters came home starving: had a huge lunch, then four o'clock tea for which my grandmother baked daily the most magnificent cakes, then dinner and still everyone always was ready to eat! Fathers remained at their jobs back in Shanghai. Some came for a week or so during the summer.'

She remembers hiking, swimming, 'inventing adventures' . . . and more eating.

I gently prodded Rena over the Internet. She replied with charm and tantalizing tidbits.

'Bobby and Leisha Hekking and their mother also spent one summer there with us. I danced with Bobby on the Villa Victorella balcony to "I'm Just a Vagabond Lover" on the gramophone. He held up my shorts with one hand behind my back because my shorts kept slipping down!!! I think we were the same age – around 13 or 14. Never had a crush on Bobby. He was one of my cousin Abe's best friends.'

Hang on. Villa Victorella? So Rena and her family had been guests or perhaps summer tenants of the Grosses in the beautiful spooky house deep in the woods behind the White Cloud Hotel. That made sense, she being Russian. The house was haunting me.

Tess Johnston publishes coffee-table books of old Shanghai. One of them is called *Nearer to Heaven*, a photographic

153

comparison of past and present Kuling, Moganshan and the North China beach resorts.

'You see the photograph on page eleven,' Rena asked me in an email, 'the big group of people outside a house in Moganshan? That's me in the floral print dress standing to the right of the middle. My mother is beside me on the right as you look at the picture.'

I looked up the photograph in my copy of the book. The sepia tones have faded, or else the photographer overexposed slightly, but it is perfectly clear. There are thirty-one people of all ages. Most are in white; short-sleeved dresses for the older women, like nurses, and white shirts for the boys and men. Only Rena and four other girls of similar age are wearing patterned print dresses, a gentle token of teenage rebellion. At least half of the people in the photograph are children.

Almost obscured by the group is the front door of Villa Victorella, House 495, my favourite derelict. In place of chest-high scrub there is a stone path bordered by the edge of a manicured lawn. It stretches out of the shot to the right. Above the house, instead of tall dark pine trees and the scraggly branches of the giant sycamores is a clear sepia sky. I had never realized the picture was of House 495. It was far too tidy and bright. Suddenly I appreciated that Moganshan, despite the basically unchanged buildings, had looked very different in the old days.

I sent Rena my digital photographs of the derelict that Villa Victorella has become, reluctantly. It seemed a shame to spoil her memories.

Rena's innocent reminiscences of Moganshan, while they did not answer my questions, confirmed what I should have asked her. She had only been a teenager. The question should have been: was Moganshan 'A Children's Paradise', the most common term used to describe the place in the reports I read in the *Daily News*. From what she wrote it seems it was.

There were children's concerts, a Sunday school, organized picnics, hikes to bathing pools in the streams than run down the mountainsides or further afield to the 'Dragon Pool' at Bi Wu village in the valley that runs across the north of the hill. The swimming at Bi Wu had to stop when the locals complained that the scantily clad foreign women were upsetting the dragon's spirit. And there was the annual stunt night, whatever that was.

The swimming-pool was so popular a quota system was introduced – children in the mornings and evenings, adults in the afternoons – and strict membership applied. By 1930 there were five public tennis-courts, with pagodas for spectators and the annual Moganshan Tennis Tournament was covered on a daily basis by the *Daily News* in its sports pages. Senior students from the Shanghai American School dominated the rankings.

The Shanghai Baden Powell Boy Scout Troop held their annual camp here for many years. They pitched it on Mt Clair as they called it then, the spur that juts out to the north-east of the mountain now known as Wulingcun. The scouts spent their days tidying the campsite, buying supplies from the local market and entertaining the local worthies with songs around the camp fire.

The village truly was a paradise.

It was a haven too. Moganshan remained an island of calm in an increasingly turbulent China.

From 1900 to 1949 the country went through more changes of government and suffered more internal strife than ever

155

before in its history. It started promptly with the Boxer Rebellion of 1900, followed in 1911 by the downfall of the Qing Dynasty and the founding of Sun Yat Sen's Republic. For the remainder of the first half of the century China was wracked by civil wars, banditry, famines, droughts, floods, warlords, anarchy, a brutal Japanese invasion, anti-foreign riots in the treaty ports, student movements, gangsters, drug wars, corruption and massacres. It was not a stable country. Kuling, which had been reclaimed by the Chinese in 1936 to become the summer seat of the Nationalist government of Chiang Kai Shek, suffered a full-scale Japanese land and air assault in 1939.

But Moganshan remained above it all. The house owners gently pottered up the canals from Shanghai each summer, opened up their villas and began their rounds of tea parties, swimming excursions, church conferences and annual festivities for American Independence Day (teetotal) and British Coronation Day (alcohol permitted within reason). Coverage in the *Daily News* was limited to the varnishing of the church pews, the concreting of the bottom of the swimming-pool and the number of books in the library. And the results of the tennis tournament. Nothing much happened in Moganshan. The Summer Resort Association only failed to hold its annual meeting twice, the first time in 1900 thanks to The Boxer Rebellion and then in 1927 when Chiang Kai Shek's Northern Expedition from Guangzhou passed by.

The main threat to Moganshan's idyllic existence seems to have been typhoons. They destroyed the early buildings, which were made from mud and wood, and regularly damaged the stone ones which replaced them. Retaining walls collapsed and roofs were torn off. Landslides kept the Road Committee busy.

1922 was a particularly bad year. A typhoon battered the mountain for a solid week. Within a couple of days a Mrs Ware died of heart failure while her house collapsed about her and on the last day of the storm the hillside above the swimming-pool collapsed. It took the Methodist Episcopal Ladies' Home down with it.

Poor Revd Percy J. King of the Church Missionary Society was in the deep end at the time. His wife and another young boy were also in the pool. According to a dramatic eye witness report in the *Daily News*, King heroically shouted out a warning but before he could save himself 'was shot headlong over the side and then carried along in the rush of water down past the new Sanchiaopu Road, some 200 ft. away, where his dead body was recovered very soon afterwards. His skull had been crushed in and death must have been almost instantaneous.'

Mrs King scrabbled out of the way but 'the Wilson boy was thrown by the force of the water up on to the bank against the terraced stone seats; how he managed to get out of the mass of mud and the wreckage of the ladies' bath house no one knows.' For Wilson, the son of a reverend, the horror of getting caught in a landslide can only have been compounded by his landing in a tangled wreck of ladies knickerbockers.

There was one other dramatic death of a foreigner on the mountain, the famous, amongst the few who know of it, Felgate murder.

Lao Han had mentioned it to me once. 'Some Chinese servants got fed up with their master and killed him,' he

157

informed me with an air of authority that did not quite ring true.

Everyone likes a murder story, and this one seemed to be the only real drama in Moganshan's short history. It was exactly what I needed to spice up my impromptu lectures to our inquisitive visitors.

I delved back into the *North-China Daily News* in the Shanghai Library and uncovered a couple of brief reports. Then I did what anyone looking for dinner conversation does. I Googled Felgate.

Robert Joseph Felgate of Kentish Town, London, gave up a promising career as a carpet salesman and left for China to become a missionary in 1894 at the age of thirty-four. He was married with two small boys.

Felgate's religious zeal only lasted five years however, its disappearance coinciding with the Boxer Rebellion of 1900, when several of his colleagues had their heads chopped off or were burned alive. Felgate resigned from the Inland Mission and moved to the safety of Shanghai, probably along with a few of his parishioners, where he started work at the Seamen's Mission. There he set up a profitable restaurant for the sailors that evolved into the Shaftesbury House lodging house. It was in Shanghai in 1907 that he heard of an opportunity in Moganshan.

For several years the Summer Resort Association had been looking for a resident manager to relieve them of the onerous burden of running the place during their holidays. In the years up to 1907 every report of the annual meeting repeated like a bashful plea for help, 'failed to find a resident manager'.

Felgate took the job at a salary of 150 Mexican dollars per

month. But it does not sound like the Association was prepared to give Felgate the full executive powers which they were dying to rid themselves of. I can't help thinking they did not entirely trust him. Perhaps this mistrust was prompted by Felgate's character, which was later described by the British Consul in Hangzhou as 'somewhat restless and highly-strung'.

Within a year of his appointment Felgate was engaged in an acrimonious dispute with a workman in the village, Carpenter Li. It was about money, one thousand dollars, a huge sum in those days. The case was straightforward. Li thought he was owed a thousand dollars and Felgate did not agree. His excuse for withholding payment was shoddy workmanship.

The dispute was taken to the Mokanshan Summer Resort Association Judicial Committee by Li, interestingly enough, not Felgate. The case dragged on for some time. At last in 1911, having already reduced the claim to four hundred dollars, the Judicial Committee finally got both parties to agree to two hundred. Felgate paid one half of it and openly boasted that he was never going to pay the other. Felgate's wife had left him in the intervening years, taking their two sons to America.

In the winter of 1911, apart from a missionary's wife and her two children who had stayed on after Christmas, Felgate was the only foreigner on the mountain. He displayed increasing signs of paranoia that Li was out to get him. The carpenter had already threatened to burn his house down but Felgate had three by now and he moved between them, sleeping in different rooms, with loaded guns beside his bed, every door and window locked and three guard-dogs downstairs. The front door of his main house was fitted with

159

a special mechanism that required the removal of a small a pin before it could be opened. He also made an impromptu will on a piece of notepaper. He cut out his wife and sons, who he must have felt had betrayed and abandoned him, and left his entire estate to his sister in England.

Felgate's behaviour shows every sign of a man who knew he had it coming.

On the night of 6 January 1912, it came. A gang of six robbers broke into his house, somehow without upsetting the guard dogs nor waking the servants in their shack a few metres away. The burglars were looking for money and valuables, perhaps the guns they had been told Felgate kept. No one can know for sure how or why exactly, but during the robbery Felgate was bashed on the head, bundled up in a blanket and thrown out of the house into the freezing night. By the time he was found in the early hours of 7 January he was dead, either from blood loss, shock or exposure. Maybe the murder had been accidental. Perhaps the robbers had only wanted to shut him up. Chinese criminals – down the ages and into the modern-day – prefer scare tactics and focus on collecting the loot. They did not find much because they could not break into Felgate's strong box.

One of the first on the scene, denying responsibility, was Carpenter Li. He was sent off to the Chinese magistrate in Hangzhou and nothing is known of what became of him. I suspect he quietly bought his way out of trouble with one hundred dollars. Two of the robbers were caught in March and executed.

Straight after the murder the local magistrate in the nearest town openly expressed his terror that the British would send a gunboat up the canal to seek revenge. The memory of the

'Great Powers' retribution after the Boxer Rebellion – the pillage of Beijing and crippling demands for reparation – would have been fresh in his mind. A quick public execution of a couple of culprits was the obvious preventative measure. The other four were never apprehended.

The foreign residents of Moganshan were obviously upset by Chinese bandits murdering of one of their number. The *Daily News* ran a series of outraged reports over the following weeks, as you would expect. An obituary of Felgate however, was prominent by its absence.

By the 1930s Felgate was a distant memory and the foreigners on Moganshan had become accustomed to Chinese bandits. The 'better class of Chinese' had by now followed them up the hill and built their own villas. Among them were the two biggest gangsters in Shanghai.

Du Yue Sheng, also known as Big Eared Du, and his confederate Zhang Xiao Lin between them ran Shanghai's illegal opium trade. Their gang was called the Green Gang. It operated openly as the 'Three Prosperities Corporation' and effectively held the key to governing Shanghai outside the upright and up-tight International Settlement. They were patronized and even funded indirectly by the French, and Chiang Kai Shek had a mutually beneficial understanding with them.

The pair ended up with villas in Moganshan more by accident than design. The honorary boss of the Green Gang, Pockmarked Huang, whose day job was police chief of the French Concession, upset the warlord of Zhejiang Province. One of Huang's bodyguards had got into a fist fight with the warlord's nephew and the nephew had come off worse. So the warlord, no doubt at the request of his nephew, had Pockmarked Huang kidnapped.

Zhang Xiao Lin went to plead for his release. As a sweetener for the warlord – I appreciate this sounds extravagant, but you must remember we are talking about the 1930s equivalent of Colombian drug cartel barons – Zhang took with him the blueprints of a villa he had built in Moganshan, up the road from the warlord's 'seat of government' in Hangzhou. It was to be a gift.

The warlord was touched by the gesture but he had aspirations. He sought official recognition for his political abilities. In other words he was trying to go legit. He told Zhang that the generous offer was 'too much'. Nonetheless he released Pockmarked Huang. And Zhang Xiao Lin was left with a villa on Moganshan.

He liked it so much he got one for Big Eared Du, right below his.

Zhang Xiao Lin was in the mould of Al Pacino in *Scarface*. But for the difference in country and years, he could have been the inspiration for Tony Montana. He was a thug who clawed and fought his way to the top and then went over it. He also did drugs in a big way. When he was eventually shot dead by one of his own bodyguards he was off his head and incoherently paranoid. While he was alive and enjoying life in Moganshan he kept tigers and peacocks, built a tennis-court and a swimming-pool and used to be met at the bottom of the mountain by a police reception committee who would let off fireworks in his honour. Village myth says he fed one mistress to his Moganshan pet tiger and locked up another in a grotto for playing around with one of his bodyguards while he was away on business in Shanghai.

Big Ears on the other hand was constantly striving to throw off his gangster persona. He longed to be a member of the political and cultural elite. He also tried to put his ill-gotten gains into respectable business. He set up one bank (his first major client was the French Consul General) was appointed director of another and went into the flour trade and shipping business. When he came to stay in Moganshan he donned a scholar's gown and once mused out loud to his favorite mistress that he wished he could write poetry. Being a Beijing opera star, she obliged him by running off some lines. But he had a fearsome reputation in private. On his first visit to Moganshan he naively brought every one of his mistresses with him. They bickered so much that he boxed their ears to shut them up. They were lucky. One day in Shanghai, so another story goes, the brother of a crony of Chiang Kai Shek's complained to Du Yue Sheng that a dancer he had enjoyed a fling with and whom he had got pregnant was getting out of hand, demanding money. Du told him not to worry, he'd set up her up in the water-lily business. Then he had his men drown her in a Shanghai river. He did have a sense of irony.

Unlike Zhang, Du died peacefully in exile in Hong Kong in 1951.

Both Du and Zhang's villas are still standing and open to overnight guests. Zhang's, the 'Immense Sea', is run by the provincial government as a state guesthouse. Du's has been taken over and restored by a Hangzhou Chinese-foreign joint venture hotel. True to the character of their original owners, the brasher types frequent the 'Immense Sea' and eat behind closed doors and shuttered windows, while the hotel chain which runs Du's villa aspires to be a classy boutique hotel, yet sadly fails. Zhang's tennis-court is a tree nursery, his waterless swimming-pool is full of leaves and the animal cages have rusted away, leaving red brown stumps of metal in their concrete floors.

The 'better class of Chinese' who came to Moganshan were not all bad, or at least not *that* bad. Another distinguished resident was Chiang Kai Shek's foreign minister, Huang Fu. He hosted the newly-wed Chiangs at his villa on their honeymoon, the first of the three times Chiang came to Moganshan. It was also in Huang's house that Chiang met Zhou Enlai, Mao Zedong's right-hand man, for secret talks. The locals tell me that the two men arrived via secret tunnels, which I think if true was an excessive precaution in such a remote spot.

The purpose of the meeting was to see if the Chinese Nationalists and Communists could unify against the Japanese invaders in 1937. But it was all for show. Neither side had any intention of working with the other. Huang Fu faded into ignominy soon afterwards, when he signed a treaty with the Japanese that gave away a vast amount of northern China.

Huang professed a sincere love for Moganshan and claimed to have grand plans for the area once it had reverted to Chinese control. He died of cancer before he could realize them and was buried on the hillside. During the Cultural Revolution Red Guards destroyed his grave.

Chiang Kai Shek's 'Evil Genius', Zhang Jingjiang, also built an enormous villa in a prime location on the mountain. He was better known as 'Curio Zhang' thanks to his immensely profitable export business in Chinese antiquities. His star faded before he could use the villa and he went to live in exile in New York, having spent only one summer there.

The Jian brothers who founded Nanyang Tobacco, the Chinese equivalent of Benson & Hedges, built villas on the mountain, and so did rich textile and silk merchants from Hangzhou and Huzhou, including Zhou Qingyun, a wealthy scholar official who wrote reams of awful poems about the place and had them published at his own expense. There were many other wealthy Chinese, less notorious and probably perfectly respectable, with houses in Moganshan.

That's why I wanted to ask Rena my question about the foreigners and Chinese. There were some very important, very rich, and not a few very bad Chinese who had villas in Moganshan, right in the middle of the long-faced missionaries, gambolling children and wealthy gentlemen like Colonel Francis Hayley-Bell. It's a small place and they must have been constantly running into each other on the narrow winding paths. I can't help wondering how they got on.

The answer is that they probably led entirely separate lives. The missionaries for sure would not have cared for such Chinese. They were concerned with the peasants. And the foreign merchants and municipal officials, deprived on their holidays of their compradors, the Chinese right-hand men who served as their go-betweens and interpreters, are unlikely to have attempted direct contact with this 'class of Chinese' about whom they understood so little. Besides, extraterritorial foreigners and Chinese, especially the wealthier and influential Chinese, viewed each other with a mutual disdain and self-satisfied arrogance that was irreconcilable. China had always believed itself to be the most superior civilization known to man. The Chinese word for China means 'Centre of the World'. The upper classes of China regarded the foreigners' presence on their soil as a temporary anomaly.

The first signs of change for the foreigners on Moganshan

appear in 1923. As is the Chinese way, the initial moves were indirect.

A new tax was announced, a police tax. The Moganshan Summer Resort Association reacted predictably: 'The attempt by Chinese officials of Chekiang to collect a police tax . . . is certainly a serious matter for the Mokanshan community present and prospective; and as an example of the attempts, of which there are now too many, to override and deny foreigners' well-established and reasonable rights, it deserves attention. [The foreigner's had no 'rights' to be on the mountain at all] . . . No one on the mountain, of course, desired to exclude Chinese or deny them equal share in the pleasures of the resort; but there is no gainsaying the fact that it was originally allotted [I think not] to foreigners as a place where they might seek recreation in the summer, managing for themselves and after their own fashion, always with due regard to the Chinese neighbours. Such it has always been and the Association, reinforced by "old custom", naturally wish to keep it so. The best solution would be to remove the police.'

See what I mean about foreigners doing what they liked in China? Imagine the Chinese restaurateurs and residents of Gerrard Street in London refusing to pay taxes and telling the Metropolitan Police to get lost and let them look after themselves.

Moganshan was not an official concession. It had never been ceded in an Unfair Treaty. The only tenuous claim the foreigners had to their property was that it had officially been purchased by Church missionary societies, but it was patently obvious that many of the house owners were not churchmen.

By 1928 the police tax was openly referred to by the foreigners as a 'protection tax', and 'the spectre of confiscation

'All colours, every hue and many luminous shades leapt harmoniously into billowed mist and cresting cloud-bank.' A description of the view from the summit of Moganshan in 1901, from the pages of the *North-China Daily News.*

Miao Qian, one of the villages on the lower slopes of the mountain, where British and American missionaries rented rooms in the late 1800s, before they found their way up to the deserted mountain top, and built their own resort.

(*above*) The garden shed and radio shack that we converted into our (highly flammable) guest cottage.

(*below*) The brothel that we converted into a coffee-shop.

(*top*) The viewing pagoda beside Sword Pond. Mr Shi and his wife have a temporary stall above the waterfall that sells soft drinks and snacks in the summer.

(*middle*) Mr Shi's wife crosses the stream above Sword Pond, with her day's supplies, on her way to set up shop.

(*bottom*) Locals of San Jiu Wu village, the highest on the mountain below Moganshan village itself, enjoy the cool evening air after supper, which will have been eaten at around five o'clock.

(*top*) Joanna and I outside our coffee-shop.

(*middle*) Mom and Pop with our children, Isabel and Tristan.

(*bottom*) Joanna's parents 'heat retreating' from the steamy south of China in the summer of 2005. Tristan looking on.

bove) Moganshan in its heyday, circa 1930: no trees, no bamboo, all round ~~v~~ews. Our house is pictured on the top right and the guest cottage is either ~~o~~bscured or not yet built. The large building on the crest, in the centre, has ~~va~~nished, almost without trace.

2008. More bamboo, fewer views. The conical roof surmounts part of the Lu Hua Dang Hotel, where Shanghai Mayor Chen Yi's 'cadres lined the windows'. The pink roof at the lower right end of the ridge was Colonel Francis Hayley-Bell's house.

The tennis courts during what seems to be a children's sports day in the early 1930s. Only the stone base of the viewing pagoda is still standing today.

Rena Krasno with her family and friends on the steps of Vil Victorella, 1937. Rena stands in the floral-print dress to the right of the centre of the phot

(*below*) Rena Krasno in 2007, looking at the derelict villa, and letting the memories floo back.

Singing carols with family and friends outside the locked up church, Christmas Day, 2007.

(*above*) The swimming pool packed by spectators, probably for a race meeting, in the 1930s.

(*below*) The swimming pool, deserted, with one curious onlooker, Tristan, in 2008.

(*above*) The world I left behind. Mark Kitto: 'mini media mogul' in my office in Shanghai, photographed in 1999 for a profile in the Shanghai Star.

(*below*) The buddies who helped me get through it all, and set fire to my house. Seated, from left to right: Jozef Van Beeck, Jules Kwan, Kirk Jobsz, Scott Barrack. Standing beside me, Mark Secchia. The shot was taken on my 'farewell' trip in Xinjiang Province, whose independence I was accused of encouraging. Inset: Brent Beisher in the kitchen.

of private property [was] stalking about the mountain', according to a letter in the *Daily News*.

The inevitable drew closer. In 1930 Weihaiwei, one of the coastal resorts in Shandong, was handed back to the Chinese. Kuling went in 1936.

Yet Moganshan still managed to muddle through, on the one hand by dragging out the negotiations with the new Nanjing government, which had more pressing matters to deal with such as looming war with Japan, and on the other by quietly transferring the official ownership of all foreign-built property to the American Baptist Foreign Missionary Society.

Even in 1939, by which time the war with Japan was raging across eastern China, Moganshan was left alone, apart from one Japanese air raid when a single bomb was dropped.

In November that year the *Daily News* published a report on the situation in Moganshan under the title 'Peace in Mokanshan', as if the mountain really did belong to another world. 'Skirmishes between the Japanese troops and guerillas take place occasionally at the foot of the mountain but the tide of battle never ascends the hill. The slopes of the mountain are entirely free from banditry, thus enabling the residents to go to sleep at night secure in the knowledge that unwanted visitors will not be prowling in through their open doors.'

To leave your door unlocked at night when a world war is being fought a few miles away must be the best advertisement for a peaceful holiday resort ever written.

Chapter Nine

Seven Years Between Scylla and Charybdis

'Due to the enterprise, energy and vitality of certain good people, on an August the third a hundred years ago, we are here to-day to celebrate the 100th anniversary of the "North-China Daily News" ... I think, maybe, we owe our survival, over this span of years, to a combination of strength and resilience, such as might be symbolized in the characteristics of the oak tree, and of the willow tree ... and our ability to have steered our little ship between those two danger spots, the "Scylla of triumph" and the "Charybdis of disaster".'

Replying to Mr Morriss's speech, the head of the worker's union said: 'We should unite strongly, labour and management, with concrete deeds.'

North-China Daily News, Front page,
lead story, 4 August 1950

In April 1951 the *North-China Daily News* was shut down by the new Communist government of China, its property was confiscated and its 'director' thrown out: a concrete end to one hundred years of publishing.

Beside the article quoted above, there's a photograph.

H.E. Morriss, the director, is standing in the middle of a group of Mao-suited workers. He is the only foreigner in the shot and towers over the men beside him. He looks thin, gaunt even, and exhausted. And old. In the autumn of 1949, when the Red Army liberated Shanghai, he had lost control of everything he had built over the past forty years. His family had acquired the paper in 1907.

Then he lost his job. He was also thrown out of his Shanghai mansion and into its gatehouse to live in a tiny space that had been the bedroom of one of his servants.

I stared hard at the image of the Englishman. I had read between the lines of his speech, the oak and willow innuendo. I knew what he wanted to say and couldn't. But it was in his haggard face that I saw something that gave me a nasty shock. I saw myself.

A few months before I came across the story of the *North-China Daily News* and stumbled on that centenary issue front page, I too lost everything I had built in China.

It so happens that what I had built was the modern-day equivalent of the *Daily News,* a series of English magazines that covered the three main cities of China: Beijing, Shanghai and Guangzhou. You could say, at not too far a stretch, that I was Morriss's spiritual heir. For many years – nothing like a hundred – my magazines were the best-known publications of their kind in China, and possibly still are. In their prime they were without question the most profitable. I had even been described by the *Financial Times* as a 'mini media mogul'.

Like Morriss I lost control, then my business, and finally my career. The Communist Party has ensured that I will never work in media again in China.

I know how Morriss felt. Reading the article and looking at that picture twisted a knife in my fresh wounds. I got up from the reading desk in the archives and went downstairs for some fresh air.

It all began in 1998.

My business partner Kathleen Lau and I had begun working together in Guangzhou, in south China across the border from Hong Kong. There we had taught ourselves how to make magazines with an expatriate rag that Kathleen, a forty-something American–Chinese, had set up called *Clueless in Guangzhou*. Its content was kick-started by the 'wanted' and 'for sale' advertisements from a notice board in the ramshackle restaurant that she had been running for a year.

Within six months we had made *Clueless* popular and profitable. But Guangzhou was a small market, our readership limited to foreign teachers, students and factory managers on what were still considered hardship postings in those days. We wanted to do something bigger and better, a real city magazine, so we started looking for a bigger and better city.

That year Shanghai's renaissance was just beginning. The city's miraculous rebirth as the commercial centre of the Far East was yet to overexcite the headlines of the western media but inside China, if you had half a finger on the pulse, you could not help knowing that Shanghai was about to explode. We flew up to have a look and carry out our own particular version of market research. We wandered the streets looking at bars and restaurants and asked friends of friends what they thought of our idea for an English-language city magazine for anyone who could read English, not just expats. One afternoon in the garden of the Ruijin Guesthouse, a sprawling mock-Tudor mansion with vast lawns, banks of shrubbery and a stable block built (you guessed it) by H.E. Morriss, we made our decision.

We did not make a business plan. We knew as little about them as we did about the man whose garden we were sitting in. The investment for our project was decided in a poker game without cards.

'How much you got?' Kathleen asked me, holding her coffee-cup to her chest with both hands. Her long frizzy hair was held in a bun by a chopstick, her big round glasses high on her squat nose. It was a sunny day in late March, warm enough to sit outside. The grass was still brown from the winter, the tips of the trees' branches speckled with pale green shoots.

'Ten thousand US,' I replied. It was all I had saved from my few years as a China trader. 'Can you match it?'

'Yes.'

'Think twenty will be enough?' I asked.

'You need a salary?' she asked back.

'Not for the moment.'

'Nor do I.'

'We go for it then?'

'Yes.'

If only it had been that simple.

Three months later in July 1998, with our twenty thousand dollars, a tiny office in the library block of the Shanghai Music Conservatory and five permanent staff, we launched our first issue. We had no publishing licence, vital in China where media is the most tightly controlled yet loosely regulated industry there is, and our corporate structure was non-existent. We would deal with all that later.

For the moment we were obeying the unwritten rule that governs all China business: forgiveness is easier to find than permission. We would get stuck in and then wait for the authorities to come and find us. We were confident that if we could publish a couple of issues we'd be able to prove our innocent intentions and find a way out of trouble.

Our *that's Shanghai* magazine was shamelessly inspired by London's *Time Out*, the best in the business. I had argued with Kathleen that listings, events, and city information would be the key to our success. She had grand ideas for deep and meaningful articles about art and architecture, and social change and interviews with important people. We agreed to disagree. Kathleen was already thinking about opening another restaurant in Shanghai. I only had to wait.

On one matter however Kathleen and I did agree, entirely. At the risk of sounding as naïve as those missionaries a hundred years ago, we wanted to show the immature and until recently purely propaganda-driven Chinese media industry and reading public that it was possible for a magazine to be objective, create its own content, and make money. It would be difficult, but our readers and advertising clients would appreciate our efforts if we survived long enough.

We were fired by a slightly different kind of missionary zeal. I sincerely believed that we had a chance to do something good for China and its nascent media industry, at least set a good example. We were media virgins. Neither Kathleen nor I had published anything more than a post-it on a fridge door before we started *Clueless*. If we came across as naïve I was not bothered. Once again, rather like those missionaries, I suppose.

Luckily for us, that naïvety paid off sooner than we could

ever have dreamt of. It normally takes a magazine two years to break even. It took us three months, almost. We were in the right place at the right time and we worked like madmen. Without a salary I kept myself alive on sushi bartered for advertising. It was another year before I could look a dead fish in the eye again.

When our third issue was about to hit the streets, the one that would put us in the black and pay for a decent cooked meal, what we were expecting to happen happened. Actually it was a little worse. We were shut down.

That was my first and most traumatic experience of dealing with Chinese government officials, my baptism of fire. Nine of them, all in uniform, from four bureaux: police, immigration, industry and commerce, and the Shanghai News Bureau, put me through a nerve-wracking four hours of Kafkaesque cross-examination, hypocrisy and double-talk. My only friend in the room was Kathleen's Shanghainese cousin, in whose name we had launched our local company to shortcut the complicated rules about foreign investment. Hence she was legally responsible for what we were doing. It can't have been pleasant for her either.

But we got through it. We were told that what we were doing was illegal and we had no hope, none whatsoever, of finding a way to continue with our magazine. Finally we were given a phone number.

When we called it the next day, the man from the Shanghai News Bureau on the other end of the line, who happened to have been the one in charge of the raid, invited us over for a quiet chat. In his office he explained how we could get round the rules, who we should go to for 'support', and how to take care of a few minor details like company registration, visas for our foreign staff and other sundry matters. We did not pay him a cent. But the publisher he introduced us to and to whom we paid a small fortune in what are quaintly known as 'administration fees' in return for a publishing licence, also happened to be under his direct authority.

We had obeyed the rules to the letter – by completely ignoring them. And when we were caught we said sorry, paid our dues, and carried on as before. The fourth issue of *that's Shanghai* appeared a couple of weeks late.

From that day on, for the next seven years, we were never out of trouble. But we survived. In fact we thrived. The magazines kept growing in popularity and making money, and every fight we fought with the authorities we won, often at the last minute.

Our reviews of bars and restaurants, the previews of shows and events established *that's Shanghai*'s reputation for integrity. I shall never forget the day an American walked into our office with a copy of our first issue open at the page where we had published an acerbic and honest review of a place that the whole town was talking about.

'At last!' he said. 'A real magazine that writes real reviews!'

Half an hour before I had been holding the phone away from my ear while the owner of the restaurant in question screamed at me, called me a traitor, cancelled his advertising contract and before he slammed the phone down rounded off with: 'And your magazine is not going to survive more than a couple of months in this town if this is the kind of thing you do!'

I was not worried, but when that American walked in and said what he said in front of my staff and then booked ten times more advertising than I had just lost to the petulant restaurant owner, I felt – understandably I hope – vindicated. And there was plenty more fun to be had.

Our increasing number of competitors pulled tricks on us, spreading persistent rumours every month that we were about to be shut down again. We played jokes back on them. We entered another's travel-writing competition and won first, second and third place with outrageous stories of cock and bull which no reader with a jot of common sense would believe. They were all published. So we printed a notice offering the winners a job.

We ran headlines that would make a *Sun* reader cringe, such as 'Up Shitzu Creek without a Poodle' above a story about pets. One of our spoofs was picked up and reprinted in earnest by the distinguished *Far Eastern Economic Review*. We played word games with our government censors, passed on carefully-placed errors to people who were copying us, and gave away a double bed as a prize for a Valentine's Day poetry competition.

All along we stuck to our principle about advertising rates: no discounts. Our clients soon realized that if they paid for an advertisement with us then our competitors would give them a free one, and bigger too. The money kept pouring in. We also threw parties that have passed into Shanghai urban legend.

The battles with bureaucracy grew fiercer in direct proportion to our popularity and financial success. It did not take long to find out who was after us.

In early 1999 the Shanghai Municipal government had announced a plan to launch an English-language daily newspaper, the *Shanghai Daily*. To prepare the ground, the Shanghai News Office – not the News Bureau, which is a separate entity – employed a standard tactic of commercial enterprises who also have regulatory powers: shut down the potential competition.

That's why the posse had come to see us in September 1998, and why every time we came out with an issue of the magazine from then on, a complaint went up to the General Administration of Press and Publications, also known as GAPP, in Beijing and then back down to us via whoever was 'supporting' us at the time. I would feed our government partners a line to pass back to the top of the chain and wait on tenterhooks to see if we had got away with it, yet again.

I was accused of being a pornographer, a pimp – thanks to our personal classified adverts – a China splittist, a Falun Gong supporter, an advocate of independence for Taiwan, and even, once, simply 'a foreigner'. That last one was hard to refute.

We were investigated by every bureau that had the remotest link to publishing, advertising, or plain business: the Administration of Industry and Commerce, the Labour Bureau, the Police, Immigration, News Bureau and News Office, Tax Bureau, Culture Bureau, Cultural Investigation Bureau, Foreign Affairs, Propaganda ... the list, and the attacks, went on. Sometimes it was a city's district bureau, sometimes municipal. The level and intensity depended on our enemies' connections, the infamous Chinese *guanxi*, and the favours they could call in. The apogee and our final accolade was the State Security Bureau investigating me under suspicion of being a spy. When your enemies accuse you of spying you know you have made it. They have nothing left to throw at you.

But with every victory we moved up another level in the

matrix of Chinese bureaucracy. Eventually we reached the top, where Party and State finally come together at the State Council. You could call it 'cabinet level' and you would be close. It is actually a little higher. Thanks to the help of one of our staunchest official allies, we secured the support of a publisher who came under the direct control of the State Council Information Office, the highest authority in the Party that governs media and information – i.e. propaganda, higher even than GAPP.

My proposal to them, not that I was in a position to negotiate, was simple.

'Let me do your propaganda for you,' I said, 'but let me do it my way, the way that works for foreigners, and let me control the business. You get the credit from your political masters and in return you look after me and my long-term interest.' They promised they would. There was another 'administration' fee involved. I was to pay for the privilege of doing their job for them. The fee was cabinet level too.

In April 2004 *that's* magazines, now *that's Shanghai*, *that's Beijing* and *that's Guangzhou*, one for each of China's three biggest cities, were issued with their very own brand spanking new publishing licences. It was a first in almost fifty years. In fact it was unbelievable. For an independent foreign publisher who had struggled so hard to get this far it was like having a bus pass upgraded to free first-class flights anywhere in the world for the rest of my life. Our Shanghai enemies backed off in awe. We were safe. But there was another price to pay.

I had long ago bought out Kathleen and married Joanna and now I had started a family. It was high time for a little job security.

Unfortunately that's all I got. Soon after I began working with the State Council's publishing company, one of my old enemies who had not quite got the message had a last go at us. I flew to Beijing to call in the big guns. In the course of the meeting with my new partner, a government official slipped in a few extra words. He meant them to be reassuring.

'Don't worry, Mark, now you are with us you will always have a job.'

With a sickening sense of dread I realized what he meant. I had stepped into the dragon's lair. Seven years of hard work and countless battles to build the most popular magazine of its kind in China for fifty years and I was going to get a job out of it.

My status was clarified eighteen months later when my partners launched a knock-off of 'our' brand – *that's China*.

'*Mei banfa,*' they said. 'It is expected of us by our leaders. How can we produce a magazine in each of China's main cities and not a national one?'

The cannibal magazine was filled with long articles about pig farming – I think one of the officials had a relative in the pork business – and the alphabetically ordered listings were lifted straight from my city magazines, but only from A to G. They did not have enough pages for the rest. When I protested, with perfect commercial logic, that the free advertising they were giving my own clients in *that's China* was affecting my ability to pay the astronomical 'administration' fee, and devaluing 'our' brand, I was told, with a completely straight face: 'But Mark, how can we be harming you commercially? We are not making any money.'

I was caught between the proverbial rock and a hard place. If I stayed with my powerful publishing partner I would never reap anything remotely like the reward I thought I deserved, the one I had been working towards, which was a solid stake in a profitable media business. But I could, if I played my cards right, make as much money as possible, in as short a time as possible, up to the point when my partners decided I had served my purpose. Until, in other words, they sacked me. And my chances of corporate raiding would only last so long as my partners did come out with too many more pig farming manuals. I could also throw away all self-respect whilst I was at it

The hard place was just as intimidating – if there was one. What were the chances of finding another powerful partner and persuading them to look after me, secure my interests, and, by the by, fight off the furious attacks from the State Council publishing company which I was sure to bring on their heads if I jumped ship? There was a lot of senior 'face' involved by now. For all the 'act first and ask forgiveness later' principles which I had employed up until now, these guys were not just ordinary government officials. As one of them told me on another occasion: 'Mark, I make the rules.' They would view my desertion as high treason.

While I was still reading the depressing writing on the wall, thanks to a remarkable fluke I met a senior executive from a major Hong Kong media company. Only later did I find out that they had been watching my progress for years.

He was hoping to expand on to the mainland. If not powerful in the purely political sense, the company had connections to the very top and was influential enough to access the same level of 'support' I was currently 'enjoying'. Yet at the same time it was commercial, with a corporate structure that I could comfortably slip into. Best of all, it was based in Hong Kong, nominally in China but at the same time governed by international business practices and rules. If I could make a deal with them, I would never again have to worry about securing my interests, nor all the other corporate and political stuff which I hated because it distracted from the job in hand that I was good at: building magazines.

Over a series of meetings I offered the executive half of my business, for free. He was surprised. I gave him the benefit of seven years experience working inside the Chinese media industry, from the ground up. Then I put my demand on the table. In return for half the business, he had to make the whole of it safe. He was getting the idea. He made some calls and told me he could line up a publishing partner of the same seniority as my current one, also with cabinet level connections. So long as we moved first we would be OK. Together we came up with a plan to keep my soon-to-be-ex-partners happy, to give them all important face.

The negotiations were progressing smoothly when I imagine he made another call to Hong Kong. At our next meeting he had changed tack. He told me his company was more interested in Chinese-language media. I showed him the numbers.

'Chinese yuan?' he asked.

'No, dollars,' I replied.

He made another call.

A few weeks later the deal was signed.

I had made it, almost. The exhausting years of fighting for survival were about to end with an expensive victory, but victory no less and a sacrifice I was more than happy to make. Not even Rupert Murdoch had got this far in China.

I summoned my longstanding senior managers from across

180

China to a secret meeting in Moganshan. I was about to start my last major battle. It was going to make me extremely unpopular with some powerful officials but I was confident we could win. All we had to do was stick together, as we had over the past seven years.

My family retreat was the perfect place to brief my loyal lieutenants. We dispensed with secret tunnels but I could not help thinking of Chiang Kai Shek and Zhou En Lai's meeting and the gangster conferences which I am sure Du and Zhang held in Moganshan.

Half a dozen of us sat around the dining-table on the terrace. It was covered in papers, notebooks and mugs of coffee. The August sun was behind the house, shining brightly on to the pale green tops of the 'hairy' bamboo that covered the hillside. We were dressed in shorts and T-shirts.

My plan made everyone nervous. That was understandable. They had reasonably secure jobs. I had given them the jobs and I paid their salaries, but they knew how powerful the State Council publishers were. Now I was asking them to take a risk on my behalf, to come with me on one last adventure. It helped that they also knew what the result would be if we did not escape from the dragon's lair. They had seen *that's China*.

The setting worked in my favour. No one could disappear to a bar or coffee-shop to discuss an alternative amongst themselves. We were stuck with each other on a remote mountain, and we had to talk it through there and then.

My chief financial officer, a Shanghainese who had been with me almost from the start and at my side through many a bureau raid, asked up front: 'But Mark, if this plan fails, the magazines will die. It will all be over.'

'If you had a choice,' I replied, 'Would you prefer a long, slow painful death, or a quick clean one?'

'The long slow one,' she said.

The majority of people on my terrace were foreigners, Americans and British. That answer helped me get them on my side and we prevailed. The only other person who expressed reservations was my national sales director, also a Shanghainese. Thanks to Mark Secchia's clever commission system it was not unusual for him to take home a larger salary than me. He had a lot to lose.

When I saw an opportunity for a quiet chat, I pulled him and my finance officer aside and went through the whole plan again, right from the beginning. As I spoke to them my own confidence in it grew. I knew it would work.

By the time the team dispersed back to Shanghai, Beijing and Guangzhou, I was more confident than ever. And I was tremendously excited that at last I was going to own a stake in what I had built.

In the last days of August 2004, Hong Kong executives in smart suits made daily visits to my company headquarters in Shanghai. We were in the final stages of due diligence. The numbers had added up and they were happy. The new publishing partner in Beijing was lined up and ready to go. Everything was set.

At the last minute, on 6 September, I was locked out of my office.

You never think it will happen to you, rather like a house catching fire. Again it was a surprise more than a shock.

Inside was a government official, my key contact at the State Council Information Office. He was at the head of my boardroom-table, surrounded by the fifty staff of *that's*

Shanghai magazine and he was telling them that it was illegal to work for me. Either side of him were the two people who had invited him to chair the meeting, my chief financial officer and the national sales director. The official explained to my staff that they, the sales director and the finance officer, were now in charge, with government support. It was a government-backed commercial coup.

I lost everything in one traumatic day. My managers in Beijing and Guangzhou were threatened with the sack, in one case jail, if they did not play along. Several staff left on the spot but most had no choice.

My life's work was taken from me in one fell swoop. It was the best thing I have ever done and I had put my heart and soul into it for seven frantic years. I was devastated. I always acknowledged the risk that I might lose my battle for true ownership. I had, after all, chosen the most precarious industry in China. But it was the manner of losing, and the betrayal, that really hurt. And we were so close to making it. So close. I cried for the first time in many years.

Joanna was wonderful, and she was very angry. She was also about to give birth to our son – my son and heir. But of what, now? That focused our attention. Once Tristan was born she turned, as Chinese wives do, to righting the wrong her family had suffered. She flew to Beijing and queued for hours to speak to the equivalent of the Citizens' Complaints Bureau. She came back with harrowing tales. She wrote to government officials. She called in every *guanxi* she could find, and their *guanxi* too. She visited the bureaux in Shanghai and Guangzhou as well as Beijing. In her home town we managed to impound an issue of *that's Guangzhou* at the printing factory. Not for long though. Someone made a call.

Much as I admired Joanna's efforts, in my heart I knew they were ultimately useless, particularly the *guanxi*. They only work when you can find someone who is senior to your opponent, and there was no one senior to mine, apart from the President of China. Still Joanna wrote to him.

As for me, once I had recovered from the shock I did exactly as every entrepreneur who has lost everything is supposed to do. I started again from scratch. For a year I had been toying with a side project, a travel magazine that had nothing to do with the State Council publishers. I saw it as my chance for a comeback.

There was a difference this time however. I was a marked man. I had lost the low profile that had let me get away with so much before. My erstwhile government supporter, the pig farmer, followed my every move.

At last, after months of attrition, I found a new protector. The match was perfect and the arrangement absolutely legal. That was rare for Chinese magazine publishing. Nonetheless, out of courtesy I warned my new supporter that working with me could be troublesome.

'Don't worry,' the Shanghai representative replied with a calm and confident, almost patronizing assurance. She was a charming lady. 'We have friends in high places too. You will be safe with us.' I appreciated her concern. That was nice.

One week after our first publication together, the call came. It began with a hysterical, high-pitched scream: 'You never told us you were THAT much trouble!'

Once she had calmed down the lady described how her boss had been summoned to Beijing by the State Council. He had been told that while his company's arrangement with me was completely legal, flawless even, he was to stop it immediately. If he did not, he would lose his position and his own magazines would be shut down. As I had been warned. They made the rules.

'They said it was working with you that's the problem,' the woman explained without a hint of irony. 'They said you were a Muslim separatist sympathizer.'

'A what?!' It was my turn to sound hysterical.

'A Muslim separatist,' she repeated.

That was a good one. I had to give it to them. They sure knew how to play games. China had recently signed up for the War on Terror.

'Mark,' my contact was explaining, 'you realize this puts you one step short of a terrorist. If you were Chinese you would be in jail.'

Then she added sweetly, 'I am sorry about this. It's rather embarrassing.'

Over the years I have been called a few names; Kit Kat, for obvious reasons, and Kippo, thanks to an embarrassing habit of narcolepsy in the army. I have also been accused with varying degrees of justification of a variety of misdemeanours, and been thrown out of one or two institutions.

'Dangerous sense of humour,' the school headmaster had explained to my parents in his book-lined study, 'Potentially fatal.' Then he expelled me.

'Saboteur!' my ex-Red Guard 'Responsible Teacher' at the Beijing Language Institute had screamed in my ear, flecking it with her spit. (A Responsible Teacher was a cross between a housemaster and a parole officer, and it was only ten years since the end of the Cultural Revolution.)

It is not necessarily a bad thing to have a name for

185

something, even a derogatory one, and I had always taken them in good humour, including the accusations over the years that came my way at *that's* magazines. I have dined out on some of them ever since. I am particularly fond of recounting how in revenge for the 'pornographer' label I contrived to get a photograph of myself, naked, into the magazine. My back was to the camera.

But getting thrown in with the Axis of Evil was not funny. Besides, I was older and wiser, married with a family, and had long since given up the pranks.

My contact had not finished. 'One more thing the State Council said, Mark.' I braced myself. 'As my boss was leaving their office they told him: "And we're going to get that trademark from him too."'

So that was it. That's why they wanted me out of the media industry in China, and out of the country too most likely.

Only after I had been kicked out of my business did I tell them that I owned China trademark number 3290466, 'that's', category 16: 'for use on books, printed publications, magazines (periodicals), newspapers, photographs . . .' and just about anything else that you can print and read. It was the only asset in my media enterprise that as an individual and a foreigner I could legally own outright, and had long been my zealously-guarded secret. It was also worth millions of dollars by now. Even when my government partners had technically infringed my rights by producing *that's China* I held my tongue. The reason was simple. If they had found out about my trump card while we worked together, there is no question whatsoever that they would have made me hand it over, by withholding permission to publish our next issue, for example. That's how they worked.

Confronted by this major hitch in their hostile takeover, the State Council people made a pretence of sitting down to negotiate a licence agreement. But that was only a feint. At the same time they were secretly applying to the National Trademark Bureau for a formal dispute to be registered. The Bureau accepted the request and our sham negotiations came to an abrupt end. The irony did not escape me that the dispute was registered and formally launched on the day of my birthday in November 2004. I lost. Of course I did. The decision came precisely one year later, to the day.

During that year I was promoted from terrorist sympathizer to 'threat to the financial benefit of China'. Then, when I appealed to the courts to get the trademark back and raised a stink in the international press, a letter was sent out on State Council notepaper. It was circulated internally, which probably makes it a 'state secret'. A sympathetic official showed it to me. Now they can call me a spy if they want.

The letter described my behaviour as 'a case of a foreigner interfering with the serious work of China's external propaganda'. It ended with an appeal to the addressees, government bureaux in charge of protecting trademarks, 'to bring your departments in line'.

It was me against China. Sympathetic officials told me my phone was tapped and my emails were being read. Friends advised me to leave the country for my personal safety and that of my family. I replied: 'This is not Russia.' In China unwanted foreign annoyances do not get arrested, shot or poisoned.

The Chinese are more subtle. They make life impossible, at the very least unbearably awkward. The pressure builds until you go crazy or leave, or both. A bit like H.E. Morriss. I do not think he went mad but his grandson, when I met him at a party in Cambridgeshire, was still pretty mad at the Chinese.

So far I have not gone crazy, I think, although my sense of humour took a serious knock. Nor have I left China. The thing is; I still love the place, despite the grief.

There is a tradition in China, a much older one than the annual escape by foreign missionaries and drug dealers from the heat of the plains. It is the tradition of retreat from public life.

I had led a dangerously public life. I had got right to the heart of the Chinese propaganda machine, on my own terms, just. My name was well-known amongst the foreign community and in the municipal and national news bureaux, cultural bureaux and a few more bureaux besides. The brand I created is known to almost every foreigner who spends more than a couple of weeks in China and many Chinese too. It's a cliché, and ironic considering the comparison I made with missionaries when we started out, but *that's* magazines were referred to as the 'Bible' by foreigners and Chinese alike. I preferred it when people called us the '*Time Out* for China'.

But I flew too close too the sun and got burnt. In China it is called the 'fat pig' syndrome. Get too fat, you get eaten.

Many friends and acquaintances assumed that the takeover of my business was motivated by the magazines' profits – which up until then I had been reinvesting – or that I had upset the censors with one too many cheeky jokes. I was sorry to disappoint them.

My real, particularly Chinese problem was face.

It is impossible to define face. It is perhaps easier to give an example. Here's mine, how face brought about my downfall.

Over the years I gave a lot of people a lot of face. Not directly mind. I do not mean to say I had arse-kissed my way to success. Quite the opposite. I never held back from telling certain Chinese officials under certain circumstances exactly what I thought of them. I think they secretly appreciated the honesty. It was a refreshing change. But thanks to *that's* magazines, many Chinese officials won an awful lot of face. I did the work and they took the credit. That's how it had to be and I was quite happy to play along if I was looked after, which in the end I was not.

The credit came in the form of promotions, praise and hard cash. A reliable source told me *that's China* was launched with a government grant of three million yuan, approximately two hundred thousand pounds sterling. I have a strong suspicion that it did not get spent on research into the pork industry, let alone office space, editing and design, or much printing either. In fact I can safely say I know it didn't because I met the American editor. She told me the magazine's staff of three were crammed into a tiny spare apartment that belonged to one of the officials in charge of it and that the designer had been told to copy my original *that's* template. After six months *that's China* ceased publication. With the same investment (including fines) my team and I had created *that's Beijing*, which grew to a staff of thirty, an office which took up half a floor of a tower block, a circulation of 40,000 magazines a month and had also made an international reputation with its annual guidebooks.

Thanks to my *that's* magazines, propaganda officials'

careers were improved and pockets lined. If I had moved in with the Hong Kong company there would have been a tremendous amount of egg on many faces. It would have become apparent that those taking the credit for my work had actually done nothing but take money off me. So the State Council Information Office had to take over my business and drive me out of China. In a pseudo-masochistic way I take that as a compliment. Cruel, but a compliment nonetheless.

When the Muslim separatist call was made, I realized I could never work in publishing in China again. I handed over the management of the travel magazine to one of my staff and accepted that my career was over. I had crossed a line and there was no going back. My fundamental error – apart from choosing the wrong industry in the first place – had been to believe that I could beat the system, a system that would happily have accommodated me on its own terms. But I was not prepared to accept those terms and, not to put too fine a point on it, my obstinacy, considering I was an Englishman trying to build a business in China, was bloody rude. If I had played by my hosts' rules, as most guests in any foreign country sensibly do, I might still be a 'mini media mogul', at least outwardly. I might have been looked after too, their way. But I turned them down. And I paid.

As the *Financial Times* quoted one of the Chinese officials as saying at the time: 'This is quite natural. Mark is a foreigner and doesn't have a wide scope of knowledge. He should first comply with Chinese law.'

The fact that the man the paper was quoting also happened to be the government official who had started the Muslim separatist rumour that finished me illustrates my point perfectly.

There's face for you. Now back to the other Chinese tradition.

Throughout the dynastic history of China officials used to resign their posts in protest; at corruption, nepotism and imperial folly. They would retreat to a remote bamboo-clad mountain and there take up residence in a cave or a reed hut where they would live as simply as possible and write poetry, a gentleman scholar's pastime.

Thanks to the classics-based, literary-leaning examination system they had been through to win an official post in the first place they were competent poets. Usually they rejected requests to return to public life or at least made a show of doing so. Once or twice they gave in and one or two famous ones bounced between their two lives, as recluse and government minister, until they settled forever in the countryside or had their heads chopped off.

Confucius started it. In his opinion one should only serve in government so long as the ruler followed 'The Way', the Dao of Daoism. If a ruler strayed from The Way then his ministers were expected, by Confucius at least, to resign. Since The Way is impossible to describe, specify or quantify there were plenty of excuses for unhappy ministers to hand in their notice and head for the hills.

The most famous scholar official cum hermit-poet in Chinese history was Tao Yuan Ming, also known as Tao Qian, who lived from 365 to 427 during the Jin Dynasty. Tao truly lived the authentic life of a Chinese peasant when he returned from his thirteen years in the 'dusty snare', as he called it, of life in the capital. He ploughed the fields by hand, went for days without food and drank himself stupid.

His imitators followed his example with varying degrees

of hardship and alcoholism. The eighth-century Tang Dynasty poet Li Bai, also known as Li Bo, perhaps China's greatest poet, carefully cultivated an image of himself as an itinerant recluse who did not want to be tied down by an official post – ignoring the fact that he was unemployable – and he famously enjoyed a drink. According to myth he drowned when he tried to embrace the reflection of the moon in the Yangzi River. It is more likely he died of liver failure. His contemporary Du Fu, frequently mentioned in the same breath, likewise preached about the beauties of the simple life.

A third significant poet, Wang Wei, balanced the life of a senior minister and hermit with consummate false modesty. His hermitage was no humble reed hut but a country estate which he retired to at weekends, ostensibly to get back to nature, more likely to go hunting in his grounds.

I am no poet and I was certainly not a government official, although I was invited to behave like one. But I did study Chinese poetry at the School of Oriental and African Studies, where I wrote my undergraduate thesis on Wang Wei. So I know something of reed huts and mountain retreats.

In September 2004 I faced a similar choice to the one which those famous poets had to make. I could re-enter the rat race – uninvited – or retire to the hills and write, and grow vegetables. My hitch was that the rat race would have to be outside China. I was only interested in publishing and it had been made clear that I would never get my name on a masthead again if the State Council Information Office had anything to do with it. And they have everything to do with it.

So I chose the hills. I had a lease on two houses on one of the nicest hills in China. It would be a shame to waste them, especially after what Joanna and I had gone through to find them and keep them.

Then in the winter of 2004 an American business publisher asked me to write a book about my experiences in China. Not exactly poetry but a book nonetheless and a stroke of luck for someone without a job, career or business. And where better to write it than our terrace above the weed-covered tennis-courts of Moganshan?

Chapter Ten

Retreating Further

There are numberless valleys running in every direction
through the hills which cluster around the mountain, and
every one of these repays exploring. It is advisable, however,
to take a mountain coolie to carry one's provisions, camera
etc., and to act as a guide on the return journey should
one become bewildered and lose the way.

North-China Herald, 28 May, 1933

They say that Moganshan is the easternmost point of a
string of mountains that leads to the Himalaya. It is a stretch,
in both senses of the word, but on a small scale map it is
just possible to find and follow a wiggling line of hills and
mountains all the way to Everest, and beyond of course. It
was a comforting fancy to think I could head west and stay
hidden in the mountains the whole way back to Europe. But
first I had to get to know my own backyard.

I took a juvenile delight in finding secret – or so I liked
to think – paths through the forest, hidden clearings in gullies,
plunge pools in rocky streams. I struggled down steep ravines,
fought through the tangled thickets that ran along the
streambeds and scrambled up to rocky outcrops that I had

glimpsed from miles away. I searched for viewpoints, picnic places for the family, or a place I could call my own secret hideaway, where I could sit in the sun with a bottle of beer and a good book. There were no decent maps, especially not for hiking, so I had to find the routes for myself.

It was not difficult to work out the principles of the mountain paths. The overriding one is that Chinese country people do not travel on foot for pleasure. Their trails are practical, from one village to the next by the shortest route, or up to a source of firewood, the edge of a bamboo plantation, perhaps a remote tea field or high altitude grazing, and no further. The idea of climbing a mountain to enjoy the view is quiet alien to them – perfectly understandable for a population that has struggled for centuries to make a living from the hillsides.

Countless times on my early scouting trips I set off up a bamboo slide or well-beaten path thinking it would lead to the top of the next hill on my list, only to find the trail stopped far below the summit. Across my path would be a bank of impenetrable bush. It was always densest at head height where the branches and twigs made a mesh like an untidy stack of wicker furniture. I tried to find ways through and always failed. Vicious thorns snagged and tore my clothes, cut my hands and face and once split one of my trouser legs from crotch to ankle. Joanna said that I returned from my hikes looking as if I'd had a fight with a 'flock of cats'.

Over a period of months I worked out which trails went somewhere and which ones didn't. The trick was to find the well-paved paths that led towards a saddle or pass between two peaks. These generally crossed over the ridges, down into the next valley and eventually a village. Before the days of surfaced roads and public transport they were the byways that connected communities. Nowadays to travel from one village to the next the locals catch a bus down their valley and back up the next one. If I came across a cattle herder or bamboo cutter up in the hills and wanted to confirm I was walking in approximately the right direction they always pointed back the way I had come. They were sending me back to the bus stop.

I learned to resist the temptation to follow small branch trails that looked as if they led up to the hilltops either side of such a trail's highest point. I would only be letting myself in for another cat fight. If I was lucky I might find a gap in the bamboo or a small meadow high enough to get a view.

With surprising regularity I came across people in the middle of nowhere or what seemed like it. Someone is always out there somewhere, chopping or picking. They were mostly bamboo cutters and usually worked in husband and wife teams. Each carried a short machete with a curved tip like a stubby scimitar, sheathed by a crude block of wood that hung off a belt in the small of the back. If they were harvesting the tops of the bamboo then the machete was tied on to a long pole. Its blade is razor sharp, especially in the crux of the curve. A quick tug at the right angle with the right section of the blade and the wispy top of the bamboo floats down to earth like a fairy from the top of a Christmas tree.

The other cutter's tool and badge of their trade is a long strip of fresh bamboo bark, coiled and carried over the shoulder like a climbing rope. The cutters use lengths of them to tie up the thick bottom ends of the bamboo when they are cutting whole ones down rather than trimming the tops. The bamboo poles are at least fifteen metres long and a bundle might hold a dozen or more, depending on their thickness. It is all in a day's work for a woman of five foot nothing to shoulder the bundle at the heavy end and carry and slide it downhill to the collection point on a dirt track below, where a truck will be waiting with a foreman counting off the poles.

You hear the bamboo cutters and collectors at work everywhere you go in the hills. When the lengths of bamboo are thrown down on to the road, then up on to the trucks, the wooden staggered clap sounds like a hesitant round of applause. It carries for miles.

The tall and hairy bamboo, *maozhu*, is the main local product, source of income and provider of jobs, as you can plainly see from the swathes of it that cover the surrounding hills and the fact that it's grown in every available space in Moganshan village itself. The Administration Bureau, who have the monopoly of the local crop, earn about one million yuan every year from it, almost seventy thousand pounds. That's an awful lot of money round here. Hence their looks of horror when I suggested that they cut some down to open up the views from a few of the village's best villas.

Maozhu satisfies two of mankind's most basic needs: food and shelter. You can eat the shoots, either fresh in March or dried throughout the rest of the year, and what you don't dig up and eat will grow at the rate of about one foot per day into a strong and durable pole, plank, rafter, beam, roof tile, floorboard, chopstick, bowl, cup, tool handle . . . You can build a house with it, and furniture, brooms, baskets, whatever you want to make. Nowadays the big stuff is mostly used for scaffolding.

Bamboo is a valuable commodity, and it makes for pleasant and shady walks, short ones. On longer hikes it can become claustrophobic. Sometimes I have almost gone stir crazy 'down there' in the forest. It all looks exactly the same and it never seems to end. I once got lost and walked in almost a complete circle for a whole day, popping out above the forest at the precise moment a tremendous thunderstorm brought to an end a day of glorious sunshine. Well, the early morning had been glorious and I had not seen the sky all day so I cannot be absolutely sure of that. I felt like a submariner surfacing after months under water.

There is only one thing missing from my walks in the wilds: wildlife. In the *Daily News* letters pages of 1920 I came across a fierce debate between the British and American residents of Moganshan about open and closed seasons for hunting game, mostly muntjac deer. Predictably, it was the British who had accused the Americans of hunting out of season. The Americans won with the simple argument that the Chinese farmers obeyed no season, so why should they? The American residents also started the tradition of the annual Moganshan wild boar hunt. By all accounts the men rarely shot or caught any boar. I don't think they meant to. I guess they too were looking for a retreat from a retreat.

An open season that lasted for a couple of centuries, capped off by the famine of the Great Leap Forward in the 1950s and the food shortages of the Cultural Revolution, has obliterated anything like a significant population of wild animals, especially in eastern China. There were even tigers in these parts once.

Wild boar are rarely if ever sighted in the woods today, despite – or more likely because of – the number of traps put out for them. The only wildlife that seems to thrive are birds such as wild partridge, tricky to catch or shoot, and the red-billed azure magpies that fly around the village: inedible.

And snakes. There are two basic varieties of snake in and around Moganshan, wild ones and the ones that escape from restaurants. The latter are usually harmless, although the moment of their break for freedom always causes a minor rout on Yin Shan Jie, the village high street, otherwise known as Shady Mountain Street. The forest snakes are usually both inedible and lethally poisonous.

The most infamous native ophidian is the *wubu she*, the five step snake. It bites you, you take five steps, and then you drop down dead. It is not as lethal as its name suggests however. I have heard of a forestry worker surviving an attack. The not-so-pleasant part of that particular story is how the snake did not let go once it had got its fangs into his leg. At least that helped the hospital identify it and find the right serum.

A close second in unpleasantness is the *zhuye qing*, the bamboo green snake, better known as a pit viper. These little bright green numbers fall out of the bamboo on to your head if you are unlucky enough to shake the wrong tree. At night they come down of their own accord to hunt. They like the toads which breed like rabbits and grow almost as big through the summer.

I used to happily walk home from Yin Shan Jie after dark without a torch until one evening I fell in with a village gatekeeper who told me how foolish I was. He explained that the snakes like to stretch out on the warm tarmac of the road during the night. He also had a very large torch. I told him I was not afraid, which was a complete lie.

The very next day, on the exact same stretch of road where

we had met, I came across a long and silver strip of ex snake, squashed flat by a car. From that day on I have always carried a torch and stamp my feet every few steps.

A favourite place that I keep going back to on my daytime hikes is a high pasture on the next mountain to the north-west, Tian Quan Shan. It is a vast expanse of grass by local standards, almost Alpine. A couple of cowsheds and a simple mud and wood shelter are hidden behind some trees at the far end. A pair of cowherds usually loiter around the hut. Their faces are so wizened with sun and age that I am never sure which is which. Both of them wear old and threadbare blue Mao jackets with buttons missing and tattered caps, and they speak with such a heavy local accent that I barely understand a quarter of what they say. To herd and guard the cows they keep mongrels of the most mixed up breed I have ever seen, oversized corgis with big rotund bodies. They look like brown barrels with legs. Throughout our chats the mutts yelp around my feet.

On our first encounter the men asked me where I was from, so I told them.

'An Englishman bought this hilltop once,' said one 'But the water was not right. It has too much *unintelligible word* in it.' I tried hard to remember it so I could ask Lao Han when I got back to Moganshan. 'So he never built anything here.'

'When was that?' I asked.

'Nineteen-forties,' the man said.

I guessed that whoever it was had been unlucky. He must have bought the field after the Second World War and before the collapse of the Nationalist regime. The real reason he did not build anything was more than likely because he was kicked out of China.

'Nice shoes,' said the other. He was studying my hiking boots with obvious envy. 'Bit big for me though,' he added.

I asked where they came from.

'Down by Fushui village,' replied the chattier man, who was not so interested in my feet.

'And you live up here for how long at a time?' I asked.

'Oh no,' the same one said. 'We walk up and down everyday.'

Fushui village was a long way round the side of the mountain and right at the bottom of the valley. I knew the trail. It was my turn to stare at their footwear. One was wearing cloth slippers, the other cheap Wellington boots.

'And what do you do up here?'

'Watch our cows,' he replied, then expanded, 'We walk them over there,' he pointed, 'and then we walk them back again. Sometimes we spend the night up here in the summer.'

I looked over his shoulder into their hovel.

'And this is where you eat?'

There was a smoke-blackened wood burning stove built of bricks and clay with a small wok resting in its hole. Beside it on a dusty shelf were flaking cloves of garlic, a moldy stem of ginger and some sad spring onions. There was no table in the room, only a couple of bed frames with rope mattresses and two small wooden stools. Every object and piece of furniture was covered in grey dust from the mud floor. One of the dogs had leapt up on to the broad window-sill and was barking in my ear. The chattier man shouted at it. It took no notice.

Opposite the hut a row of larches led away to the southern side of the broad dell where the meadow lay. Beside it a small vegetable plot inside a wicker fence had gone to seed. The view across the pasture back to Moganshan was spectacular. Where the sides of the bowl drew close at the edge of the flat field they framed the mountain perfectly. I could see why a foreigner had wanted to build here.

'Who does this field belong to now?' I asked.

'That's a good question,' my friend replied.

He reeled off a list of local villages and a couple of counties. The mountaintop fell right in the centre of all of them, so they all claimed ownership.

The fantasy which had taken only seconds to form in my mind, of the perfect house, built in Moganshan style with real stone and a tiled roof, a tennis-court one year, a swimming-pool the next while a landscaped garden gradually took shape, would have to stay a fantasy. Even if I had the money and the guts to take another chance on a China investment, it would be a nightmare to work out how to get hold of such a no man's land. Besides, I noticed how beneath their caps the men's heads were balding in ugly patches and their few surviving teeth were black, rotten and twisted. They looked like they had radiation sickness. The water was definitely not good.

I bade them farewell. Even if it was possible to buy the land it would have been a shame to bring to an end their Arcadian livelihood, though they probably did not see it in such rosy terms.

'Be careful you don't go into the woods over there,' the more sociable one shouted after me. He was pointing down one side of the dell that was covered by a long copse of pine trees. 'Hunters have put traps in there for wild boar.' And then he waved.

I cut down the middle of the meadow. The ground was

202

boggy. The strong odour of cowpats reminded me of a British farmyard. The flat space would be perfect for a garden once it had been drained. The tufts of grass came up to my knees.

A large bull with a crude bell hanging from its neck walked over to take a closer look at me. A few metres away he stopped and stared. Then he let rip a torrent of steaming piss right into one of my fantasy rose beds. It was only when I reached the lip of the bowl and was about to descend back into the bamboo forest that I heard his bell clang as he turned.

The old man's last words were still ringing in my ears like a cowbell too. I had learnt about boar traps the unhappy way.

On one of my longer hikes I had climbed to the top of a high ridge above Geling village, a beauty spot about four hours walk from Moganshan via one of the ancient inter-village highways. The attraction was a narrow valley that led out of the back of the village. It was lined with steep cliffs along one side and in their middle a dried up waterfall dripped into a shaded pool. Beside it was a cave where, according to legend, a Taoist recluse had lived with his pet tigers – every Taoist recluse seems to have kept a pet tiger, as if they were big housecats. The other side of the valley was steep and scattered with outcrops of rock.

It was winter and I deliberately climbed up the opposite, wilder side of the valley for a good view of the cliffs. A thick layer of snow covered the ground beneath the bamboo whose bushy tops drooped under the weight, some of them right to the ground. As usual I had reached a dead end, retreated, taken another path and again come to the end, but this time there was a faint trail discernible as a slightly wider space between the bamboo stems. There were no footprints. It lead across the hillside at a tangent but ascended

203

slightly. I was striding along it when I had my first encounter of that day.

I heard laboured breathing and the crash of what I took to be a man lurching up through a thicket below me. I waited for him to appear. But it was not a man. A beautiful female sika deer, her coat a deep reddish brown mottled with white splashes, stumbled on to the path barely five metres in front of me. She was about four feet tall and looked well fed and healthy. She stopped dead in her tracks and stared for perhaps three whole seconds, then suddenly she bounded up the hill towards the crest of the ridge. I was relishing my amazement when the reason for the deer's flight appeared. A beagle, as pure bred as any I have seen in China, tongue hanging wet from its mouth and its face a picture of eagerness, sprang up on to the trail. It too stopped and stared at me. The question was written plain across its face.

'That way,' I said in English and pointed up the hill.

The dog's eyes said 'Thanks,' its tail wagged and it ran on after the deer.

'Well, I'll be buggered,' I said out loud. To find a rare surviving deer living a happy if not entirely hassle-free life so close to a Chinese village and a thoroughbred beagle enjoying some sport, with no sign of a hunter, was, to put it mildly, one of the freakiest experiences I ever had in the hills around Moganshan. And I guess they are still at it. I was relieved to see the beagle lose the scent and head off in the wrong direction.

Soon after my Bambi moment I found exactly what I had been looking for, a rocky outcrop with a gently sloping platform a few metres below the crest of the ridge. I scrambled up on to it and looked back the way I had come. Immediately below me I enjoyed a panorama of the cliffs of Geling. A small blue-roofed pagoda clung on to to them where the locals had built a shrine for the Taoist's spirit. Where the cliffs fell away to the right I could look over their shoulder back to Moganshan, some fifteen miles away. It was a grey white hump in the distance. The bright specks of the houses flashed in the winter sunshine.

I spread the contents of my rucksack on the rock, set up my stove and started heating up lunch. The cliff above the platform made a perfect sun trap. The peace and quiet was amplified by the thick snow. I was warm and happy. I sat back and celebrated my find.

Then the howling began. I fretted for a moment that the sound came from a pack of hounds surrounding a deer at bay. Then I realized the noise was not excitement. It was pain, or fear. I wondered if there was a hunter after all, with more dogs, one of which had got stuck on the rocks below me. I had my rope with me and imagined for a while that I would abseil down, tie it on to my back and then deliver it to a grateful local at the bottom.

A few minutes delay would not matter though. I still had to finish my lunch and smoke a cigarette. I had walked a long way for this moment and I needed the rest after the yo-yoing up and down the ridge to find the rock. I packed away the stove and dirty saucepan, sat back against the rock and lit up.

Then another dog began to howl with the same plaintive tone. This one sounded closer, though it was hard to tell. The noise was beginning to grate on my nerves and my conscience. Two animals were obviously in distress. The howls seemed to be calling and responding like an echo.

The white man's other 'burden', an inexplicable affinity with the canine species, was too much to bear. I cursed, stubbed out the half-smoked cigarette, and pulled on my rucksack.

It took me over an hour to narrow down the source of the howling. As I got close the dogs stopped, or another started, or so I thought. The folds and rises of the hillside warped the sound, played tricks on my ears. The terrain was difficult to cover too. In unlikely places the well-spread bamboo suddenly ended at a line of dense scrub. I tried to work my way round the thickets but then I found myself going too far downhill or getting dangerously close to the top of some frightening precipices I had spotted on the way up. At one point I decided the only solution was to go all the way down, turn up the valley and try to spot the animals from below. Maybe I would have to climb up to the shrine and look back from there. But as I was halfway down a fit of howling started up agonizingly close. I thought I had a fix on it so I turned back uphill and lost it again. I was getting tired and frustrated.

At last I thought I had worked out where the dogs were, roughly, but my intensely physical echo-sounding had brought me to the edge of one of the densest thickets I had ever seen. Short pines trees were packed in so tight that their branches interlaced. Beneath them like a rabbit fence was a mesh of the brambles I knew well from our garden. They are impossible to uproot and have well spaced thorns up their rigid stems. They can grow to at least five metres, tangling themselves in tree branches above. I had nicknamed them bastard brambles. Among the knotted low branches of the pine trees and the high brambles was a back up of chest-high 'spring' bamboo, the type that looks pretty in a patch at the end of an English suburban garden but which roundabout Moganshan spreads like a weed, which it is.

Somewhere inside there were the stranded dogs. I still imagined they were stuck near the top of the precipice that I knew was in there too and which I worried I might plunge over as I pushed through the mess. I assumed that the dogs had been hunting deer or boar. It was an ideal hide for wild animals.

I dropped my rucksack on the ground, zipped up every zip and pocket on my jacket and prepared for battle. I took one last walk up and down the thicket looking for a gap, couldn't find one, and plunged in.

Progress on my feet was impossible so I dropped to my hands and knees and crawled. It was like fighting through a giant toothbrush. I had already begun to wonder if the attempt was futile when I found a boar track, a small boar but a boar nonetheless. The tunnel it made through the brush was a couple of feet high.

'Why am I . . . Bastard! . . . doing this?'

Talking to myself helped. The dogs kept howling.

I found the first one where the slope started falling away. It was not stranded on a cliff. As soon as it saw me it stopped howling and started barking, barring its teeth and growling with blatant menace. The end of one of its forelegs was dangling uselessly from a trap. The rusted metal device, two semi-circles of barbed iron, was tied by a thick wire to a tree. It looked like a medieval torture instrument. The dog had dug itself a basin at the foot of a tree whose bark it had either eaten or scratched away in its fury and hunger.

'It's OK,' I said gently. 'I am here to help. Good dog.' I approached it slowly. 'Don't worry. Good dog. Keep calm.' I kept coaxing it.

The answer was plain: 'Come within my reach and I'll tear your arm off, you human fucker. Just you see how you like it.'

I have never seen such fury in an animal. It must have been semi-wild, or a very fierce guard dog. And it had plenty of energy left. Dragging the trap on its broken leg, it used the other three to lunge towards me. The attempt to attack was sad and frightening. I backed into the bush to the right and heard a howl from further down the slope.

'OK, mate. Have it your way. I'll go and see if your neighbour is more amenable. Perhaps that'll show you I only want to help.'

Keeping my distance I crawled past the frothing beast and passed on. The slope was getting so steep that I had to flip on to my backside and skid down through the boar run feet first.

Dog number two was not far away and in a much worse state, almost starved to death.

'Bastards,' I said, not to the brambles this time. How could the local hunters be so cruel and careless? Or maybe, the thought flashed through my mind, they were actually after dogs too. It was winter after all, prime season for dog stew. But, judging from the state of the dog, they had not cleared this trap for weeks.

It whimpered as I approached. This one was domesticated, a family pet. Again it had worn a hole in the ground where it had been struggling to get away from the trap. And the lower branches and trunks of the trees and bushes within its reach were stripped completely bare. It had eaten everything.

Reciting my dog calming mantra, I got up close. There

208

was little room for manoeuvre in the bush. I prayed the dog was as calm as it looked. It was a black mongrel bitch. She looked up at me sadly. I put my hand under her nose and she turned away. I stroked her head. No reaction apart from another forlorn look from her misty eyes. I pulled a bar of chocolate from my pocket, broke off a chunk and held it under her mouth. Chinese dogs do not get chocolate drops for rolling over. The dog turned away again.

Now I could see the trap up close I studied it for a release catch. There wasn't one. Obviously there was a special tool for the job, perhaps a simple crowbar, something I did not have.

'All right,' I said to the dog, 'I am going to have a go. Believe me, this is going to hurt me more than it hurts you.'

I grasped the jaws of the trap. There was just enough space to get my fingers in where the mashed bone of the dog's foreleg left a gap. I pulled gently, afraid to hurt the animal as the teeth came out. The jaws did not budge. This was going to require a superhuman effort, and I am no superhuman.

'OK, we'll try it like this,' I said.

Trying not to twist her injured leg I laid the trap on the ground and inserted the heel of my boot into the gap. Then I stood upright as far as possible under the bushes, grabbed the upper jaw with both hands and pulled with all my feeble might. It moved.

I gasped with the effort. With a heave I pulled the trap apart enough to release the dog's leg. Holding on tight with one hand I gripped the dog's elbow with the other and pulled it gently. It came free from the teeth of the trap. The dog did not flinch.

'Oh shit.'

I had not allowed enough room for the paw. It wasn't going to fit through the gap. But I couldn't release the trap and give it another tug with both hands. That would mean shutting the jaws on the dog's foreleg and breaking it again. I almost cried with frustration. I would not be able to hold the trap open much longer.

There was only one thing for it. With my one hand on the trap I pulled with every ounce of strength I had in me, simultaneously pulling the paw towards the threatening gap, which I was widening a fraction. It fitted through.

I collapsed on the dirt, panting for breath, and rubbed the deep imprint the trap had made in my fingers. The dog lay motionless at my feet. Both of us were at our limit.

'Now come on, girl. I know dogs can walk on three legs. Up you get. Time to go home.' She did not even look at me.

'Please. Get up. Come on. You can do it.' She moved slightly, but only to lick her wounded leg, then laid her head back on her good paw. I got my arms under her and pulled her on to her three feet. She flopped straight back down again. The poor thing had no fight left in her at all.

'Bitch,' I gasped. 'No, not you. Sorry. This situation is a bitch.' I stroked her head, hoping for a reaction. There was none.

Now for the unhappy bit.

I weighed up my options. There was about an hour of daylight left. Already it was growing dark underneath the dense mass of branches over my head. The wild boar track carried on downhill through the bush but I had no idea if it led safely to the bottom of the hillside or came to a dead stop above those cliffs. It looked like it was getting smaller too. That was too difficult and dangerous.

210

Whichever way I went, up or down, there was no room to stand and carry a dog. If I was to get it out of there I would have to drag it like a dead weight. It was going to be painful for both of us and what if the dog took a dislike to me – the only way would be to hold its injured leg above the break, and the other foreleg for the drag – and it bit me? I looked upwards, back the way I had come. Steep, very steep, and somewhere up there was a rabid dog who would assume I was bringing it dinner, or I was dinner. I would have to detour round it again through impenetrable bush. Then I would have to carry her down the path, in the dark and I was already exhausted.

Then I thought about what I would do with the dog if I did get it down the mountain and back to the village. I had a good idea of what the locals would think. 'Stupid foreigner. Why go to all that effort for a dying dog?'

The rural Chinese have a remarkably, to us, heartless attitude to animals. Animals are for work or the wok. Giving an animal sympathy or love is about as soft and stupid as if a British builder apologized to a brick before chopping it in half with his trowel. I would be laughed at and as soon as I had gone the dog would be bashed on the head and thrown on the rubbish heap. It was too far gone to fatten up. I thought back to a conversation I had had with one of the Moganshan minivan drivers we had got to know. He was tremendously proud of his dogs. He had five of them. Once I was chatting to him about them and tried to confirm how many.

'You've got five dogs, haven't you, Mr Qian?' I asked.

'Oh, no. Only three.'

'I am sure you had five though,' I protested.

'Did have,' he replied. 'Ate two of them last winter.' My look of horror was completely alien to him. He stared straight through it, didn't even notice.

I turned to the black bitch curled up in her dustbowl at my feet. 'I am very sorry, my friend. Very very sorry. But I can't help you if you can't help yourself a little bit. And I have no idea what'll happen to you, and I can't look after you at home. Call me heartless but I simply don't want a three-legged dog. Besides, I am half in Moganshan and half in Shanghai . . .' I was making up excuses, I know.

I gave her one last pat on the head and turned her to face downhill. Maybe she would find the energy somewhere to struggle down on her own. With a last shameful apology I turned and scrambled back up the dirt tunnel. I felt angry, guilty and sad. I was also spent and now had to walk four hours cross-country and back up Moganshan. I would arrive late after dark.

The other trapped dog, the wild one, frothed at me as I passed it for the second time.

'Sort yourself out, you ungrateful fucker,' I growled back.

So I know about boar traps. And whenever I see a three-legged dog I feel a sharp stab of guilt.

Chapter Eleven

Permanent Life

The Ice King seems to have taken advantage of the short ice crop of last winter and successively raised the price, first to $1.50 per hundred, then to $1.60 and now up to $2. And this also is at his own weight, his own accounting and his own slow coolie delivery ... This matter should have the attention of the incoming Executive Committee before the season closes, and some agreement should be reached concerning the ice supply for the new year.

North-China Daily News report on the
annual general meeting of the Mokanshan
Summer Resort Association, August 1921

No one says 'Good morning' in Moganshan. The first greeting of the day is either, 'On your way to market?' or 'On your way back from market?' It depends if you are walking up or downhill and what you are carrying.

The market opens at 7 a.m. and shuts almost two hours later at 8:50 sharp. Most of the village meets there, in which case the greeting is: 'So you're at the market then.'

The market, such as it is, comprises two butchers and two grocers. Their stalls are concrete tables – polished to a deep grey sheen by years of blood, vegetable juices and broken eggs – which form a line under the eaves of the open basement of a large souvenir and instant noodle shop on the street above. Behind the stalls in the depths of the basement, dried mushroom, bamboo shoot and local tea sellers will lay out their shriveled wares for tourists later in the day.

Whatever the weather a couple of smallholders will be lingering outside the market in the parking lot like black market dealers, which they technically are, a couple of chickens strung on a motorbike's handlebars and a basket of vegetables on the ground beside them.

The concrete stall on the far right downhill end belongs to Mrs Hu. She has prime position. Anyone coming up the hill has to pass her by and many coming down get pulled towards her by momentum. Mrs Hu keeps her fragile goods, such as beancurd, wind-dried duck and chicken, and her smaller fish and prawns, on the counter beside the electric scales that she plugs into a thin extension which hangs from the rafter above her head. The rest of her produce is laid out on the paving stones to her front, open to the weather. Large plastic sacks spill their contents over the ground, eggplants, cabbages, *bai cai*, potatoes, tomatoes, gourds and pumpkins. And a big polystyrene box half full of water and flapping fish beside a straw-lined blue plastic crate of eggs. Customers step through the display, squat on their haunches to pick through the vegetables and place them separately into thin plastic bags. Eggs are sold by weight, in the same fragile bags, forty Chinese cents for a *jin*, a Chinese pound, a little more than an English one.

Next up from Mrs Hu is Mr Zhang, the shorter and more muscular of the two butchers. In the summer he wears a

214

dirty white singlet or more often than not goes shirtless. His brown biceps bulge like enormous coffee beans and you could sharpen a knife on his smooth whetstone of a chest. The way he wields his curved chopper brings to mind a hero from the *Outlaws of the Marsh*, the classic tale so regularly hammed up on the radio. The eager grin on Zhang's beady-eyed, weather-beaten peasant face is positively roguish as he slices and hacks through flesh and bone.

Third in line is the more gentlemanly butcher, Mr Yu. As tall and languid as Zhang is short and muscle-bound, Yu is quicker with his wits and charms you into alternating your custom between himself and Zhang, although at first I couldn't help worrying that switching allegiance for a pound of pork would cost me a hand to Zhang's chopper. Yu and Zhang actually work in tandem, chucking lumps of meat and bundles of small change to each other like brothers-in-arms.

At the end of the line, tucked in the corner against the post office is Lao Xu, the other grocer. Xu's set up is sophisticated. He backs his truck to within a couple of metres of his stall and in wet weather stretches a blue tarpaulin from the cab, over the flagons of cooking oil, sacks of peanuts and baskets of fruit in the bed of his truck and over the vegetables on the ground between the truck and the stall. The awning adds a touch of class and keeps his customers dry. I think the short, rotund and jovial Lao Xu does the best business. His hardware store in Yucun, the village at the foot of the steep front road up Moganshan, takes up half a block.

By the time I arrive at the market the older locals will have gathered for their daily gossip on a low wall across the paved parking lot. They place their blue plastic bags of meat and vegetables at their feet, rest their walking sticks between their knees and turn their faces to the sun. If it is raining they move inside and prop themselves up on the mushroom sellers' stalls.

The first person I see every day is another Lao Han, our caretaker Lao Han's brother-in-law. Lao Han and his wife, my oldest friends on the mountain, by chance share one of the Chinese 'Hundred Names'. Women keep their maiden name after marriage in China.

Lao Han, the street sweeper – in a Welsh village he would be 'Han the Street' – spends the day ambling up and down the ridge-top road, his broom under his arm. Sometimes it makes contact with a pile of leaves or a piece of rubbish. On my way down the five hundred steps from our house to the market I usually find him at the halfway point where I cross the road. He'll be sitting on a concrete bollard, looking up and down his patch and wondering which direction to start off on. We exchange the standard greeting.

'Going to market?' he asks.

'Going to market. You starting work?'

'Starting work,' he replies and I pass on.

Han the Street has a colleague at the bottom of the steps. I don't know his name and I can't ask him because he is mute. He looks after Yin Shan Jie and a stretch of road below it. We smile at each other and I slow down if I catch him a few minutes before 8:30. He will also be sitting on a wall, planning his day's work. Then we both hear the echo of a bus chugging up the hill. The sound bounces back at us from the far side of the bowl where the heart of the village is.

The fifteen-seater is one of three buses that bring the Administration Bureau staff up from the valley every day. You can set your watch by them. Two of them stop off lower down at the Administration Bureau offices and the third on Yin Shan Jie, right at the steps. As the echo of the bus's engine becomes the real thing, the street sweeper springs to his feet and starts brushing, head low, elbows pumping from belly to chest. I slow my pace to a dawdle.

With a final long drawn out belch of exhaust the bus heaves up round the steep corner by the post office and comes to a halt right below us. The doors flap open and the commuters starburst in both directions along the road and past me up the steps. When they are a safe distance away the sweeper stops as suddenly as he began and sits back down on the wall. He pulls out a packet of cigarettes, puts one his mouth and lights it.

Once I have skipped down the last few steps and caught Mrs Hu before she loads up her van to return down the hill, I stock up with food for one or two days, pile the useless plastic bags into a shopping basket that once held a Christmas hamper from London and head back up the steps.

Everyone I meet peers into my basket and feels obliged to comment. One day there was a loose onion on top of my pile of plastic bags. An old man leant over my shoulder from a doorway beside the steps. I could hear women's voices in the house behind him.

'The foreigner has bought an onion!' he shouted at the top of his voice like a town crier.

Occasionally I buy a fish, live and flapping in another flimsy plastic bag. The trick is to put enough green vegetables on top to stop it jumping around the basket and keep it from breaking the eggs, but not so much that I kill the thing before I get it home and drop it into a large saucepan of water.

Han the Street will have moved a few yards along the ridge road to another bollard by the time I return.

'Been to market?' he shouts, a little louder than before.

'Yup, been to market,' I shout back.

And I walk up the final two hundred steps to the house. Through the summer of 2005 I was alone in our Moganshan house, except for the weekends when Joanna and the children came out to see me. The family home was still in Shanghai. Isabel had started nursery school, we had half a year left on the lease of the flat – a bargain thanks to Brent – and we had no idea what we were going to do next.

We also had Tristan. Moganshan was too remote and wild for a brand new baby and Zhou Aiyi, our longstanding Shanghainese maid and nanny, had made it clear she did not like the place.

'Moganshan's too quiet,' she had whispered on her first and only visit, as if she expected to see a ghost any minute.

'Shanghai's too noisy,' I pleaded with Joanna when we discussed where I was going to write the book for the Americans. Apart from the distractions of a screaming baby our flat overlooked a busy intersection where the cacophony of blaring horns and squealing brakes ran non-stop from dawn til late after dark. I did try working there for a couple of days, with headphones, but it was impossible to concentrate.

Besides, I enjoyed the liberty of having no job, career, or business. I might as well use it. So I retreated from the 'dusty snare', as Tao Qian described it, and disappeared to Moganshan to write my poetic business book.

To complete my sense of isolation, a couple of articles in the international press about my fall from grace had rounded

218

off their reports with the neat ending: 'Mark Kitto has gone home.'

I let the rumour spread.

Not without reason I had begun to suffer a mild persecution complex thanks to the repeated concerns for my personal safety from my friends and the straightforward manner in which my last ever publishing partner had explained that the State Council guys were 'out to get me'.

When I went to Beijing to see my lawyers about the trademark case, and they introduced me to someone who might have been able to help, I was told that I was not who I said I was.

'Mark Kitto has been thrown out of China,' the woman declared with conviction. She was a board member of the British Chamber of Commerce.

'That's good to hear,' I replied.

When Joanna and the children did not come up at weekends, I went down to see them in Shanghai. Joanna was remarkably tolerant of my deserting her. No matter how well I believed I was taking my recent disaster I am sure I was not the most cheerful company, so perhaps it was best for both of us. And the trademark case, which Joanna was helping with, put a strain on our relationship that often made me wonder if I should not drop it altogether. Weekends when both of us concentrated on having fun with the children were a perfect distraction.

If I ran into a curious acquaintance or old client while I was stocking up for my hermitage from the supermarket across the road from our flat, I explained that I had just flown in from London, or Hong Kong, or wherever else I felt like.

'Dropping by to tie up some loose ends,' I said. They believed me.

Moganshan was the perfect writer's bolt hole, and an ideal sanatorium where I could recover from my commercial shell shock, which is not a bad way of putting it. My business had exploded in my face and my career been blown to smithereens.

The tragedy had also brought to an end seven years of relentless battles, behind-the-scenes attrition and the nightmare of building a business in a Chinese 'grey area' – half-legal, half-illegal, forever at the mercy of powerful friends and enemies.

I had survived quite well, or so I thought. But the stress had still been immense. It was good to be rid of it. Not that it vanished overnight. Getting it off my chest and on to a computer screen helped.

My days fell into a pleasant rhythm. Up early and walk down to the market, keeping Han the Street up-to-date on my progress. Back for breakfast, then into the morning sun on the terrace with my laptop and sheets of notes. The words came easily. I was writing a simple saga that was fresh in my memory and I was used to deadlines. The only difficult bits were the adjectives. I rather overdid them when describing the people who had ruined me.

Lunch, a spell in the garden weeding and clearing underbrush, then back to my desk for a couple of hours, first to remove the morning's adjectives now I had cooled down a bit, then polish the rest and prepare for the next day's work. With an hour or so to go before sunset I went for a walk round the hilltop, usually out to Queer Stone Corner.

At the top of the jumble of giant rocks there was a hollow that made a comfortable seat. I looked across the valley towards the glowing sky in the west, made notes for the book and considered my uncertain future. Mind a little clearer, I returned home through the pine trees. The needle-covered floor beneath them was burnt a deep red by the setting sun, like a terracotta carpet. I cooked myself simple suppers and ate them in front of pirated old movies.

I tended to watch war movies or ones with fights in them. Any fight would do: a legal fight, cowboy fight or a simple battle between good and evil. I liked it when the good guys won but there was one movie which held a special place for me, when the good guy lost. That was *Cool Hand Luke*. I could not help identifying with Paul Newman's character's futile fight against authority, and the film's most famous line, 'What we have here is a failure to communicate', could have come from any one of my countless arguments with Chinese government officials. I smiled with tears in my eyes when I heard it. But it made me feel better.

I lived the quiet life at the end of a sinuous path. I rarely saw anyone at all. Occasionally I was driven indoors by a passing typhoon but for the most part the weather was hot and fine. Every mid-afternoon the cicadas started singing. I could distinguish them individually as they began, then the solos merged into a chorus that worked up to a deafening and continuous crescendo. By the time I went to bed the noise was such a uniform roar, like a jet engine warming up for take off, that it drowned out my thoughts and drove me to sleep.

It was a pleasant life and an unusual one for China. No one leads a quiet life here. The world's factory is a noisy place.

Everyone who buys a newspaper has read about China's frantic progress towards becoming a world power, possibly *the* world power, how the country's booming economy is driving up the prices of raw materials and its factories turning them into unbeatably cheap exports. What the media makes less comment about is the obsession with personal wealth that has seized China's vast population. No report can accurately portray the greed, the hunger for material gain, and the mayhem it has created. For all the graphic descriptions, the newspaper columns and television documentaries, the enormous facts and figures, it is impossible to grasp without seeing it for yourself. China is a shambles, a ruthless cut-throat shambles where every single man and woman's aim is to amass material wealth. I know it is wrong to generalize, and of course there are exceptions, but where else in the world would you find a public notice from the police that says: 'Attention all thieves! You will get a better return if you play the stock market.'

Every time I returned to Shanghai I felt further removed from the commercial chaos of the growing city. The buildings grew taller, both in reality and from my own rusticated viewpoint, while my world grew smaller.

I realized that I had never really liked the city. I remembered with mild surprise how in my early days in China, in Beijing and Guangzhou, I had sworn I would never end up in Shanghai. No one in China outside of Shanghai likes the city or its people, and the Shanghainese look down their noses at the Chinese who live anywhere else. The reasons are complicated and founded in the city's foreign-dominated past. Yet the place had ensnared me, as it had so many other dreamers, especially foreign ones. I had betrayed my promise to myself. Now I could put things to rights. The chapters in my manuscript about Shanghai took on the tone of personal revelation, tinged with bitterness that I had been conned into spending the most productive years of my life there.

In Shanghai I had also lost much of my affection for China. In Moganshan I have learned to love China and the Chinese again.

The people of Moganshan are country folk to start with, generally guaranteed to be more genteel and generous than city ones. Take Lao Gao for instance, the accountant in the Administration Bureau.

You would never guess Lao Gao's job from looking at him. He is short, maybe five feet five, sixty-five years old, and his thinning grey hair comes down over his shoulders. He has a wispy beard like an ancient Chinese sage and his brown eyes sparkle with kindness and a childish glee. Lao Gao is also superbly fit, with a body like a martial arts master. He runs marathons, wins prizes for his calligraphy, and gives my children peaches from a tree in his garden. He is a good neighbour.

Sometimes I meet Lao Gao on bright winter mornings on the road behind our house, jogging down it with a bundle of firewood under his arm, shirt hanging from a belt around his old and faded tracksuit trousers, his bare torso tight and spare arm pumping like an aerobic instructor's. His house and vegetable patch above Yin Shan Jie are beautifully kept, almost fictionally perfect like Mr McGregor's garden. He keeps white geese in a wicker fenced yard in the bamboo behind it.

He also he plays the flute like Pan. I was walking along Yin Shan Jie one summer evening, having missed the market in the morning, and treated myself to dinner in a restaurant. Stars were shining brightly in the moonless night. No one was outside. A window was open in the hardware store above me and from it came the flap and crackle of *ma jiang* tiles.

Then I heard the most haunting flute music. It was a long time since I had heard an instrument. It sounded as if it was coming from another world. I picked up my pace towards it, but then all of a sudden it was behind me. I turned and ran back. Again I missed it. Thanks to the bowl in the hillside the gentle notes were floating back and forward over my head, teasing me. I rushed up the steps to the window of the hardware store and thrust my head through it. I recognized one of the *ma jiang* players.

'Lao Huang, who is that playing the flute?' I asked, rather too desperately.

The four men looked up at me with surprise. One of the older ones cocked his ear as if he hadn't heard anything yet.

'Oh,' he said after a moment, 'that's Lao Gao.' And he looked back down on the table as if it was perfectly normal to have a neighbour who lived like one of China's mythical immortals.

I pulled back from the window and two at a time walked up the steps through the bamboo to Lao Gao's place. The music grew clearer and yet more entrancing, as if it was sucking me out of the waking world. Lao Gao was playing what I assumed were folk tunes though they were not simple and there were hardly any repeats that I could make out. The melodies were long and fluid, meandering in stately codas from one extended phrase to the next. Gao was embellishing them with soft taps and rolls like a tin whistle player yet at the same time there was a classical virtuosity to his playing. He was very good.

I stopped short of the house and sat on the steps in the

deep shadow. The music brought to mind fair maidens in long silk dresses sitting in moonlit pagodas, cow herders asleep on boulders in paddy fields, ragged Taoist monks wandering from village to village, mumbling crazy yet perfect allegories at anyone who stopped and listened. I was away with the fairies.

There is a famous poem by Li Bai, 'Hearing a flute on a spring night in Luoyang':

> *From whose house secretly floats the sound of the*
> *   jade flute,*
> *Carried by the east wind across the city?*
> *On this night the tune sounds like a breaking willow.*
> *Hearing it, who could help but think of home?*

A broken willow branch signifies a longing for home and old friends because the character is a homonym for 'stay', as in 'at home'. For two friends or lovers to break a willow twig and each keep one half was also a traditional parting gift and symbol of loyalty. The halves will only make a whole with each other.

I wish I could say that I recited the poem to myself and thought of a distant home and old friends as I sat in the darkness outside Lao Gao's house. But that would be too poetic. I had to look it up when I got home and make my own translation.

Then Lao Gao stopped abruptly in the middle of a tune. I was disappointed and resented the silence but it was somehow right and fitting. My secret audience would not have been so enthralling if it had lasted too long.

I have never told Lao Gao that I heard him play his flute. I have never heard it again either. Lao Gao is not exactly a

225

typical resident of Moganshan, but he does personify the spirit of the place.

For the most part the permanent residents are simple people, ill-educated children of peasant refugees who came to the mountain to work for the foreigners and 'better class' of Chinese in the 1920s and 30s. Their own children, the middle-aged generation, have left for towns and cities, so the average age for a Moganshan native is probably about eighty. But they are surprisingly healthy, just to reinforce the myth I am trying to create that Lao Gao is an 'immortal'. It is said that everyone lives to a hundred in Moganshan thanks to the clean air, the spring water and regular and unavoidable exercise.

But it cannot be an easy life for an old person. Living in a falling down stone house with no central heating that is swathed by damp cloud for much of the year can't be good for old bones.

One characteristic of the Moganshan locals that surprised me is their acceptance of a foreigner in their midst. I rarely hear the word *laowai* that so often is shouted at our backs elsewhere in China. The reason is that they were brought up amongst foreigners. There is nothing special about us here. They ask me if I have been to the market as if I have lived here my whole life or I was just another grandchild of a former resident. This too is pleasant and unusual for China.

It is a shame for me that the old locals retain their thick Anhui dialects, handed down from father to son with the carpentry tools. I wish we could chat more freely. I have to keep asking them to explain themselves and often miss much of the conversation, especially in a group. Then there is the added complication of the antiquated Chinese. For example

I get asked if I have 'moved my body', *dong shen le*, instead of being asked if I went away recently: *chuqu le*.

There is a Moganshan saying: '*Yi shan yi gong.*' It means, 'One mountain, all together.' If someone needs help then he will get it. Many locals are related by blood or marriage. There is a community spirit you do not find in a city and which is also rare even in the countryside of China. I think one reason for it is the hard times the locals have been through, and they were very hard, as I would find out later.

So everyone knows everyone. They can tell you whose sister works in which hotel, the factory where a younger brother is a foreman down on the plain, and what he did before that.

There are clannish connections between the hotels and restaurants. Hotel managers are commonly surnamed Huang and Chen, the restaurant owners Shen and Wang. I have lost count of the Hans. The wife of the manager of the Empress Hotel is the deputy manager of the White Cloud. The owner of the popular Xing Long Hotel set his brother up in business with a small guesthouse down the road. Everyone seems to have worked everywhere at some point in their career. One summer's day I shared a ride in a minivan taxi to the local town with Mrs Wang, mother of one hotel manager, one deputy manager, the Administration Bureau office cleaner and a son who has emigrated to Chile where he is a chef in a Chinese restaurant, so he does not count.

Mrs Wang was born in the early 1900s. She is not sure when exactly. She speaks with an accent thicker than the bamboo forest and is tone deaf in her left ear. I did not have a translator or notebook and I was sitting on her wrong side.

While the minivan swept and swayed down the steep road to Yucun, Mrs Wang gripped her walking stick as if it was the only thing stopping her falling out through the window. I had a burning question to ask her. It was about Mao Zedong's visit to Moganshan.

One of the villas in the complex of the Empress Hotel is known as the 'The Mao House'. It is a museum with one exhibit: a metal bed frame. Mao slept on it, so the story goes.

I had already established that the Great Helmsman's sleep was not an overnight one, though the guidebooks would have the tourists think otherwise. He had taken a snooze after a boozy lunch, then left the mountain in the evening. But the Mao myth has enormous pull in China. I longed to hear about his visit from an eye witness. Mrs Wang must have been there.

After some small talk about her family, I began with a nod towards historical research: the date.

'Auntie Wang, I suppose you were in Moganshan when Chairman Mao came to visit. When was that exactly?'

'What?'

I raised my voice and repeated the question.

'Ah yes, Chairman Mao,' she shouted back. 'Never saw him!'

That was disappointing. She must have been away when he came. But she had not finished. 'It was in '44,' she enunciated clearly, as if I was the deaf one.

But that could not be right. Mao did not take control of China until '49. He would hardly have made a public visit to the mountain – and I was sure it was a proper visit – when he was a guerilla living miles away in a cave in north-China. Or had he? Maybe I was wrong.

'Forty-four?' I asked Mrs Wang. 'You're sure?'

'Absolutely. I was there.'

Hang on. She had just said she never saw him. But she hadn't finished.

'Yes. I was there all right. Everyone was locked up for the day. They got us out of bed at 5:30 in the morning, told us to cook some food and to put it in a lunch box, then they took us down to a big house, Number 62, and shut us in. The whole village. The builders and workmen from outside were sent down the hill to Yucun. No one saw Mao, and he saw no one either.'

Thinking of the propaganda posters of Mao meeting the peasants, shaking hands with factory workers and waving to the masses, I was indignant to hear that the Great Helmsman would intern an entire village so he could have the place to himself. I wondered if the house arrest was on his express command or had been ordered by an overzealous bodyguard. Whatever the case it was a mildly shocking and juicy tidbit.

The driver of the minivan took the short cut from the San Qiao road across to the 104. The long and straight country lane was bordered by hedges of pink oleander bushes. Behind them regimented fields of cactus, privet saplings and patches of turf for sports pitches stretched south towards Hangzhou and north to Huzhou. The local nursery garden industry benefits from the local spring water too. We passed through the tiny hamlet known simply as '54'.

We would soon arrive in town, so I moved on to Chiang Kai Shek. I had already met an old man who as a boy remembered seeing China's other 'great' leader of the twentieth century in Moganshan.

'Ah, Chiang Kai Shek.' Mrs Wang smiled. 'I remember him coming up the mountain. Yes. Of course. He used to walk around the place with his guards and that wife of his,

229

what's her name? Song something. They used to have parties, and dances. All very lively it was when they were about. Must have been '27 or '28.'

'Nineteen Twenty-seven?'

This time I was sure she was wrong. Chiang Kai Shek was only just setting out on his Northern Expedition in 1927. He was nowhere near Moganshan and he was not married.

As politely as I could, I leant across her front and shouted into Mrs Wang's good ear. 'Auntie, it can't have been 1927! You must be wrong!'

'No, I am not!' she shouted back, not obstinately but with absolute certainty. 'It was the twenty-seventh year of the Republic!'

Her dates suddenly made sense. As was the custom since dynastic China began, 4,000 years ago, Mrs Wang dated everything from the year of accession. To her Sun Yat Sen's Republic, founded in 1911, was just another dynasty. I wondered if she took 1949 as yet another dynastic debut. But that would make the date of Mao's visit much earlier. I was going to confuse myself again.

'Aha!' I smiled. 'You mean the Republic of 1911!'

'Yes,' she replied, clear as a bell.

My mind was spinning. How could she know the date of the Republic, put it correctly according to standard practice, but then refer to every year after it as dating from it. I let out an internal scream and decided to gloss over the fact that the maths still did not add up. I put that down to another quirk of Chinese counting whereby everyone gets a year older on New Year's day, and accepted that Mrs Wang's dates were ten years, if not eleven, early. Or was it late?

230

'So Mao came in 1954, just like I thought,' I shouted with all the respect for a sweet old lady that I could muster.

'That's right, '44.'

In our last few minutes together in the minivan I discovered that Mrs Wang's eighty-three-year-old husband was the son of the Moganshan Ice King, a Mr Wang You Fang, who had supplied the foreigners with ice throughout the summer. With so many Americans on the mountain it must have been a big business. He made a fortune, not least thanks to his habit of charging according to the weight of the ice when it left his ice house, as opposed to when it arrived at its customer, severely depleted by the hot walk of half an hour or so across the mountainside. The family fortune was lost in 1949.

The minivan dropped Mrs Wang off at the hospital where she was going to visit a friend. Her eldest son was going to pick her up in his car later.

By October 2005 my own story of making and losing a China fortune was finished and with the publisher.

'The only manuscript I have read in one sitting for ages,' the boss of their Asia office told me over the phone from Singapore. 'Exactly what we are looking for.'

I was sitting in the sunshine on the wall in front of the house, my back to the trees and looking at the desk on the terrace where I had been slaving at my computer for the past three months. It felt good. I might be a hermit in my hideaway but I was in touch with the world. The self-indulgent dream of living the life of a literary recluse was coming true, even if it was a business book.

The editing was done by Christmas. We started on the cover design and a marketing plan. The head office in New York doubled its order for copies when a top executive dropped into the Asia office and saw the work in progress. It would be on the shelves in a matter of months. Things were looking up.

I went down to Shanghai to spend the weekend with Joanna and the family. I had an idea for our next life I wanted to discuss.

For once I was happy to be back in the big city. I was on top of things again. I looked at Shanghai as if over my shoulder. I was about to leave it for ever. When I bumped into people I knew and they went through the usual round of sympathy I surprised them with my cheerfulness.

On the Saturday morning I sat down with Joanna in the large study which also served as a piano, laundry and guest room. My unused desk stood against the back window, forsaken for a table on a terrace in Moganshan. A massive bauhinia tree blocked out the white-tiled building across the yard underneath the window. A couple of dirty white blossoms tried to look beautiful.

The apartment where we had lived for four years in Shanghai was the envy of our friends and I did love it. But after a summer of silence in Moganshan the traffic seemed even louder and the top of the Portman Hotel, only a block away, was shrouded in grey smog. There was no comparison between our two homes.

A delivery truck backed into the yard below the window. I had often wondered what went on down there. It seemed to be a freight forwarding depot. The sound of boxes being dropped on to the truck's metal floor, amplified by the emptiness of the container, thumped through our conversation. There were shouts and cries from the yard, the street, the building site across the road and the landing outside our front door. I flinched.

Isabel and Tristan skipped and tottered into the room, pulled on our hands and begged for attention. We promised them lunch in our favourite restaurant and a trip to the park and then asked Zhou Aiyi to distract them for ten minutes.

'I am going to be an author,' I told Joanna once we had been left in peace, sort of. 'The book is going to be published.'

'That's great news.'

'And I'll earn some money from it. I am not sure how much, but it will be a start.'

'A start of what?'

'Well,' I hadn't thought through how I was going to say this. Joanna had married a successful entrepreneur. She still wanted me to fight a fight, that I knew was pointless, to recover my business.

I carried on. 'I was thinking, now I am an author, maybe I could write another book.' I watched her face carefully. 'A second one. A happy one to follow up on the story of *that's* magazines. Once you've got one book out I hear it is much easier for the second . . .' Joanna was looking receptive.

'So how about we leave Shanghai? Go and live in Moganshan, as a family, permanently. It's a perfect place for writing, and for the children.'

'Except there are no schools,' Joanna slipped in quite reasonably.

'Yes, true. But the children are young enough for us not to worry about that *too* much yet. We'll take them on nature walks . . .'

'And how are we going to survive? Earn a living?' Joanna asked, again with good reason.

'From my writing,' I replied confidently.

'And how much will that bring in?'

'Um, as I say, I am not sure. But a friend who has published a couple of books told me I might get about fifty thousand US, over time.' My wife likes numbers. So I was making them up.

I was doing all right but I was not doing brilliantly. Joanna clearly had reservations about leaving the city, my giving up a chance of a well-paid job, the convenience, the social life, the shops. She had spent all her life in big cities.

After a moment's silence, she asked, 'And what am I going to do?'

There she had me. I had not thought about that. In my dreams she was going to live a life of healthy country leisure, make a home of our big house while I made books in the small one. She was going to lay out a garden, grow vegetables, raise chickens, collect eggs, walk a dog, play with the children, bring me cups of coffee and cook me lunch. Do the shopping in the market. Keep busy.

I realized that if I said all that right now I was going to be in big trouble. I thought hard and fast, back to my first ever visits to Moganshan with Brent and Leona, and – looking away from Joanna's gaze – Crystal. The car trips, the Hans, the breakfasts and whiskies ... Suddenly I had it.

'I know. Why don't you open a coffee-shop?'

'Great idea!'

I could have wept with relief. Joanna's face had lit up as she said the words. She meant them. She really did think it was a great idea. We hugged.

We fleshed it out a little. I would be the cook in the evenings and for breakfast, either side of my writing. Joanna would be in charge and run the bar. The more we talked about it the more obvious it seemed. There was nothing like it in Moganshan and I had always wished there was. The number of foreign visitors was on the up – boosted by our own friends – and I was sure others had missed a glass of whisky or a decent cup of coffee.

It would be a small business, nothing on the scale of what I had done before. There would be plenty of time for writing and gardening and nature walks with the kids. We only needed enough income to keep us in noodles. Keep it low profile. A family business, just what Joanna wanted, she and I running an American-style Mom and Pop shop, serving good food, drinks and answering questions about Moganshan.

We pencilled in a launch date for the following spring, once the worst of the winter was over, and I went back up to Moganshan to scout locations for a coffee-shop and plan my next book.

Chapter Twelve
Back in Business

The Mokanshan Assembly Hall was formally opened at the regular five o'clock service yesterday afternoon . . . In none of the summer resorts in the Far East can there be found a community building, or a community centre, more complete in all of its details.

North-China Herald, 21 July 1923

Chinese tourists, of all classes, had been coming to the mountain for years, mainly on day trips and in organized groups, taking in the village's few tourist spots: the viewing pagodas, the dried mushroom and bamboo market and the 'Sword Pool', but I was beginning to see more and more curious and independent foreigners, just as I myself had been in 1999. These visitors wandered the pathways during the day and found their own secret hideaways at night. There would surely be many more in the future. The place had been built for foreigners after all, and no matter how Chinese the infrastructure, the restaurants and the services, it would be foreigners who truly appreciated the old buildings built by their predecessors, and the place where they had put them.

On my trips back to Shanghai I couldn't help being surprised at the number of foreigners on the streets, in bars and restaurants, train and bus stations, everywhere. Riding a taxi through certain parts of town I could have sworn that every other face was a white one. And those were the Caucasians who were easy to spot. A well-dressed Chinese was as likely to be an American or Canadian 'banana' – yellow on the outside, white on the inside – or a Hong Kong or Taiwanese, or an overseas-educated returnee Shanghainese, as they were to be a local white-collar worker.

Almost a decade had gone by since I first arrived in the city. The changes were astounding. The number of bars had multiplied a hundredfold, as well as restaurants and nightclubs. I used to know them all, their owners and managers and many of the staff. Now when Mark Secchia or Brent suggested a place to meet, I had to ask: 'And where is that?'

'There's a really useful magazine that has all the bars in its listings pages,' they teased. 'You should check it out . . . oops. Sorry.'

The foreigners moving into Shanghai in 2006 were different to my friends from the old days. The new arrivals were professionals. They knew what they were doing and earned their high salaries not because they were prepared to suffer the inconvenience of living in China, but because they were good at what they did. They weren't expats. They were world citizens. The days of the Sinophile amateur like me were coming to an end and Shanghai was turning back into the international city it was born to be. The 'old days', my ones, were long gone. Shanghai was returning to the *really* old days of a hundred years ago.

The new class of throw-back foreigner in Shanghai would

be looking for weekend escapes, I was sure of it, especially in the summer. Even with air conditioning Shanghai will always be a sweatbox from July to September. By 2006 it was clear that, once again, Moganshan needed a place where visitors, particularly western ones, could get together. If history repeats itself, and the *North-China Daily News* says it does, then it was time that Moganshan had a new community centre.

Over the years since Brent and I first fumbled our way to the mountain, the roads from Shanghai to Moganshan have made a leap in progress, the equivalent of going from boat to air travel.

The Shanghai to Hangzhou motorway has been widened from four lanes to eight. Advertising hoardings run its entire length at intervals of a couple of hundred metres. In places they are ranked two deep.

Junction eighteen of the motorway – it'll be in the twenties by now – connects with the new Hangzhou ring road, which brings you to the new four-lane Hangzhou Nanjing highway, the 'Hangning'. The Moganshan exit from the Hangning is only half an hour from the village.

The journey by car from Shanghai to the top of Moganshan can now be made in less than two hours. The only hold-up might be an accident, as ever. The roads are still fearsome but, thanks to the number of lanes, the crashes are fewer and getting past them is easier too, unless you stop for a photograph.

Joanna and I watched the trickle of friends – and friends of friends – coming to Moganshan become a regular stream. During the summer our cottage was used every weekend. Word was spreading.

If so many people were coming thanks to word of mouth then how many more would come if we set up a business that we could advertise openly? Probably enough for a small hotel. But we did not want to get ahead of ourselves, nor did we want to compete from day one with our new neighbours. That is not the path to a peaceful life in China. If we could make enough money to live off, keep the locals happy by passing on custom for their hotels and guesthouses and get into the good books of the Administration Bureau by bringing more visitors to the mountain, then we'd be happy, so would our neighbours, and I would have time for writing and the garden.

The design and style of small coffee-shop was obvious, a no-brainer. Quite apart from the impossibility of finding a decent cup of coffee in the village, there was nowhere for a visitor to sit other than a hotel room or balcony, especially on a wet day. The alternative was an uncomfortable wooden chair in a white tiled restaurant on Yin Shan Jie, where you could drink tea or Moganshan Spring Beer and enjoy an atmosphere with as much charm as a doctor's waiting room.

The Chinese can sit over a dining table for hours and are happy to play cards in a hotel room if it is raining, or even if it isn't. Weekending westerners are different. They like to lean on a bar or sit round a table and meet people like themselves.

And we foreigners like our coffee-shops small and cosy, and old. Chinese tend to like big, bright and new. So we would create a place that harked back to the old days, that looked and felt original, Moganshan original, and that meant unashamedly western. For the Chinese tourists we would create a living museum. Once again we were going to step into the cultural divide.

239

The exterior was taken care of because every building in the village is old and western. All we had to do was find one that was available for a reasonable rent. Inside, we would just have to use a little imagination and some authentic furniture. We had plenty of the latter in our Shanghai flat thanks to Mr Yang and nowhere to put it in our houses thanks to Mr Zheng, all made at the time of Moganshan's heyday. A couple of modern touches, like a television and DVD player for rainy days, and an Italian coffee-machine . . . the more we thought about it the simpler it sounded. The burning question was where in the village to put it.

In the dead quiet of January I started my search.

Beside the old swimming-pool and a small chapel, near the hub of village life and every visitor's arrival point, there was a building I had often dreamt of restoring. It looked like it might have been the original post office. There was a deep, south-east-facing veranda that cried out for rattan chairs and gin slings. It led down on to a broad swathe of weed-covered concrete. Across that a retaining wall dropped down to the street through a couple of giant sycamores that could be trimmed to open up the view. It was close yet removed from the main drag. Perfect.

Sometime between the 1950s and 80s I knew the place had been the village school. Now it was the unoccupied office of the Moganshan Residents' Committee, or so said the characters down the side of the door, black on white in government typography. What they meant was: 'Wasted Government Property'. During the summer, extra staff for hotels and restaurants used the place as a dormitory.

I made enquiries via Mr Shen, who owned the restaurant below it.

'No,' he came back with a few days later. The Administration Bureau had vague plans for the place – like Mr Ge's museum of the secret police, perhaps, which had remained derelict ever since we asked about it seven years ago.

I had already come up with another idea, so I thanked Mr Shen and moved on.

At the other end of Yin Shan Jie there is a hotel called the Songliang Shanzhuang, the Pine Tree Grain Mountain Resort. The name is derived from the pine trees across the hotel's front and the fact that it was built in the sixties by the local Grain Bureau as a staff rest house. Today it is leased and managed as a hotel by a Mr Wang, one of the sons of Mrs Wang – same Wang sound, but written with a different Wang character in Chinese.

I had noticed that some of the ground-floor rooms in one wing of the hotel were not being used. They had been a 'hairdressing salon' until the year before last.

There is a reason for the inverted commas. You do not visit such places for a haircut. At first glance they do look like barber's shops, with chairs, mirrors, and bottles of shampoo on their counters, but that is where the resemblance ends. The staff are young girls, some of them passably attractive, who sit in the window. In the interior of the 'salon' there will be curtained off cubicles, possibly a passageway leading to private rooms where you will find massage benches. The girls are not professional masseuses either.

The Songliang's 'salon' had gone out of business. The candy-stick hung askew under the eaves but never turned. The location had one significant advantage – in addition to the conversation starter that it had once been a brothel – it was above the road and had a broad area across its front for outdoor seating. Our foreign clientele would be looking down on the passers-by, not the other way round. This was incredibly important.

A bonus attraction for Chinese tourists at popular destinations across the country is the opportunity to watch foreigners. And we're not talking about people watching from a café.

'Look, *laowai*!' passers-by shout with glee and at the tops of their voices to friends and children; especially children, the way parents do at the zoo.

It can get on your nerves.

A junior official from the Administration Bureau had shown me another vacant 'massage' parlour directly below Yin Shan Jie, precisely underneath the stretch of road where local tour companies unload their coaches. The building was a good size and had a potentially pleasant garden. But there was no doubt that our customers would be driven mad when every few minutes another fifty gawping Chinese tourists in baseball caps would peer over the stone balustrade and scream with delight as if they had found the pandas.

So it was vital be above the street, out of sight of the pedestrian traffic, yet close enough to be accessible. The wing of the Songliang was perfect, better in some ways than the unused Residents' Committee hall. The hotel was shut for the winter so Joanna and I arranged to meet the owner at a teahouse in town.

Wang Rong An is easy to like. He smiles a lot, talks straight and runs his hotel professionally. The professional girls, by the way, were nothing to do with him. He had leased the wing to a local pimp.

Joanna and I explained our idea to him and his wife. We

had brought Isabel and Tristan along as if to demonstrate from the start that we meant to set up a family business.

Once he had heard us out, Wang's reaction was a perfect illustration of the cultural gap – both the chasm and the opportunity.

'I think I could lease that space to you,' he said, 'But I am very worried.'

Joanna and I exchanged looks. 'What about, Mr Wang?'

'Are you sure it will work?' he replied. 'In my opinion it is bound to fail. No one drinks coffee in Moganshan.' He did look concerned.

'We think it will work,' Joanna replied.

I was keen to tell Mr Wang not to worry, we were good for the rent and he could leave the running of our business to us. But that would have been far too foreign and rude. I sat patiently while Joanna went over our concept again, being careful not to sound too confident.

When I thought the time was right I chipped in, 'We hope of course that we'll attract more foreigners to Moganshan and we'll be very happy if they stay in your hotel, Mr Wang. That makes it more likely they'll come to our coffee-shop too.' I expanded on the theme of mutual benefit, a standard phrase which usually goes down well in these situations.

Mr Wang patently did not believe me.

Joanna and I pressed on. Mr Wang was open to letting us try and we knew that he didn't have a better plan for the three neglected rooms. He reluctantly agreed to let us draw up a draft contract, leaving the space for the rental fee blank. He'd think about that later.

Leasing an ex-brothel from Mr Wang had another major advantage. He was a local of some standing. His family had

243

been on the mountain for generations and he knew how to handle the local officials. He was the perfect buffer. He was also businesslike. If or when he saw the benefits a coffee-shop would bring to his hotel, he would look after us. Dealing direct with the Administration Bureau or Hangliao, particularly for a building which we wanted to use for a commercial purpose, as opposed to privately, was fraught with the risk of excessive rent, official interference and ultimately having them take over the place for themselves.

My gut instinct also told me Mr Wang was a decent man. We would put a non-compete clause in the contract to be sure. If he accepted it then I could rest assured, almost. My scars were still raw.

Wang left us with a warning. 'If you go ahead, you absolutely must have your renovation work finished before the season starts and my hotel opens. May the first.'

'We certainly shall,' we replied. 'It's in our own interest too.'

The anxiety had not left his face for the entire meeting.

Our life, which had been dawdling for almost a year, picked up speed again: China speed. In ten days we had a contract agreed with Mr Wang. It was unsigned, the length of the lease was open to question because it depended on Wang's own lease for the hotel, which was due for renewal in three years, and the price was still blank. We had vaguely agreed on two thousand pounds a year. That was a good enough basis for us to start the renovation.

I made a rough business plan. Start-up costs, running costs, turnover required to keep us alive and pay the bills. The numbers were small. The business would be cheap to start and would work financially, but we were not going to make a fortune. That was fine by me. One China fortune had been enough hassle. I was going to be a writer anyway. Joanna would run the coffee-shop, I would help out, and the children would have a healthy country upbringing.

We fixed a date to hand over our Shanghai apartment, pack up and leave the city forever. I had long since left in spirit. Cities are tough enough places anywhere in the world, but Shanghai has a particular ruthlessness, a lack of soul. But for the fact that my children had been born there and the opportunities the city had given me, I had no attachment to the place. And Moganshan was near enough to keep in touch with close friends.

As soon as we'd finalized the contract with Mr Wang, Joanna and I made an irrevocable commitment to country life. We bought a car.

I had not owned a car for ten years. Living in Chinese cities I had never wanted or needed one. They were more trouble than they were worth. Taxis were cheap and plentiful and trips outside the city could easily be made by train, bus or Brent. In Moganshan we were going to need one.

I suggested to Joanna that we wait until we *really* needed it, once we had moved. By now I knew many of the minivan drivers who scoot up and down the mountain and had hitched lifts with all sorts, from the truck that delivered Moganshan's spring water to Hangzhou every morning to the luxurious limos of foreign chief executives all the way back to Shanghai. I had even walked down to Yucun one winter when the roads had frozen over. In fact I had walked up and down the hill many times, and everywhere around it. I enjoyed my morning exercise to and from the market, the greetings and the villagers sticking their noses into my shopping basket. I could

245

not help thinking that a car was going to spoil our rustic idyll.

Joanna was right however. We needed a car for the children to go to school and to make supply runs for the coffee-shop. And there was no point in waiting.

So we purchased a brand new 'Great Wall' in Hangzhou. It is a diesel seven-seater and looks like a four-wheel drive but isn't. In London it would be called a Chelsea tractor. The price, if we had put it into the books for the new business, would be a third of our total start-up costs. Cars are still expensive in China and starting a business still cheap.

Despite my hesitation about a vehicle taking something away from our pristine country existence, when I got behind the wheel and chugged out of the showroom on to the open road I felt like a cowboy who has got his horse back, as if my real life in China had begun. I now had a complete family unit: wife, kids, house and car.

So this time when the three removal rucks arrived at our flat in Shanghai we did not give the drivers directions and cross our fingers. We pulled out ahead of them in our shiny new green jeep, packed to the roof with leftover luggage, two children and their dear Zhou Aiyi – who was braving her fear of high mountains and open spaces and coming to help us settle in – and led the slow-moving convoy out of Shanghai, on to the highway and, four hours later, up the mountain.

We arrived in daylight and the removal men, who had been briefed on the path through the woods and how to unload one truck at a time, got everything into roughly the right room and pretty much the right house without a hitch. The furniture we had allocated to the coffee-shop was put into a warehouse until the renovations were complete.

Those were going surprisingly smoothly too. We had the benefit of experience and the immeasurable advantage of daily supervision. While Joanna had remained in Shanghai to wrap up our old life I had been the advance party for the new one. My main concern was the deadline. We did not want to upset Mr Wang before we had even opened for business.

I'd asked Pan Guang Lin if he wanted the work. He told me he was busy into the summer. I had my doubts and I couldn't entirely blame him. I had to find a new construction crew.

There was one right on my doorstep, restoring Hangliao House 21, the villa at the bottom of our steps that had been marked for demolition. One morning, after the ritual thrusting of cigarettes in each others' faces, I asked the foreman if he would be available for a quick job on three hotel rooms.

The foreman was yet another Lao Han and working for him was his elder brother, referred to as Lao Lao Han, Older Old Han. That meant three Lao Hans, Builder, Street and Caretaker, and one Double Lao Han were working within a stone's throw of each other. My morning greetings had recently become rather repetitive.

'We'll be finished here on the back of a horse,' Han the Builder told me, using the Chinese expression that can mean in the next five minutes or any day in the next month. 'Let me come and have a look this afternoon.'

'Can I see what you're doing here first?' I asked. I wanted to check out his work and also see for myself how far along it was.

Han the Builder showed me round. The work did look near to completion and the standard was not bad. I was particularly keen to see the woodwork. We were planning plenty of it in the coffee-shop: wainscotting, floors, shutters and, of course, a bar.

There was a private dining-room in an extension at the back of House 21, built entirely of wood. I studied it closely and was impressed. The joins were neat, the finish smooth.

'This is very good, Lao Han,' I said.

'We didn't do it,' he replied.

At least he was honest.

'Back of a horse' was a week later. Lao Han's demolition men started at dawn without telling me. It was Mr Wang who called my mobile and suggested I went down.

I had made detailed drawings and gone over them with Lao Han; separate ones for floor plan, water and electricity, and especially careful ones of the bar itself from every angle and with precise measurements. I had even knocked up a passable three-dimensional sketch of the general impression. Nothing had been left to chance. Lao Han had a hand-copied set.

I drove down to the Songliang Hotel. The familiar sound of hammering came from our wing. I stepped in through the glass doors under the candy stick. Behind them was the corridor where the barber's chairs had sat and to its right were the hotel rooms we had rented. The idea was to knock the whole lot into one.

There was a large hole in the first wall and a pile of rubble on the floor. The air was thick with dust. Two old men in blue Mao jackets, dark trousers and army issue gym shoes were smacking it down with hammers. They did not use chisels.

I greeted them and asked for Lao Han.

'He's not here yet,' one of them replied.

'Has he told you which walls are to come down? Did he give you the drawings?' I asked.

The old man pointed at the bathroom at the end of the corridor. 'You want that out, don't you?'

'No.' It was going to be a small office and storeroom.

'And you want us to leave that one?' he pointed through the hole in the wall to the bathroom in the first bedroom. It was exactly where the bar was due to stand.

'No.'

'And you want this wall down.'

'Yes, but I want a buttress left at the end.' I realized I had left my copy of the drawings at home in the rush.

'Which end?'

'Tell you what,' I said, 'I'll go and get Lao Han. You knock this wall down to about here,' with a broken brick I made an orange mark on the white wall, 'and you can take the windows out.' That should give me enough time to track down Lao Han and get things straight.

Over the next four weeks I went to the Songliang twice a day, morning and afternoon. I joined in with the simple work like removing the tiles from the bathroom walls. This taught me why Chinese workmen never bother with precision tools like chisels. The tiles were cemented on so hard and fast it was much easier to thwack them to bits with a hammer.

'You're very capable,' the workmen told me with the standard face-giving overstatement. When my blisters grew too big despite my gardening gloves I went back to my writing desk at home.

By mid-April the space was beginning to look like a coffee-shop. Lao Han's carpenters were good craftsmen. We went to town together and bought the timber, nails, hinges, glass for the windows, stain and varnish, everything we needed. The diesel jeep proved its worth, chugging up the steep switchback hill in first gear, laden with boxes of kitchen tiles and timber. Thanks to my being on the spot to supervise every step and make every purchase, the process was fast, cheap, and the quality was not bad at all. I was confident we would be finished in time.

With four days to go to, all that was left to do was paint the walls.

By now Joanna and the children were with me. Our country life had begun. Zhou Aiyi had returned tearfully to Shanghai after a week with us. She still did not like Moganshan but promised to come twice a year for the children's birthdays.

Joanna was pleased with the coffee-shop. That was a huge relief for me and Lao Han – though he did not know it – and I was glad she was here for the final stages, specifically the painting. Mr Wang had made it particularly clear that he did not want the smell of fresh paint upsetting his guests, so we didn't have any time for mistakes.

We intended the coffee-shop's walls above the wainscotting to be a pale yellow, but not too pale. When the emulsion and pigment turned up, which I had selected from a colour card at the paint shop recommended by Lao Han, approved by Joanna, we mixed them and slapped on a test strip. The result was a sickening yellow that was almost fluorescent, like luminous golf balls.

I asked Lao Han's young painter, 'Why is this nothing like the yellow on the colour card?' I pulled it out to show him. 'The man in the shop said he could produce this exactly.'

'Which shop did you go to?' asked the painter. I gave him the name card.

'That guy can't make paint according to colour cards!' he exclaimed. 'He hasn't got an electric mixing machine for a start, let alone the right pigments!'

Joanna and I rushed to town. The young painter came with us. He took us to a professional paint shop and helped us select and supervise the mixing of the right colour. Then we sent him and the right paint back up the hill by taxi to get on with the job while we returned the wrong one to the dodgy dealer. In my careful planning I had neglected to allow time for the final coat of varnish on the wooden floor, which had to wait until the walls and ceiling had been painted. We were still going to make it, by the skin of our teeth, but now every minute counted.

On our way back up the hill we stopped off to see how the painters were getting on with the better quality and significantly more expensive yellow. I was horrified.

With indisputable logic, they had started with the ceiling. It was almost finished. They smiled and pointed out how little was left as we walked in the door. But we did not want a yellow ceiling. No one wants a yellow ceiling. Ceilings are white. I had told Lao Han so some days ago. I was sure I had. But I had never written it down.

We had furniture, bar equipment, kitchen equipment, a coffee-machine and fresh coffee, pictures to hang on the walls, everything scheduled to arrive in strict sequence and just in time for us to polish off the whole effect for 1 May. We also had an impatient landlord who was pestering us whenever he saw us, which was about every half hour. Now we had to wait a whole day for a yellow ceiling to dry so we could paint it white again.

If you ever come to Moganshan on a sunny day and look closely at the ceiling of our coffee-shop, you will notice that in places it has a slight yellow tint. Those are the bits I couldn't reach with Joanna's hair-dryer.

Everything came together in a madcap last minute rush. Our green car yoyo'd up and down the mountain on runs to collect supplies and vital bits and pieces I had forgotten, like a sign to go over the door, and then, on 30 April, we suddenly had a coffee-shop.

It looked almost exactly as we had wanted it to. A couple of structural pillars had spoilt my plan for broad arches to lead from one space to another, the inner one slightly narrower to give a sense of perspective and draw customers in, an idea I had picked up from a local interior designer. Han the Builder had said he could take the pillars out but that the long-term effect would be 'not too good'. In other words the wing of the hotel would eventually fall down. So the pillars stayed, one of them slap bang in the middle of what would have been a graceful open arch.

In the middle space we had erected the bar and shelves for bottles and glasses, made to measure and moveable in case Mr Wang could not renew his lease and we had to find a new home. By the central window, recessed by the balustrades left in the two walls, was a long dining-table, one of Mr Yang's original treasures. He had restored and stained it beautifully. This would be our communal dining-table. It could seat twelve.

In the snug inner space we had made a sitting-room with some original leather sofas, also from Mr Yang, a coffee-table and a pair of tall bookshelves made by Han the Builder. My books made a respectable if eclectic library. Dr Spock's *Baby*

252

and Child Care sat beside a biography of Mao Ze Dong. I would organize them later.

Across a narrow corridor behind the bar I had made a small kitchen, equipped for breakfasts, cake-making and simple lunches and dinners. People were not only going to eat at the same table, at the same time, but they were also going to eat the same thing. It added to the homey feel we wanted and made us more of a meeting place, the community centre that Moganshan needed.

We called it the Lodge. The name suited the look and allowed us to move on and offer accommodation in the future, if and when the time was right.

Everyone in the village thought we were mad, including the officials in the Administration Bureau and the police. That helped with the red tape. They imagined we would be shut within months, at the latest by the end of the year. The local tax bureau took one look, presumed we were going to fail, and set our annual tax bill at a couple of thousand yuan paid in advance. That was fine by us. We were confident that once word got around, we would bring home the bacon.

There remained only one major problem: the bacon.

Key to the whole plan were decent western breakfasts. If there is one imported western luxury money cannot buy in modern-day China, it is decent bacon. The foreign goods stores in most major cities have cold shelves stacked with imported vacuum-packed pink streaked meat which says bacon on the label, and it does taste like bacon, but throw it in a frying pan and by the time it's cooked it will be half its original size and swimming in fat and water. Call me fussy but I like bacon to look like a slice of meat, in the pan and

253

on the plate. Call me patriotic but I am talking about proper British bacon.

What there *is* plenty of in China is pork. It is the staple meat.

There was only one thing for it. I had to learn how to make bacon. I went to the obvious place to find out how, the web.

'Two parts salt, one part brown sugar, and a dash of potassium nitrate, otherwise known as saltpeter, commonly used for making gunpowder,' the Internet told me. 'For a dry cure, rub into the pork bellies three times over a period of ten days, keep the juices drained, then hang in a cool place for another ten days.' It sounded so easy I kicked myself for not trying to make my own bacon sooner. Ten years is a long time to go without.

The first customers to taste the result were some Brits and Americans from Hong Kong and elsewhere in China who had come to compete in the inaugural Moganshan Adventure Race, held on 6 May 2006. They had set off at dawn. Twenty-four hours later, the last of the mountain biking, cross-country running, boat paddling and abseiling masochists crawled back up to the village. The organizer had kindly mentioned our breakfasts in his pre-race briefing.

The Hong Kong Brits were first through the door. If anyone could tell me how authentic the bacon was, it was them. I laid the plates in front of them: eggs, bacon, fresh kidneys, tomato, mushrooms and toast, and hovered nervously behind the bar, my ears straining to hear their opinion.

'Amazing bacon,' the first man to finish remarked. 'We can't get this in Hong Kong even. How on earth did you find it in mainland China?'

'I made it myself.' My chest swelled a fraction.

'Where the hell did you learn to do that?'

'*Blue Peter* of course.'

He was British, so he got the joke. And after their prize-giving they came back for another round. I'd discovered one of the secrets of our success.

There was something else I discovered in those early days of my new career. Being a cook was damn hard work. I had done my time in bars and restaurants as a student and thought I could easily slip back into it. It was a fun job, or so I remembered it. But I had forgotten that I was now twenty years older and used to sitting behind a desk. On a Monday morning after a busy weekend my legs ached as if I too had run an adventure race, my back was sore, and my hands cut and burnt.

Joanna and I did everything ourselves. She was front of house, making coffee and serving drinks while I stayed in the kitchen knocking up breakfasts with a greasy spoon and in the evenings cooking the few dishes I knew: roast chicken with bread sauce, roast pork with crackling and apple sauce, beef curry, spag bog and fish pie. The home-cooked formula worked. We made no claim to *haute cuisine*. We did not even call ourselves a restaurant, just a coffee-shop and bar with a kitchen.

'We'd like to order dinner this evening,' foreign mothers with children and maids and husbands in tow would say as they grabbed a menu from the bar. Then they would reel off a selection of dishes.

'It's chicken,' I would reply. 'I can fit you in, just. Seven-thirty.' And I'd leave Joanna to work out the seating plan and go back to my stove.

For someone with no formal training or experience I like

to think I did a pretty good job of creating a professional kitchen. It had been fun to work out the ergonomics and a real pleasure to buy all the proper equipment. I have always enjoyed cooking. But I did make a couple of mistakes.

The worst was to think I could do without an extractor fan. The stove sat between two windows so I had naively assumed I only had to open them to let the smells and smoke out. It did not take long to find out that bugs and flies could come in by the same route and had a nasty habit of landing in the soup. So I shut the windows and put up with the smells, but then whenever I opened the door they would flood out into the corridor, up the back stairs and into Mr Wang's hotel rooms.

'Smells delicious, what are you cooking?' the chambermaids asked with sweet smiles as they passed along the corridor with the laundry. With perfect Chinese manners they were actually saying: 'You are stinking out the hotel. Please stop it.'

They had further reason to complain when I set the kitchen on fire. It was only my second roast, but there were more customers than the first time so I used a large roasting dish that had come with the shiny new oven. Brent had come up for the weekend and was helping out, bringing me cold bottles of beer and serving behind the bar.

I had no idea that what I was filling with oil and fat was not a roasting dish. It was a deep baking tray, designed for biscuits, with unsealed corners through which hot oil and fat could easily escape.

As you do with a roast, I had put the pork in at a high temperature to get it going and then left it for twenty minutes. Twenty minutes of chatting to Brent and some customers at the bar.

He smelt it first and slipped away to have a look. He was back in a flash.

'Mark, I think your oven is smoking a bit. Want to come and check it out?'

'Nothing to worry about,' I replied. 'Quite normal. I've got it at a high temperature to get the crackling started. The fat in the pan gets a bit hot and smokes, that's all it is.'

'OK, but does it normally smoke *this* much?' Brent was standing in the doorway at the back of the bar as smoke wafted out of the kitchen behind him.

'Yes, it does,' I tried to reassure myself. I was already on my way to join him.

Smoke was pouring out of the back of the oven.

I squatted on my heels and put my hand on the oven door. When I pulled it down a sheet of flame shot out and stopped millimetres short of my eyebrows. It retreated to the back of the oven.

'Shit! The oven's on fire!'

I pulled the pork out, slammed the door shut and turned it off. I reached up on to the wall and pulled the plug.

'What the hell do we do?' I asked Brent.

'Well,' said Brent slowly, in his unflappable way. 'I read somewhere that when you have burning oil in your oven you put flour in there to douse the flames and soak it up. You got any flour?'

'Course I have. This is a kitchen.'

'You wanna try it?'

Mr Wang's sister, who helped run the hotel, appeared in the doorway. 'Mark, I think you have a problem in your kitchen. There is smoke all along the corridor upstairs and it is going into the rooms. We've had to open all the windows to let it out.'

Brent and I stood up straight and tried to look as innocent and in control as possible. 'Just something burning in the oven, Wang Aiyi,' I said. 'We're dealing with it. Won't be a minute.'

We smiled and slammed the door in her face.

'Right, close the windows and let's try the flour.'

I stuck my hand into the sack, pulled the door of the oven open and threw in some flour, then some more. I started shovelling it with my hands. At first the flames seemed to devour it in mid-air but then it worked.

We wiped the sweat and grime from our faces with a tea towel, slipped back into the bar as unobtrusively as we could and grabbed a couple of beers. No one raised an eyebrow. By some fluke the smoke hadn't crossed the corridor.

'Er, dinner's going to be a little later than expected,' I announced.

'That's fine,' replied someone very nice. 'We're having a good chat here.'

That was something else I noticed about the Lodge, and Moganshan too, once the foreigners began to return. It attracts 'nice' people, the ones who long to get away from their city lives, who do not stay there and party all weekend and struggle through the first days of the week with a monster hangover as I had in my foolish entrepreneurial youth. We rarely get awkward customers, drunks, or people who complain. The most common problem we have are new Shanghai-based foreign families who mistakenly believe that Shanghai standard international service, convenience and comfort are available across China, which they are not. As I keep repeating to them: Shanghai is not China. They learn fast.

Throughout 2006 we played host to all walks of life: estate

258

agents, advertising executives, consultants, investment bankers, normal bankers, website designers, teachers, textile exporters, sourcing agents, floor makers, PR people, marketing executives, commodity traders, wives, children, visiting grand-parents, diplomats, wine merchants, yacht salesmen, meat importers, hotel managers, entrepreneurs, writers, potters, artists, car makers, car-parts makers, car upholsterers . . . We even had a couple of modern-day missionaries.

They came from the UK, America, France, Belgium, Canada, Germany, Holland, Italy, Israel, Spain, South Africa, Argentina, India, Singapore, Malaysia, Taiwan, Singapore and Hong Kong. Most lived in Shanghai and worked for foreign companies or joint ventures and they had one thing in common: they longed for an escape. The expressions on their faces as they walked in the door were heartwarming. We had created exactly what they were looking for: a small dose of home comfort in a peaceful village on top of a picturesque mountain in the middle of the madness that is modern China.

Thanks to our pushing people together at the large dining table strangers got to know each other – if they had not already run into each other on the trails around the village – and were soon chatting like friends. From what I hear I think we have created something of a social circle, the 'We met in Moganshan' crowd. And I know of at least one modern Moganshan romance which began during an evening in the Lodge.

You could even say: 'Old friends, acquaintances and nodding acquaintances here meet in happy informality and get to know each other more intimately and so carry away the happiest impressions.' Which is how the *North-China Daily News* had described the summer community of Moganshan in 1926.

One of our earliest guests was an American engineer from an industrial city up country from Moganshan. He was effusive in his praise, as Americans can be: of the Lodge, our website, our help getting him a room in the village, our advice on where to go for a walk, my potted history of the mountain and also the fact that he had met such a nice crowd of people.

When he was about to leave he turned and said, 'You guys sure know how to help foreigners feel comfortable in China. You should do more with your website, or guidebooks or something. You could help people get much more out of this place.'

My heart quietly bled. The creed I had laid down for my magazines was: 'Help English speakers get more out of China, and put something back into it.'

I smiled and told him I'd think about it. I didn't tell him I was on the point of publishing a book about trying to help foreigners in China, and trying to help China too, and being shafted for my efforts.

The book was about to go to press. Or so I thought.

At the last minute the publishers sent a copy of the manuscript to their Beijing office, the people responsible for expanding their business in China.

'We think', the Beijing office replied immediately, 'that if we publish this, we will be in serious trouble and it will hinder our attempts to expand here.'

'We do not want', the boss of the Asia office of the large and well-known American publishing company told my editor, 'to risk our Beijing staff to go to jail.'

'We are chicken shit,' my editor told me over the phone. 'And we will not be publishing your book after all. I am very sorry.'

260

My dreams of becoming a poet-recluse who wrote business books in a (large) hut on a Chinese mountain were over.

When the children were in bed that night I sat outside on the terrace with Joanna. 'The book has been dropped.' I told her. 'I'm very sorry. We're going to have to rely on the Lodge for more than noodles now.'

My poor long-suffering wife. She married a successful entrepreneur, a mini media mogul no less, and she had ended up with a cook.

And I was back up Shitzu Creek without a poodle.

Chapter Thirteen
Add Seasoning and a Large Legend

... It is the moral effect of a typhoon which most appals.
The remorseless, ceaseless roar, the general sense of mad
violence and one's own littleness produce in one a
weariness, a kind of mental paralysis such as the hardest
day's work does not bring.
... Will the wind never cease?

North-China Herald, 11 September 1920

The Moganshan year begins punctually on 1 May, May Day, in Chinese still referred to by some as the 'Workers' Festival'.

As with the Lunar New Year China shuts down, only for a shorter period this time. To give the workers a clear seven-day break the government makes the weekend before or straight afterwards a working one. This complicates the workers' lives because China's growing private industry and its international companies prefer to take weekends off like the rest of the world and work for the two extra holiday weekdays, while government institutions work on the weekend and shut for the official holiday – except for those with private business interests, which is quite a lot of them. So some people get nine days' holiday, most have seven, and the unlucky get only five.

They come in their coachloads, from Shanghai, Hangzhou, Wuxi, Huzhou, Nanjing, and even Hong Kong. The village is overrun as Margate once was by cockneys. The steep switchback 'front' road from Yucun is stacked with city drivers like a school stairwell between classes. They stall, roll backwards and crunch headlights on the way up and burn brakes on their way down. The wider and gentler back road is clogged with coaches.

For years the police have campaigned for a one-way system during the holiday, up via Yucun and down along the back road, or the other way round. But the Administration Bureau fear it will reduce their May Day bonanza from entry ticket sales: eighty yuan per person, special discounts for tour groups. So they have held firm. Only in the centre of the village have the police managed to establish a short one-way system along Yin Shan Jie with a counterflow through the market car park. It does not help much. For a week the blaring horns remind me all too nightmarishly of Shanghai.

It is a dramatic irony that the May Day crowds miss the best time of the year in Moganshan by barely a week. In April the village blooms.

Along the Ridge Road and the ones up and down the mountain, giant magnolias as tall as English oaks sprout enormous flowers from every tendril. The locals call them 'spoon flowers'. They do not last long. Thanks to their size and weight the slightest wind knocks them to the ground where they lie for a day like balls of fresh snow then turn teabag brown and vanish.

Flowering camellias are scattered through the woods, beside houses, along the roads. Generally they are a bright crimson, occasionally pale pink. Like the magnolias, the flowers are fat and heavy and do not hold on for long. The large bush in front of our house reminds me of a Christmas tree. The flowers are as bright and eye-catching as fairy lights.

Among the bamboo and the fir trees along the ridge and out towards Queer Stone Corner, one tree in a hundred will be covered in delicate white or pale pink blossoms. After a spring shower, when the sun is drawing a light mist from the wet ground, it is easy to mistake – as I have done more than once – a dense white and perfectly fluffy tree for a lonely cloud floating in the treetops. Where the mountain doubles back on itself behind our houses, the tight globes of blossom scattered through the trees on the opposite slope from the road look like the aftermath of a giants' snowball fight.

Across the floor of the bamboo forest and beneath the pine trees, purple corydalis cover the ground like a carpet of bluebells in an English wood. Corydalis are native to Zhejiang, Moganshan's province. Broad swathes of the tiny flowers swell, contract and slightly shift each year. Behind our house the slope is solid with them, as if we had laid a purple rug. In the woods nearby are small clusters of wild irises, a paler purple. A drooping bank of a honeysuckle-type yellow flowering shrub lines the wall above the path leading to the house. From a distance it looks like Scottish broom.

But it is the azaleas, the cuckoo flowers, that rule supreme. They are everywhere, cultivated and wild. In the scrub that lines the gully which the steep road climbs from Yucun, the splashes of colour are like flecks of bright paint on the walls of a dull green corridor. In Moganshan village itself, carefully tended bushy banks of them hang from the roadside retaining walls. The dirt bank along the top of our garden disappears under a mass of wild ones that hang like a blanket.

Moganshan in springtime is a cliché of colour: a riot. It is stunningly beautiful. And few see it.

As the blossoms fall and the wild flowers wilt and disappear, bright green buds and tiny leaves appear on the trees. Day by day the mountain takes on 'the verdure of Japan', a simile that was often repeated by the correspondents of the *North-China Daily News*. Only now do the tourists arrive.

The local ones come for the local sights, by tour coach and private car. At the ticket gates below the village young women with badges offer their services as guides. They meet the coaches by prior arrangement and tout themselves to the private cars. They are the daughters and wives of longstanding Moganshan families and guiding is their summer job.

The girls first whisk their clients to a photo opportunity at the Green Dripping Pond where a fifty-metre high cliff is inscribed with 'the largest calligraphy in Southern China' according to the information board beside it. It says '*Moganshan Hao*', which could either mean 'Hello Moganshan' or 'Moganshan is fine'. I assume the former because the board also describes in Chinese Franglais how the inscription 'offers up a big bonjour' to Moganshan. But if it was the latter it would still make perfect sense. As a sharp-witted friend once observed, 'The Chinese travel to confirm what they think they already know. Westerners travel to discover something new.'

On the way up the mountain there is another – smaller of course – inscription in red paint on a rock that says 'Number

265

One Mountain in South China'. All the tourists will have seen it. The fact that the much higher Yellow Mountain, one of China's top international tourist spots, is only a couple of hundred miles away to the south can be conveniently forgotten for the day.

Next stop is the White Cloud Castle museum in the grounds of the White Cloud Hotel, where Chiang Kai Shek tea danced with his new bride and held his secret and pointless meeting with Zhou En Lai. After lunch at a restaurant run by a relative, where the guide picks up an extra commission, she'll take her charges round to the back of the mountain to gawk at the bed frame where a drunken Mao Ze Dong probably took his nap.

The foreign history of Moganshan is quietly overlooked. When the troops of Chinese tourists march past the weed-infested tennis-courts, no one tells them they were tennis courts or that the annual tournament was usually won by the American students from Shanghai American School. The old Assembly Hall and church is what it is, a carpentry workshop, not what it was, the centre of the community. The sad swimming-pool is ignored. No one tells the story of poor Percy King or points out where his brains were squashed on the road below. Felgate's murder is forgotten, the ruins of the Railway Hotel bypassed.

The main tourist site and the climax of a visit for domestic tourists is the Sword Pool. This is the spot that gives Moganshan its name. And after that dig about the guides skipping the foreign history, I'm a hypocrite myself for leaving so much of the Chinese history of Moganshan until now.

The Sword Pool is a couple of hundred metres below Yin Shan Jie, nestled in the main gully that leads down to Yucun.

The gully is the mountain's fairy glen, with a rushing torrent of spring water flowing down its middle. It is shaded by tall pines, there is a waterfall, a grotto and a real, properly mythical, legend.

It was here that two famous swordsmiths, Gan Jiang and his wife Mo Ye, were allegedly commissioned by the King of Wu to make a pair of swords with the sharpest and strongest blades they could possibly forge. Wu was one of the petty kingdoms in the Warring States period that preceded the first unification of China by the Emperor Qin in 221 BC. But some put the legend of Gan Jiang and Mo Ye in the Spring and Autumn period, the one before the Warring States. Others say it was in fact the King of Chu who wanted the swords, not Wu.

A commission from a king, whichever one he was, put Gan Jiang and his wife in an awkward position. Not only did he have to make the best swords of his life, they would also mean the end of it. It was a foregone conclusion that once he presented them to the monarch he'd be beheaded. Then the king could be sure that none of his rivals, like the King of Chu – or Wu – could commission an even better sword for cutting off *his* head.

So Gan Jiang, assisted by his wife Mo Ye, dragged out the process. Some say it took them sixty days, others three years. But there's another version of the story. This one describes how Mo Ye, frustrated at the lack of progress and keen to develop just the right mix of metals going into the furnace, first cut off her hair and threw it in, and when that did not work threw herself in. Hey presto! Out came the perfect alloy and the swords were made, cooled and tempered by her widowed husband under Moganshan spring water.

Yet another version of the story says that the king chopped both of Mo and Gan's heads off, either in accordance with tradition or more than likely because he was annoyed at having to wait so long for his swords.

One sequel has Mo Ye surviving and sending her son to avenge his father's death with one of the swords, which Mo Ye had hidden from the king. In a dream – no legend is complete without one – the king saw the son coming to kill him, so he put a price on his head. Arriving at the kingdom's capital, the vengeance-seeking son met a helpful citizen who warned him he was in mortal danger. The citizen also had a bright idea.

'Let *me* chop the king's head off for you,' he suggested. 'No one will suspect me.' But there was a catch. 'First I'll have to chop off your head so I can take it to the king and collect the reward,' the man explained.

The son agreed to this apparently ideal solution and even saved his new friend the trouble of chopping his head off. He decapitated himself and handed his own head over.

The helpful man took the head and presented it to the king, who immediately chucked it into a cauldron of boiling water, this being the standard procedure in those days to prevent a headless victim's ghost from haunting you.

The helpful man hung around at court, probably waiting for his reward, and noticed that after three days the head had still not cooked. So he invited the king to have a look.

The king bent over the cauldron and, you guessed it, the helpful man chopped his head off and then to round the story off, chopped his own off too.

And that's how Mo-Gan-Shan, the Mountain of Mo and Gan, got its name. The story may vary but the characters

Mo and Gan are always in there somewhere. Today there are several museums in China that claim to display the swords, and they also feature in a popular online dungeons and dragons computer game.

Beside the Sword Pool is a larger than life statue in polished black stone of the couple. Mo Ye stands beside her husband, holding one finished sword. Gan Jiang is hammering away at the other on his anvil, a large flat rock. Both of them have intricate top knots in their long hair. Gan Jiang is draped in a toga-type length of cloth that bares his muscle-bound legs and arms. His chest would get him into the finals of Mr Universe. His right arm is raised, the hand holding a hammer and his black eyes are focused on the blade in front of him. Mo Ye wears a long flowing dress. Behind them the water splashes into the pool, sparkling in the limited sunlight that reaches into the gully for a few hours each day.

A tourist knick-knack seller has a stand behind the statue. Her souvenirs of a visit to Moganshan range from a selection of swords – plastic, wooden and metal – to sun hats, walking sticks, hammocks, wooden carvings of crocodiles and cars, *ma jiang* sets, back scrubbers and Russian dolls.

The shaded Sword Pool empties into a lower pool from which a waterfall tumbles. Wild orchids flourish here. Sheer rocks rise on one side, steep woods on the other.

On hot days the Sword Pool is a cool spot. In high summer it loses some of its magic as the crowds of tourists tramp up and down the stone steps and along the well-made wooden walkways and viewing platforms. The girl guides keep up a running commentary through their megaphones.

Local men offering sedan rides congregate at a small rest area beside the statue of Mo and Gan. They are bare-chested, and have their trousers rolled up over their knees to reveal their knotted calves. They lounge with their legs draped over the carrying poles of the sedan chairs they have rented for the year from the Administration Bureau. When a gaggle of tourists come by they leap to their feet and aggressively bid for custom. The Sword Pool is a couple of hundred steps below the nearest road, and at least five hundred back up to the village.

'*Jiaozi*! Sedan chair!' they cry. 'It's a long way back up. Come on, let us take you. Only fifty bucks. Come on, take it easy, relax in my chair.'

If they can persuade one member of a group then others are sure to follow. The tourists look at the chairs with obvious nervousness.

'Is it safe?' they ask. 'You sure you won't drop me?' Then they look uphill at the steep steps, and back at the rickety bamboo chairs.

Sometimes everyone in a large group wants a chair. The carriers take them in shifts. When they get to the top they tip them out like a barrow load of coal and one of the pair sprints back down two steps at a time to reserve another rider. His buddy runs after him almost as fast with the empty chair on his back.

I asked one of the carriers what the standard rate from the Sword Pool up to the road was. His name is Lao Da, which best translates as Mr Big. He is taller and stronger than average for a chair carrier, with a close cropped haircut. In the old days he would probably have been the leader of the chair carrier's syndicate, the one that was broken up by the Mokanshan Summer Resort Association after a boycott in 1919.

'It all depends,' Lao Da told me.

'Depends on what? How heavy they are?'

'Oh no,' Lao Da shook his head. 'On how much money it looks like they've got. Or if they are nice to us, or stuck up, or are from around here or are city folk. If they try to bargain hard or are tight-fisted, we screw them. We have our ways of judging.'

'What about foreigners?' I had to ask.

'Same rules apply,' he said, and then one eye almost winked. 'But they are usually more generous.'

Chinese tourists in their own cars, of whom there are more and more every year, tend to stay in their cars if at all possible on a visit to Moganshan, only emerging for photographs and lunch. Instead of a five minute walk from one scenic spot to another they prefer a twenty minute traffic jam. The roads are all narrow and passing places few and far between.

Something I find completely incomprehensible is the way Chinese tourists litter. The custom and cottage industry of recycling might go some way to explain it in the cities – where you're actually doing someone a favour if you leave a plastic bottle or empty coke can in an obvious place – but in Moganshan there are no beggars to go rooting through the bins. It is a holiday resort.

The tasteful concrete tree-stump bins that the Administration Bureau has done an excellent job of placing along the trails are surrounded – not filled – by sweet wrappers, empty cigarette packs, tissue paper, plastic bags with half-eaten food in them, Styrofoam boxes, congee tins, fruit peel, and sheets of newspaper. After a summer weekend the paths are lined with rubbish and the hillsides scattered with it. The wind twirls it into piles in the corners of the pagodas in the woods. Their concrete floors look like the stands of a football stadium after a cup final.

The rubbish does get cleared away, however, by the forestry department workers. Every Friday the mountain is green and clean, ready for the next round.

Moganshan has another kind of visitor, much more interested in its natural environment. According to the season local villagers, people from towns on the plain and distant city folk in the know, come to reap the wild harvest. In spring it is the bright green leaves of wild tea bushes. Old ladies with carrier bags on their wrists wander through the woods, plucking the tiny green shoots off the tea plants. They sprout again overnight and the women re appear every day until the year's bounty is exhausted.

From March until April men wander through the bamboo digging up its shoots with an all-purpose mattock that every country family possesses. The wooden handles are polished by years of oil and sweat and the countrymen wield them like an extension of their arm.

They stuff the dirt-covered shoots into old grain sacks, sling them over the backs of their small motorbikes and take them to the nearest market where they will sell for about ten pence a pound. The shoots will then be stripped like artichoke hearts and sold fresh for a small mark-up, or else sun-dried and stored away to be sold in the summer at the Moganshan tourist market.

The bamboo shoots are easy to find. When they break through the earth they look like ducks diving in a village pond. They are perfectly conical, brown and feathery. But they grow incredibly fast. Within a week they will be a couple of feet high and the cute duck's bottom has become a pungee stake, threatening to spear you if you should stumble.

Nothing gets in their way. I have seen them push rocks aside as if they were a ball of paper. An ancient form of oriental torture was to tie a prisoner in place above one and let the relentless growth spear him to death, very slowly – even on the slow death scale – and very painfully.

In the *North-China Daily News* I came across a happier anecdote that described a householder returning one summer to find his bed pinioned to the ceiling by a bamboo that had thrust up through the floor.

Less lethal and quite delicious are the wild spring onions that appear after the bamboo shoots and tea leaves. They grow profusely in our garden and Han Aiyi helps herself, even though she stopped working for us when we moved here permanently.

'Have you left any for us?' I have to ask her as she stands up with a giant bundle of onion stalks under her arm. She laughs and walks off.

One day I found her weeding the flowerbeds.

'Thank you, Han Aiyi,' I told her. 'But there is really no need. Our own *aiyi* can do that, or I will when I get round to it.'

'*Yecai*,' she replied with her cheeky grin that always reminds me of the enigmatic way she answered our questions about her vegetables when Crystal, Brent, Leona and I first enjoyed her cooking.

Even our wild flowers get picked, our roses too if we are away for any length of time, but not by Han Aiyi. She would not be that cheeky. And the village idiot helps himself to my illegal pile of bonfire rubbish.

He is not exactly an idiot. He lost his mind in the Korean War. The poor man's head and face are covered in patches of grey stubble and he looks harmless enough, despite the machete that he carries. He wears the standard tattered blue Mao jacket that is the uniform of his generation and army plimsolls with holes in them. When I ask what he is doing he grunts and goes back to bundling up the twigs and branches. I leave him to it, but not before asking him to be careful how he drags his booty away. He pays no attention and walks straight through the flowerbeds.

Lao Han tells me the man is collecting firewood for his long dead wife who he thinks is still alive. He drags it down to Yin Shan Jie where he dumps it in heaps outside the post office. The street sweepers pull it to one side and burn it when it gets out of hand.

Then there are the hunters. Anything that flies or roosts and has somehow survived until today is fair game, as well as squirrels, rabbits and wild boar.

One summer's night I was sitting on the terrace with a glass of whisky, reading the latest Elmore Leonard novel that a guest had donated to the Lodge and enjoying the peace of the late evening. An owl was screeching intermittently close by. Then I heard someone approaching along the path and a light flashed across the treetops in front of me.

I stepped into the open and was blinded by a car headlight on full beam. For a split second I thought someone had brought a motorbike up the steps. Shading my eyes I went to meet the light. It was a head torch, the biggest I had ever seen. When the man wearing it looked up into the trees I recognized his face in the back glow.

'What are you doing?' I asked.

'Oh, just out looking around,' he replied.

'Looking for what?'

'Nothing much. Just anything really.'

He scanned the high branches above him as he spoke, the headlamp casting a beam as bright as a London blitz searchlight.

'Er, you mean birds by any chance?'

'Yes. Birds maybe.'

'And you're just looking?'

'That's right.'

'Not hunting?'

'Oh no,' he replied.

'Then what's the gun for?' I had to ask.

'Shooting them. But right now I am just looking, that's all.'

He followed me across the front of the house on his way into the woods. As I stepped back up on to the terrace and turned to say goodbye I was careful to place my feet in front of my pet toad. He was a small monster who used to sit under the outside light every evening and wait for the bugs to fry themselves and fall on to his tongue. We were good friends by now, although the conversation was one-sided and I am not sure he appreciated my repetitive jokes about Mole, Rat and Badger. I did not want the hunter to see him and tell me how tasty he would be with some bamboo shoots.

I have since discovered that the toads' meat, luckily for them, is toxic.

One of our neighbours puts up nets in the pine trees around her house and waits for the birds to come to her. She stopped me as I walked down to the coffee-shop one morning.

'Mark! Look at this! Look what I caught last night.' She

held up a limp brown bundle of feathers. I winced in anticipation of what was coming next.

'A baby owl! Isn't that great?' she shouted. 'Delicious.'

I had to smile and congratulate her. To do otherwise would have been pointless and impolite.

After the May holiday the city folk go back to work and the woodland scavengers disappear. Apart from the occasional packaged busload of Sword Pool visitors, even the weekends are quiet. Then, as the temperature rises in the Yangzi River valley and the metropolis of Shanghai, as it has always done, visitors begin to return, as they once did for whole summers, and the weekends get longer.

The conclusive sign that Moganshan's season is back in full swing has nothing to do with the weather, however, nor even national holidays or the flora and fauna. The oldest profession known to man comes to the village.

When Brent and I first came to Moganshan in the late nineties every hotel had a few rooms or a tucked away wing with a barber's candy-stick like the Songliang's rooms that we turned into the Lodge.

Those were the days when 'tourists' were state-owned company men on trips away from home for 'meetings'. I once overheard a party of them check into a hotel and as they left the lobby for a walk around the village, shout back over their shoulders: 'Can we have some *xiaojie* when we get back?'

The hotel clerk called after them with no hint of discretion: 'How many? And just for dinner and the evening or the whole night?'

Xiaojie are not a snack like tea and biscuits. The word strictly means 'Miss', but it is also an accepted euphemism.

But those days are over. The barber's shops have almost disappeared, the girls sent back to the small towns they came from. The state company men are now shareholders and directors of semi-privatized corporations. They can afford to bring their own 'better class' of *xiaojie*.

The market may be much smaller but one brothel still operates come June. The *mamasan* is a rolly-polly forty-something ex-prostitute with a mischievous smile and a sense of humour. I rarely see her in the mornings on my way down the hill but in the afternoons and evenings she holds court at the reception desk of her small operation. The double doors are open to the road and she always looks up and waves as I pass. Her girls are sweet to Isabel, whom they know by name. I found that disconcerting at first but it amuses me to think how I shall explain those particular 'big sisters' to her when she has grown up.

Now and again the local lads congregate in *mamasan*'s reception area, usually late at night. They drink tea and call me in if I pass by.

'Go on. Have a 'massage' Mark,' they tease me. 'We won't tell your wife.'

Prostitution is more than tacitly accepted in China. In fact it is so open that there is hardly a flicker of shame or embarrassment about it. And Moganshan has seen plenty of salubrious behaviour, be it foreign 'honeymooning couples' or the concubines of the 'better class' of Chinese.

Once or twice a year Joanna's extended family troops up to see us. My mother-in-law, a children's dance teacher at the Guangdong Provincial Dance Troupe, has Isabel dressed up in a tutu and doing the splits. Father-in-law tells me stories of his teenage years when he was a messenger boy for the Communist guerillas and we both talk with sadness about the brief but heady days of the socialist utopia that existed in China in the early 1950s. My parents-in-law come from the generation who believed they were building a socialist heaven on earth. Now they live on meagre state pensions and watch the younger generation punt on the stock exchange, drive sports cars and take expensive overseas holidays.

When the cousins from Ningbo, a nearby coastal city, arrive for their annual visit to coincide and catch up with the in-laws, I am torn between running for the hills and staying at my post for the inevitable hard-drinking and ear-bashing conversation. I do not mind the drinking. It is the conversation. Ningbo is a crowded city and the cousins only have one volume-setting: high. Then there is the subject matter:

'HOW MUCH MONEY ARE YOU MAKING, MARK?'

'HOW MUCH DID YOU MAKE WHEN YOU WERE IN SHANGHAI?'

'WHY DIDN'T YOU BUY AN APARTMENT IN SHANGHAI? IT WOULD BE WORTH MILLIONS BY NOW.'

'HOW MUCH DID YOUR CAR COST?'

'HOW MUCH IS YOUR RENT?'

But that is what Chinese people talk about, especially family. British do weather. Chinese do cash. (It is perfectly normal for a Chinese customer in the Lodge to ask as I hand him a coffee: 'So, how much money does this business make a year?')

Once we have audited the family accounts the conversation moves on to social and economic issues. It is also quieter.

'The problem with China,' one of my uncles by marriage explains after dinner, 'is that we do not have guns, like people in America. If we had guns, then we would have none of the petty thieves and scam artists.'

'No, our problem is all the fake goods,' his father interrupts. 'You can never be sure that what you are buying is the real thing. Fake cars, fake alcohol, fake policemen too. Fake food even. Did you hear that hairy crabs,' a Shanghai seasonal delicacy, 'have been faked? And then there was that fake baby food that starved some children to death in Fujian Province last year.'

It was time to lighten up the conversation.

'You now what?' I say. 'Some of my foreign friends and I when we have had a bad China day,' the family knew what had happened to my business, 'we joke that maybe all China is fake, that we'll wake up in the morning and it's just a dream.'

No one laughs. So I shut up and listen again.

'And the education system is no good either,' says the mother of a young girl cousin. She points at her daughter. 'At Xiao Qing's high school for example, the English teachers are all just young foreign students. They might speak English but they don't know how to teach it.'

Now I have a serious point to make. 'In my humble opinion,' I start, 'the problem is that Chinese schools and universities are not prepared to pay for proper foreign language teachers. How are you going to get a qualified teacher when you only pay them a couple of thousand yuan a month and give them a cheap dormitory to live in?'

'That's too true.' Mother-in-law jumps in. 'We have a couple of foreigners who teach English at the Dance Troupe and you know what . . . ? One of them is French, so how can she speak English? And the other . . . the other one . . .' she pauses to put a toothpick in her mouth, which allows for a neat dramatic pause, then she pulls it out and says with perfect timing, '. . . and the other one is black.'

I cannot not help smiling but stop short of laughing.

'Ma,' I say. 'You can't say things like that.'

She puffs up and looks at the others for approval. They see nothing wrong with her logic.

It was time to be British and talk about the weather.

July and August in coastal and southern China is the typhoon season. The storms rise in the Pacific Ocean and make their way inexorably towards the landmass of East Asia. During the typhoon season the Chinese do talk about the weather. Along the eastern seaboard people watch and listen to the weather reports as a storm approaches. The burning question is: where will it land?

Between Moganshan and the coast there are no natural obstacles, no hills to break up the force of the winds, to soak up the rain. Even a typhoon coming ashore in the next door province of Fujian will affect us. In 2005 we were hit head on by Typhoon Matsu, one of the biggest in decades. It was exciting and just a bit frightening.

In line with the maxim, there was an ominous calm for half a day before the storm arrived. Not only was nature quiet, eerily still, the birds not singing in the motionless trees, but the tourists disappeared overnight. Shutters went up and builders tied tarpaulins over roofless A-frames with ropes weighted with rocks. Sun shades were folded and put away, outdoor furniture was jammed into hotel corridors. Everyone knew what was coming.

280

The typhoon was due to arrive on Isabel's birthday, 5 August. The parents of her friends called to say they had cancelled their trips out from the city. It would be dangerous to travel and they had to look after their own properties and businesses in Shanghai. Mother and father-in-law had stayed especially for the birthday party. It was going to be a small one if we had it at all.

On the evening of 3 August the trees began to sway and a light rain started to fall. The wind built through the night, rattling our windows. None of them broke. We had closed the shutters on the ground floor and now I wished we had installed them upstairs too. The rain grew heavier and by the next morning was sheeting down at forty-five degrees. The wind seemed to have peaked however, and in the afternoon lessened a fraction.

'I think it's missed us,' I said to the family. 'I'm going to call Isabel's friends and see if they'll change their minds.' They wisely stayed put.

That evening all hell broke loose. I have sat through big storms but this was something else, completely outside my experience. It began suddenly. To announce the start of round two, the dormer window on our top floor shattered. The sound of breaking glass was almost drowned out by the howl of the wind and the lashing of rain. I ran upstairs to block the empty window frame with a kitchen tray. Water was flying in through the hole. I jammed a pillow behind the mosquito mesh to hold the tray in place and stopped the worst of it but still it pumped through. A door upstairs slammed shut with a crack like a rifle shot and Tristan burst into tears. Mother-in-law took care of him. Isabel looked worried but brave.

We sat in the drawing-room. No one spoke. It was as if we were being besieged by an axe-wielding madman. Then father-in-law picked up a newspaper and put on his reading glasses. Mother was rocking tiny Tristan.

The house felt secure, almost cosy with the shutters locked up tight. Then the lights flickered twice in quick succession and went out. Isabel let out a cry. I fumbled for a torch and went to the drawer where we keep candles. I was lighting them when the village generator kicked in and the lights came back on. No one had moved. Somewhere close to the house a branch was wrenched off a tree with a sickening tear. The lights stayed on and I gave silent thanks that the tree had not brought down our power line.

We gave Isabel her presents and sang happy birthday at the tops of our voices to compete with the howling storm.

It was hitting the house in a frontal assault. We had long ago realized that the downhill side of the house was the one worst affected by the weather. Hinges had rusted and window-sills rotted. Now we could see the process being accelerated a hundred times. Water was seeping in through the windows and under the front door, which was trembling in its frame. We stuffed some rags along the gap at the bottom and, as I stood back to see how the dam was working, I noticed something far worse. At the foot of the sitting-room doorposts, well inside the house, water was bubbling up through the floor boards. I stared at it in amazement. Where on earth could it be coming from? Surely not from under the house? There was no sign of water coming down from the ceiling, unless it was coming down the doorframe . . .

I sprinted upstairs. The rooms above the sitting-room were dry. I went out on to the balcony. My feet splashed.

The balcony was full of water, up to and over my ankles. It must have been flowing into the floorboards and then down through the door posts.

'Jesus Christ! The house is sinking!' I shouted.

I ran back down for a dustpan, stripped to my shorts and started baling. Every second throw the water flew straight back and pelted my face. The wind was ferocious. Illuminated by the balcony's outside light, the rain billowed towards me in white screaming sheets. I could have been on the deck of a sinking ship. Eventually the floor was just soaking, not flooded. I left it and went back to the sitting-room.

'We may as well go to bed,' Joanna's father said.

Isabel slept with her grandparents in their room at the back of the house, Joanna and I put Tristan between us in our bed. I tried not to think about the worst-case scenario: the house slipping down the mountain like a Methodist Episcopal Ladies' Home. I had often wondered how effective the drainage around our perch was. There were no flumes sticking out of our retaining walls, as I had seen elsewhere in the village. I could have sworn that the wall had bulged, if only a fraction, since we had rented the house. An architect friend had told me that the trees along the front of the house were there to soak up excess water as well as provide shade. That night I silently prayed they were thirsty.

The next morning the house was still standing and the storm had died down. The wind continued to blow but the rain had passed on. It was safe to go outside. We went to survey the damage.

The area around the houses was littered with branches, some of them small trees in their own right. When I bent down to pick up a fallen limb from our tallest pine I noticed that its roots on the windward side had started to pop up out of the earth. I looked up. The whole tree was leaning over. We had been lucky. If that one had come down God only knows what damage it might have done. It was on the side of the house where the children's bedroom was. I said another silent prayer, of thanks this time.

Joanna and I walked down to the Lodge. The roads were carpeted with leaves, twigs and pine needles. You couldn't see the concrete or tarmac. They looked like farm tracks.

There were no landslides but several trees had been blown over and one of them had taken out the Lodge's phone lines. Electricity was cut during daylight hours while the Administration Bureau repaired damaged cables. When it came on in the evenings we could hear the ship's engine rattle and hum of the emergency generator from our house far above it. The main lines from down the hill must have been broken in several places. It was another few days before the village was reconnected and we had twenty-four-hour electricity. Lao Han kindly helped replace our broken window panes.

On the coast of southern Zhejiang, Typhoon Matsu killed several hundred fishermen who had not received a warning in time, as well as some village school children who had taken refuge, on local government orders, in what was supposedly a strong public building. The number of deaths has never been confirmed. So we cannot say it was a bad storm for us.

Throughout the month of July thunderstorms hit Moganshan almost daily. Once you have been through a typhoon like Matsu they are nothing in comparison but they can still take you by surprise. They gather in minutes and begin with an explosion of noise. The cracks of thunder sound like artillery going off right beside your head. Further away the rolls drag on for long minutes, as if the gods are rearranging furniture. It can go on for a couple of hours without a break. From our balcony I can watch the lightning streaking up from the plain.

Then the rain comes down in a wall of water. So long as there is no wind the house gets only a good rinsing, as opposed to a thorough soaking. After the deluge, as suddenly as the storm started, the sun comes out and sucks up the steam from the plain into perfect fluffy clouds. They make a carpet of white around the mountain. The tops of the lower hills stand out like islands, a deep dark green, and so clean.

In autumn the mountain is at its best. The leaves turn brown, gold and yellow, the temperature, which hits the mid-thirties in July and August, cools to a comfortable English summer and the sky is a crystal-clear blue.

For the final holiday of the year, National Day in October, the village is overrun for one last time. There is one last collective gasp from a coach load of tourists at the statue of delicate Mo and muscle-bound Gan, and one last heave up the steps from the waterfall. Then they trickle away, like the mountain stream, down to Yucun; the tourists, the touts, the chamber maids and the hookers.

It's all over. Moganshan becomes a ghost town again, only now the ghosts can rest in peace.

Chapter Fourteen

Approaching the End

I have consequently decided in full liberty to make the government of the Chinese Republic irrevocable donation of my property as described above. I expect such donation shall be accepted in memory of the thirty-six years I have spent in China.

Letter from Dr Paul Premet, owner of Moganshan
House Number 461, to the Control Bureau of
Properties of Mokanshan, 26 June 1955

Almost the first thing the Communists did after their victory in 1949 was outlaw ownership of private property. Summer homes would have been the first to go, especially summer homes occupied by foreigners who had been raping, pillaging, bullying, forcing drugs on to, illegally occupying and generally abusing China for the past hundred years.

According to the older Moganshan locals, the last time they saw the original foreigners here was the summer of 1948. They did not exactly leave the mountain. They just never came back. The People's Liberation Army marched into Shanghai in May '49. The foreign house owners, the committee members of the Resort Association, the missionaries, the families with their broods of children, the people who had made the village what it was, were never seen in Moganshan again.

Lao Zheng, a spritely octogenarian who likes a chat, told me the full story.

'The foreigners went away in '48 at the end of the season and that was that.'

He and I were sitting in the sunshine on the low wall opposite the burnt out shell of the Hans' place. I was on my way home to do some gardening while Joanna took care of the shop. It wasn't quite the picture – of the foreigners being run out of town by a frenzied horde of Communists – that I'd been hoping for but isn't that so often the way?

'My father looked after a house for an Englishman. He was the boss of a bank in Shanghai. After '48, we never saw the man again. Our family was paid according to the going rate for rice. The inflation in those days was crazy. Soon as he got the cash my father would run to the market to buy food before the prices went up again. There was a comprador who took care of the details for the Englishman. His name was Qu. The value of one sack of rice per month was my father's salary, 150 Chinese pounds. After they disappeared we were stuck. Nothing to live off. I had to help my father cut bamboo to sell down in the valley. He made a special trip to Shanghai to see Mr Qu in early '49. Nothing came of it of course.'

'No word from the Englishman?' I asked.

'Yes, there was actually,' replied Lao Zheng, looking up. 'He sent a letter from Hong Kong, in '49. I never saw it. That's the last we heard of him.'

Lao Zheng paused for a moment, then his eyes narrowed.

'Why are you so interested, Mark? Some foreigner want his house back? Where is he from? America? UK?'

'No, Lao Zheng. I am just curious. That's all,' I reassured him.

'Because you know what?' he added, looking up and down Ridge Road to see if anyone was coming. He lowered his voice. 'Not all the houses were actually confiscated.' He looked again and whispered. 'Some were just taken on loan.'

'Really, Lao Zheng? Now *that* is interesting.' The word he had used, also bearing in mind the context, could mean 'permanent loan'. But it means loan nonetheless. 'Do you know which ones?' I had to ask.

Lao Zheng leaned back on the wall and huffed at me. 'Of course not! It's all on record in the Administration Bureau though, not that they'd let you see.'

So that's why Mr Shen had been so nervous about showing me the files.

Old Mrs Wang tells a similar story about the exodus. In 1948 she and her husband were looking after a house for a German priest, her father-in-law having long since sold the ice business.

'The priest just disappeared. Left all his books and bits and pieces. Even his priest clothes. There was nothing really valuable in his house,' she said. 'Left behind his records of his parishioners too. That caused some trouble later on.'

Mrs Wang was in a talkative mood, as ever. I had stopped by her house where she was sitting on the porch stripping gourd stalks. 'And we got into trouble too. My brother-in-law was in the Nationalist army, so my husband got locked up for forty days. I had nine members of our family to look after on my own. No money, no food. Imagine that!' she

288

said. 'Then there was the fact that we were 'bad elements' because our family had made so much money with the ice business. They wouldn't give us rice coupons. Nor oil coupons for that matter. In the end we went and sat outside the local government offices in Wukang and told them we'd stay right there and starve to death. So they took pity on us and gave us some coupons. Mind you, the officials were always changing in those days. One day to the next. So we had to keep going back.'

Somewhere in her story Mrs Wang had skipped forward to the Cultural Revolution in 1966. I had been careful to avoid asking her for dates this time. Then again, from 1948 on was pretty much the same for her anyway. It was all *ku*, a word that encapsulates bitterness and hardship.

'Yes,' she said, narrowing her eyes at me, 'it was very *ku*.'

The only documentary evidence I can find of the foreigners' departure from Moganshan is that letter from Dr Premet. It was in the back of a file in Mr Shen's office. Leading up to the liberation, the *North-China Daily News*, my main source, concerned itself with more important news than the threat to a holiday resort, and once the paper had been liberated itself it would have been in no position to stand up for or comment about the status of foreigners' property in China. Besides, the few editions that came out between May 1949 and the paper's own sudden end in 1951 were only eight pages each, a fraction of the forty-odd pages before the war.

The foreigners fled, not only from Moganshan but from Shanghai and all China. To use an apposite and suitably abrupt Welsh turn of English: 'There they were. Gone.'

They lost everything, especially the entrepreneurs: their

assets, their factories and all the machines in them, entire companies that many had built from nothing.

Last summer one of the foreign teenagers who had run wild through Moganshan in the 1940s came to revisit his childhood haunts and called in at the Lodge.

Sam Moshinsky is now a seventy-three-year-old Australian. When he stayed in Moganshan House Number 190 with his friends and family he was a stateless Russian–Jew. Like Rena Krasno, he could not tell me much about Moganshan society. He was too young. But his story of how his refugee father set up the Shanghai Cardboard Box Factory – I got the impression it would have been the Tetra Pack of its day – and then lost everything to the Communists was tragic. Sam's father took his family to the States, and remained a broken man for the rest of his life.

The China missionaries were simply told to move on and find their converts somewhere else, just as they themselves had pushed the Buddhist monks off the top of Lushan in 1897. What goes around comes around. And how the missionaries must have smarted, after all their campaigns against opium dealing, to have the Chinese Communists tell them they were being evicted for propagating 'the opium of the people', as Marx described religion.

Victor Grosse, the owner of my favourite haunted villa in the woods behind the White Cloud Hotel, had died in the 1920s. His daughter Elizabeth, whose wedding reception had been held there in 1922, succumbed to scarlet fever in the South of France soon after. Leo Grosse, her brother, had inherited the house from their father but wisely sold it on in 1947. Good timing. Unfortunately he then, not so wisely, returned to Russia, where he was imprisoned and died in a gulag. The Grosses, it turns out, had been notorious and generous benefactors of refugee White Russians in Shanghai.

Moganshan's 'better class of Chinese' knew better than to stick around as the victorious Chinese Communists approached. Big Ears Du retreated to Hong Kong to die of the effects of long-term opium addiction. His crony Zhang Xiao Lin had already had his addled brains blown out by his bodyguard.

Huang Fu, Chiang Kai Shek's unpopular foreign minister and wannabe Moganshan squire, had died of cancer in 1936. His grave on the hillside awaited its desecration in the Cultural Revolution. Other wealthy Chinese patrons of Moganshan, such as Jian Yujie, China's Mr Benson & Hedges, accepted the inevitable and donated their property to the Communist Party. Jian remained in China and became a member of the People's Representative Committee, as did many successful businessmen whom Mao Zedong deliberately retained to keep the economy ticking over. They all came unstuck once they had outlived their usefulness. Jian 'died of illness' during the Anti-Rightist campaign of 1957. He was most likely deprived of medical care.

Having been the exclusive playground of one privileged set wealthy enough to possess a villa purely for summer use, Moganshan became the exclusive playground of another privileged set: Chinese Communist Party cadres. The village was officially renamed the East China Sanatorium. Access was restricted to senior officials and their minions.

According to Lao Zheng the transformation did not happen overnight. The People's Liberation Army liberated the mountain in May 1949 and then left it alone for a couple of years while they got on with more important things. The East China Sanatorium was not officially established until 1951 and did not come into regular use until 1954, the year of Mao's visit.

At a party in Hangzhou in 2006 I was introduced to a retired university professor. He was getting on in years and had best remain nameless. He was interested to hear that I lived in Moganshan and pressed me to tell him how the place had changed. He explained that in the early sixties, fresh out of college, he had worked as a personal assistant for a senior Hangzhou party official. He freely admitted he got the job thanks to his father's connections. The official liked to escape to Moganshan for quiet weekends and party meetings as often as possible.

'It was my job', the old professor told me with a cheeky grin, 'to go to Moganshan in advance and book rooms in the rest homes which, um,' he coughed and smiled, 'had the prettiest, er, nurses.'

Hero of the Revolution and the first Communist mayor of Shanghai, Chen Yi, whose statue has replaced the British War Memorial in the English Garden – of the apocryphal 'No dogs and No Chinese' sign – was also a frequent visitor. I hear from the old ladies that he was quite a mover on the dance floor despite a war-wounded leg. He wrote a famous poem – famous in Moganshan at least – whose title is *Moganshan Hao*, as per the giant Green Dripping Pond inscription. The first stanza runs thus, in my own translation:

> *Moganshan is fine*
> *It is bordered by tall bamboo*
> *Ten thousand poles line its narrow paths*
> *with a sea of green*
> *The busy wind rises, circles and falls.*
> *The cadres line the small windows.*

I have racked my brains, the same ones that won me a first in Chinese poetry at university, and I have asked every literate local and intellectual Chinese friend to confirm it, but that is what the line says: 'The cadres line the small windows.' I think it rather spoils the verse. The rest of the poem is quite good.

I would love to know what the newly empowered Communist cadres, mostly from poor family backgrounds, thought of the foreign playground of Moganshan. Images pop into my head of proles ransacking houses, burning furniture that had been passed down for generations for winter fuel and trampling through rose beds. According to Lao Zheng and old Mrs Wang, it was not that melodramatic.

Over the years however, the natural consequences of state ownership made themselves felt. Flower beds became vegetable gardens. The hairy bamboo plantation spread uphill and filled every available space and shut out the views. Unwanted houses, perhaps because they were too remote, like 495, or too small or too big, were left to rot. Some fell down or when they were on their way down were raped of their stone which went into the construction of the village's 'Cultural Hall' where Chen Yi danced, or a cookhouse in a garden. Tennis-courts were turned into nurseries for Chinese sweet gum trees which grow fast and straight and are used for roof frames. A radar station was (not) built on the mountain's highest point.

The only foreigners who came to Moganshan were Soviet Russian technical advisers and Albanian students. Lao Gao remembers the Albanians taking full advantage of the pool. The place became a standard eastern-bloc-style Communist health resort. Milan Kundera could have set a novel here. It would have fitted perfectly.

293

There were even residents here for their 'mental health', Communist-speak for re-education. Ding Ling, a well-known female author, women's rights activist and a general pain in the neck for Mao Ze Dong, was put under house arrest in Moganshan.

The Party still comes to Moganshan. In 1984 what might have been a landmark conference was held here. The reform-minded 'Policy Advisers to the Chinese Communist Party' – a think tank where you think quietly and speak carefully – spent weeks in the Moganshan Mountain Resort, a hotel that stands out at the end of the old Mount Clair ridge like a James Bond baddy's eyrie. They came to discuss reforms that would help China's economy catch up with the world. The kibosh was put on their conclusions, which I am sure were modest, by another kind of tank – in Tian'an Men Square, on 4 June 1989.

Today's Administration Bureau chief seems to spend half his time acting as the village concierge for his provincial and national seniors. He brings some of his mid-ranking charges into the Lodge to show us off.

Soon after we opened for business we were paid a visit by the modern-day version of recuperating political commissars: the senior staff of a Shanghai district tax bureau on a jolly, the very same bureau I used to deal with in my former life.

One of them had dropped by during the afternoon to check us out. He was charming and spoke fluent English. We discussed literature and history. He was also effusive, yet gracefully so, in his praise of the Lodge. I was almost ready to change my mind about tax officials, a long shot considering what I knew of the man's particular office.

'My colleagues might come by this evening,' he said as he left. 'I'll try to come with them but to be honest I don't usually hang out with them.'

That evening at seven o'clock a dozen drunk Shanghainese settled themselves at one of our outside tables and shouted through the open window: 'Waiter! Come here!'

I was alone in the bar, so I guessed they meant me.

They had pulled up some chairs to crowd around a single table. One of the men already had a shoe off and was picking fluff from his nylon pop sock. In his teeth he clenched a cigarette. Another was so drunk he could barely sit up straight. He lolled in a bamboo armchair, backwards and forwards, and finally came to rest on his forearms on the table.

One of the women screeched at me. 'Do you have any tea?'

'Yes,' I replied, trying to smile. 'Earl Grey, Ceylon, and of course Chi . . .'

'I mean Chinese tea!' she shouted from her seat below me. 'We want Chinese tea. Ten people!' She turned and shouted in Shanghainese to the woman beside her, who took out her mobile and shouted at that. I assumed she was asking if anyone else was joining them.

'Twelve people!' the first woman corrected me.

While I was behind the bar the drunk was brought in on the shoulder of a colleague. They disappeared into our lavatory, left the door open, and I heard the sound of retching. Then they stumbled outside without a word, nor flushing.

By the time I appeared with the tray of tea a bag of sunflower seeds had been spilt over the table and the husks littered the ground. The drunk official had put his feet up on another chair, his head on his chest. Cigarette butts were mixed with the sunflower husks. The conversation sounded like a fight on a street of fishmongers' families, wives taking the lead. The pleasant man who had come by in the afternoon was nowhere to be seen.

I retired behind the bar and watched through the open window. I was having a problem dealing with the situation. Three years ago this district tax bureau, more than likely some of the people sitting outside behaving like louts and treating me like a white slave, had fined me four hundred thousand yuan, about thirty thousand pounds. They had caught me on a technicality which had been pointed out to them by my local business partner who was friendly with the female bureau chief. I had even been coerced by that partner to employ the bureau chief's son for a year. He was the nastiest piece of work I ever met in Shanghai, as he proved at a staff party when he smashed a bottle on the table and threatened to thrust it into an editor's face.

The editor was a girl. I later discovered the son had helped his mother with the tax bust too. I never met her face to face. I never wanted to.

'Waiter!' the woman called through the open window again. 'Bring us hot water!'

'Do you have anything to eat?' she asked while I filled their teapots.

'Some cakes, yes.'

'No noodles? What kind of a place is this? Oh, never mind. What cakes?'

The woman was so unpleasant I reckoned she was more than likely to be the same person who had fined me and brought into the world that vicious 'little emperor', as spoilt single children are called in China, who had behaved so foully in my employ.

The man opposite her stubbed out his cigarette in a tea saucer and hacked up a mouthful of phlegm. The ashtray in front of him was full of sunflower seeds. So he spat on the floor behind him.

I smiled at the woman. 'Chocolate and fruit cake.' I didn't think she would care to know I had made them myself.

'Bring me the chocolate,' she ordered.

At last they asked for the bill. It came to 220 yuan, almost one pound each. They had been sitting outside demanding hot water for their teapots for over an hour. The area surrounding their table looked like the floor of a hard seat railway carriage after a twenty-four-hour journey between two of the poorest parts of China. It was plastered with cigarette ends, sunflower husks, tissue paper and spit.

The queen bee came in to pay.

'Give me a discount,' she said as she approached the bar. 'And I want an official receipt.'

So she was going to claim this on expenses.

'We do not give discounts,' I replied.

'Of course you can.' She made no attempt to charm one out of me. She slapped two one hundred yuan bills on the wooden counter top.

'No, we can't.' My temper was rising but I kept calm. 'Please pay the twenty.'

She looked at me as if I had grabbed her wrist and twisted it. She paused to summon as much ill grace as she could and then threw a twenty at me.

'And my receipt?' She held out her hand.

My tiny victory was close.

'I am afraid that we have just opened, so we do not have our official tax receipts yet.' I smiled, not out of politeness

297

but because I was happy. 'I can only give you a print-out from the cash till.' She could not claim expenses with a print-out.

'Huh.' She turned her nose up at me and moved her hand closer.

I laid the useless ticket on the bar and she stormed out with it.

If you had suffered as many attacks from Chinese government bureaux as I had – precisely those people who had just treated me like a piece of chewing-gum on their shoe – right now you would be putting me up for a saint-hood.

I regret to report that drunk Chinese officials generally behave like obnoxious bullies, but there are exceptions. A few weeks after the tax bureau another drunk stumbled into the bar. He was short and wearing a suit and large glasses. With him were three lackeys, likewise off their faces on local liquor. I prepared myself for a repeat performance. But this one was not loud and obnoxiously drunk. He was a giggling and stupid drunk.

'Y'sell coffee here . . . ?' he asked.

'Speak English!' one of his companions shouted from a table. 'C'mon boss, show off!'

The man turned and laughed at the speaker. 'Can't,' he replied in Chinese. 'Too drunk.' And he giggled like a child. He turned back to me.

'. . . Cos I hear coffee makes y'sober,' he drawled. On his third attempt he got himself up on to a bar stool, leaned over the counter towards me and looked over my shoulder at the wine racked on the shelf.

'That good wine?' he asked.

I told him it was OK and stopped grinding coffee-beans for his quintuple espresso.

'Show me.'

I handed him a bottle and left my hands under his.

'Hmm, Australian. Should be all right. Been there.'

'Really?' I asked.

'Yuh, been to Australia, been to France. And Germany. Don't like Germany 'cos that's where Hitler came from. Austria. I like Austria. Austria is nice . . .' he tailed off.

'You're a businessman then?'

'Sort of,' he giggled again and fumbled in his jacket pocket. 'Here's my card.'

I looked at the job title: City Mayor.

'You're a mayor.'

'S'right! You can read Chinese!' He winked. 'Now, can you read my name?'

I looked at the character for his surname. He seemed to have a sense of humour so I said it, in English. 'Ah, and your name is Cow.'

He laughed so hard he had to grab the bar so he did not fall off the stool.

'You got it!' he shouted, also in English. 'I am a cow!' And he disintegrated in a fit of hysterics.

When Mayor Cow had regained his composure he picked up the bottle from the bar and handed it back. 'Open it, please. We'll drink ourselves sober. Promise we won't make a mess.'

I was growing to like the mayor.

'Mayor Cow, forgive me but I have to ask how come you speak English?'

'Studied in Australia,' he replied. 'Lots of us officials can speak English now. Good for business. You should come to my city. Lots of foreign investors.' He watched as I poured him a glass of wine. 'You should open a bar there, just like this one. You'd do a roaring trade.'

Mayor Cow lifted the glass and made as if to study the colour. The rim chinked against his eyeglasses.

'Looks all right,' he said, trying to be serious. He took a sip and put the glass down.

'I mean it about you opening a bar,' he said. 'My city is not too far from here either. Full of immigrants. We're all immigrants there. I'm an immigrant too. And I don't see what's wrong with having a good time. People work hard, they should let their hair down now and again, get drunk.' He was speaking Chinese again. 'I don't have any *pianjian*. Hey, what's the English for *pianjian*? Distinguish? Display?'

'Discriminate.' I answered.

'That's it. I don't disseminate against anybody. You really must come over, let me take you to dinner, show you around.'

I think Mayor Cow really was drinking himself sober. His companions were behaving impeccably too, perhaps thanks to Mayor Cow's insistence that they sipped the wine rather than knocking it back like *bai jiu*.

He leaned on the bar again.

'Can't sleep . . .' Mayor Cow said, looking straight at me as if I had the answer. I wondered where this was going.

'Bloody karaoke in the hotel.'

That was a relief.

'Music. Singing. God,' he sighed, 'I thought Moganshan was supposed to be peaceful.' He looked down into his glass

Mayor Cow was full of surprises. I put his card into my

wallet instead of the old flower pot under the bar where most of them went.

'So anyway,' Mayor Cow brightened up. 'We saw your sign and thought: what the hell, if everyone is going to make such a racket and party, we'd come and have one ourselves.'

It was the most civilized little party. Mayor Cow was a perfect gentleman. His companions were too.

The surprises kept coming. Early in our first high season an attractive girl walked past the open window where I was sitting at my laptop writing emails. I was alone in the coffee-shop. She glanced inside and smiled. Then she walked back again. I could not help admiring her looks. She was well-dressed too.

After a few more passes along the terrace she sat down below the window and pulled her mobile phone out of her handbag. She made several calls, speaking in the local dialect but with the clear tone of a girl trying to find someone, or get someone to come and meet her. In other words she sounded like she was arranging an assignation.

Then she walked in.

'Hello,' she said in English. She gave me a charming smile and then continued in Chinese. 'Do you mind if I join you for a while?'

I was running a hospitality business so I could hardly say no.

She sat down beside me and looked over at my screen. I could smell her perfume.

'What are you doing?' she asked. Her eyes were brown and deep, her hair long and curled to make it seem natural. She was beautiful.

I muttered something about being on the web and asked her if she would like a cup of coffee.

'Yes, please,' she replied. 'I'm not bothering you, am I?'

'No, not at all,' I replied half honestly, half guiltily.

I went to make the coffee and then returned to sit beside her. After some small talk about the Lodge and Moganshan she asked a question.

'See if you can guess what I do,' she said, looking straight into my eyes.

Now she had me. She was clearly a nice girl but she was on her own, extremely attractive, well-dressed, and she kept making phone calls. I could not help making the assumption. But how did I say it?

'Um,' I stuttered, 'Are you, er, in the . . .' I was going to say 'beauty industry' but that would have been too direct, the euphemism is too well known '. . . er, cosmetic business?'

It was the best I could come up with.

'No,' she smiled a beautiful smile. 'Guess again.'

I tried not to blush.

'Um, how do you say it in Chinese?' I asked. 'You know one of those places where *women*,' I stressed the word, 'go to get facials and things? You are the owner of one of those?'

'Wrong again!' She laughed, throwing her head back and running a hand through her hair as she did so.

This was impossible. How do you say: 'I think you are a high-class call-girl' politely?

'OK, I'll tell you,' she giggled. 'I'm a judge.'

With a massive effort I tried to look as if that was the most natural job for a stunningly attractive young woman.

'You would never have guessed, would you?' she said.

'Actually, that was next on my list,' I joked through my teeth.

She laughed again, gave me her mobile number and told

302

me I should look her up in town. Call me bashful, but I never took her up on the offer.

She is a judge though. I was in the middle of my legal fight for my trademark and described the case to her. She knew exactly what I was talking about. She was in Moganshan for a legal conference.

The village continues to fulfill its original legal uses too, as a convenient out-of-the-way place for isolated internment. For a couple of months over the autumn of 2005 we had a distinguished neighbour staying in one of the Hangliao houses below ours. The guest took regular afternoon walks in the company of a couple of smartly dressed young men. If our paths crossed the man, likewise well turned out and always with an ironic smile on his face, greeted me cordially. I wondered out loud one day who he was and why he was staying so long.

'*Shuang gui,*' Joanna said. 'Best not talk about it. I heard he is a deputy party secretary from Huzhou. Corruption.' *Shuang gui* translates as 'the two rules'. The rules are 'no going out, and no visitors'. In other words: house arrest.

An eerier echo of the past, thinking of women's rights activist Ding Ling being locked up here, is the modern-day Moganshan Women's Labour Camp. It is not in Moganshan itself but at the bottom of the hill in a perfectly manicured little hamlet called Lao Ling, or so I am told. For understandable reasons, I hope, I have not been in search of it. Perhaps the village is so clean and tidy thanks to the women's labour. Well-tended lawns surround a pretty little pond, the houses are always freshly painted and the roads clean. It is a true 'model' village in the Communist sense.

The Labour Camp is assigned to female Falun Gong

supporters and practitioners. Falun Gong is the quasi-religious sect that put the wind up the Chinese government in 1999 when they held an unprecedented mass demonstration outside Zhong Nan Hai, the Party leaders' enclave beside the Forbidden City in Beijing. Since then the Party has relentlessly cracked down on the sect's adherents. Temples are plastered with graphic posters of Falun Gong members immolating themselves, propaganda announcements condemn the evils of the sect, and people like us in Moganshan in the hospitality business are politely invited to grass on any customers who mention the words 'Falun Gong'. So that's the last time I'll mention it. It's another radar station as far as I am concerned.

I am straying into territory which, while potentially rich in narrative material, will not endear me to my host country if I bang on about it. Let's get back to the rosy picture stuff.

The most conspicuous and cheerful example of Moganshan's history repeating itself is the return of the foreign families.

They drive up in processions of seven-seater people-carriers with Filipino maids, Shanghainese drivers, and children, lots of children, looking for a convenient and relatively cheap weekend or holiday location for their young families. The parents troop into the Lodge and ask for suggestions for hotels, directions for hikes, where to swim, where to eat, what to eat, how to get to a cash machine.

Once we have answered the practical questions the next round starts, always along the same lines: 'I wish we had known sooner about this place . . . We have been looking for somewhere to get away from Shanghai for so long and never found it, apart from a flight to Thailand . . .' and then the inevitable: 'How can we get a villa for ourselves up here?'

The hillsides of Moganshan echo again with the cries of children in a Babel of languages. Brothers and sisters and gangs of school friends make dens in the woods and run riot up and down the paths.

For some reason the most popular play area is right behind our guest cottage. I often find tree branches I have trimmed and left in piles to clear away have been converted into brushwood barricades in small clearings. I have also stumbled on teenagers squatting around small camp fires late at night. I have words with them, all the time feeling guilty that I am hardly innocent myself.

'I am the only foreigner who lives in this village,' I explain. 'Any foreigner who does something wrong or makes trouble, I get the blame. It's as simple as that. So put it out, please.'

I am surprised by the acknowledgement I get. Young foreigners grow up fast in China.

Thanks to the return of the heat retreaters the Lodge has been far more successful than we expected. Mr Wang is happy, for us and himself. We have more than kept ourselves in noodles. In our first year, before we took on some staff to help out, Joanna and I worked like madmen. We did not have a single weekend off. From Friday evenings to Sunday afternoons we were on the go non-stop.

If I had a moment's breather I would lean on the bar and guzzle a cold drink. There was always someone keen to chat.

'So why did you come to Moganshan?' they'd ask.

'For the quiet life,' I replied.

'What a good idea,' they said. 'How you must love it.' Then another dozen people would walk in the door and I'd dive back in the kitchen to cook bacon and eggs.

Thanks to the amount of food we go through we have had

to give up the village market in favour of the local town, Wukang. There is more variety in the market there and we need more of everything, more than the locals can supply. It's a half hour drive to Wukang from the top of the mountain so I get to sit down, which is a blessed relief after standing in the kitchen for hours. I take back everything I said about not wanting a car.

Wukang is a small town, by Chinese standards, of only a hundred thousand people. In 1999 when we first passed through it was surrounded by construction sites and the shops on the downtown streets sold nothing but building materials. Since then, and in direct correlation with the development of the new apartment buildings, factories, schools and villa complexes on the outskirts, one by one those shops have shut down, re-opening as furniture and lighting stores, bathroom outfitters, electrical goods suppliers. Smart restaurants have appeared, and foot massage parlours, Karaoke joints and nightclubs. The first supermarkets opened in 2004. Now Wal-Mart is developing a site.

Wukang is a classic example of a small Chinese town's accelerated and exponential growth. Within ten years it has gone from dusty backwater to thoroughly modern small city. There might even be a good school when we need one for the children.

The market is as big as two football fields side by side, covered by a first floor where tiny booths sell cheap clothes, and is divided into areas of produce. Stretching almost the entire width are two rows of pork butchers. Half-pigs hang on massive hooks behind the stall owners' heads and the details are laid across the concrete tables in front of them: chops, kidneys, slices of belly, livers, heads, trotters. Entire pigs are dissected every morning on tree trunk chopping boards. This is where I buy the 'back' for my bacon and the joints for roasting. Now that we have got to know each other the butchers hold up the pieces they know I like as I walk between them and the shout echoes along the row: 'He wants kidneys today!' Then someone skids across the wet floor and thrusts a bit of pig in my face, constantly looking over his shoulder in case he misses another customer.

The vegetable sellers are spread around the edge. Their stalls are piled with baskets of red, green, orange and brown and their sales pitch is to ask: 'And how about some of this? Or this? Or do you want this? Very cheap at the moment. Have you tried this?' Their fingers dance across the vegetables like a conductor bringing in every section of an orchestra at the climax of a symphony. 'And the cucumbers! And the lettuce! And the carrots . . .' their trembling fingers rise towards the roof. The higher the finger the lower the price.

On the outside touchlines of the two football pitches are the bamboo shoot sellers – fresh, dried, whole, peeled, shucked, stewed. There is an incredible amount you can do to make bamboo edible – especially given how much else you can do with it. The bamboo overflows the stalls in season and out of it the sellers are fewer and the prices higher.

At the back, in the far two penalty areas, are the fish. Enormous plastic basins the size of bathtubs with oxygen bubbling from white plastic tubes to keep the creatures alive until they are sold and taken home still flapping. Prawns are sold in heavy duty plastic bags pumped with oxygen and fastened with elaborate knots of elastic bands. Walking out of the market with them feels like carrying a heavy, upside down, alive-and-kicking balloon.

In the far left corner of the market are chickens, ducks and geese, eggs, dried herbs, frozen meats and dried beancurd. And last but not least, somewhere near the centre circle of the right-hand pitch, are the 'other' butchers. They have two large stalls that make up a block of their own.

Here you find the truly local produce, the game. What is for sale depends on what has been shot or caught the day before. Sometimes there are enough rabbits to fill Watership Down. Or one of the butchers will have a deer, flayed and displayed across his entire stall. In the cold months of the year, when eating their stewed meat keeps you warm, dogs are heaped across the counters, paws furry, carcasses stripped. Above them hang partridge and pheasant. The skinned cats look macabre, like spirits from an Egyptian fairy tale. Live pigeon are kept in small cages. The goat and lamb are less shocking or would be but for their eyeless, tissue-covered skulls attached to their scrawny bodies. It is not on my normal route but now and then I cannot resist the temptation to visit the freak show. It fascinates and horrifies me, and takes away my appetite.

My usual vegetable seller's husband, if he is not at home while his wife runs the stall, thrusts cigarettes in my face and pulls out his better quality produce from a stack of boxes behind the stall. If he does not have enough of what we need he sends his sister-in-law to another stall to buy it. Prices are so cheap I never quibble. For a busy weekend at the Lodge I can buy everything I need for a thirty or forty pounds. The other stop on my supply run is the newest supermarket in Wukang, a two-storey building which looks like a supermarket but is in reality a sanitized version of the market. It is sparkling white throughout, food and bottles and cans are arranged on the shelves like in Asda, but in the meat section the animals are in cages, fish swim in glass tanks and rice is sold in sacks. The locals behave like the place is the market too. Men smoke and spit and the queues at the checkout tills are treated as a nuisance. Here I can find bread, sweet but toastable, and fresh milk and olive oil. Everything else we need, like chocolate, butter, and pasta entails an hour's drive to Hangzhou. We do that run every fortnight. Before the Wukang local paper ran a story on the Lodge the stall holders in the market presumed I was a foreign teacher, especially when they realized I was British, not French or black. Apparently the town has a school where the children are taught in English. We must go and have a look one day.

Chapter Fifteen

The Final Repeat

We were in the final days of the October National Holiday, 2006. Our first full season in Moganshan was almost over and the exodus had already begun.

One morning Mr Wang's chambermaids walked past the Lodge with bulging carrier bags in both hands.

'Throwing stuff out?' I asked as I handed a customer a cup of coffee in the sunshine.

'Back to Wukang for the winter,' they replied.

Mattresses were upended in the hotel's rooms, sheets and bedding washed and folded away, and the few surviving chickens in the hotel coop were killed off.

'It's a bit old and tough,' Mr Wang's sister said as she handed me one. 'I've been trying to catch the thing all summer. But you may as well have it. It'll be all right for soup if you cook it long enough.'

In the second week of October the husbands of the older hotel staff rode their motorbikes up the mountain to collect their wives. The women perched on the very back of the pillion seat, a bundle of clothes in their lap, and went home to help with the winter work on the family smallholding in the valley. They smiled and shouted, 'See you next year!' as they passed. It was like the end of term at school.

By the middle of October the village is eerily quiet. There is a sense of sudden abandonment, as if everyone at a wild party has been called outside for a fireworks display, or the moment at the end of a Chinese banquet when the host stands and says: 'That's that then,' and everyone leaves at once.

The sudden stillness is a surprise at first. Everyone left behind seems to stop and take a breath, a minute to stare at the empty door.

Then the gentle undercurrent of village life picks up again.

The older locals who seem to hide through the summer but only get lost in the crowds of tourists reappear on the wall above the market in the mornings to enjoy the late autumn sunshine. Hotel and restaurant managers settle down to play *ma jiang* in the village store and the back rooms of hotels. The games seem to have no end, as if the players have begun an epic, winter-long *ma jiang* tournament. They chain smoke, clack their tiles and swap stories about the season's visitors; the government officials, the fussy foreigners, the rich Shanghainese. Every one of them complains that they have worked too hard for too little income, and – as they did the same time last year – declare they're going to pack it in and start afresh in Yucun or maybe Wukang.

Junior officials from the Administration Bureau tour the village beauty spots to assess the season's wear and tear, plan improvements for the next season, and then return to their warm offices to drink tea and talk about something else. The chair carriers sigh with regret that now the weather is so cool there are no fat city folk to carry up from the Sword Pool. They too return to their small plots and tiny tea plantations in the valleys.

Then the builders arrive and the silence is broken.

After a good season a hotel will often eviscerate itself. The whole place will be gutted and the fixtures and furniture replaced. The tenant managers rarely make major structural changes or attempt a significant upgrade. They substitute. Plastic baths for plastic baths, white tiles for white tiles, paper thin veneer replaces pale veneer and everything else gets yet another coat of paint. A wooden window frame is torn out and an aluminium one appears in its place, with blue glass window panes.

It is the nature of Chinese domestic and business management to buy cheap and replace frequently. Appliances break, walls crack, thin floorboards buckle and split. If you have the cash, you replace them. If you don't you leave them broken. The false economy has the benefit of allowing for frequent changes of mind, another trait of Chinese life and commerce. If a business idea is not working, all too often the first thing to do, before you work out what is wrong with it, is change it. In a country where labour, materials and time are so cheap it almost makes sense.

I have watched some hotels rip themselves to bits and start afresh every year since we have had the houses here. General Manager Li and Pan Guang Lin are constantly on the go, particularly in winter. So is Lao Han the Builder.

If it has been a bad year a guesthouse manager will find an excuse and do nothing.

'I did not make much this year so I am just going to tidy the place up a bit. Decoration is a waste of time and money anyway. Who needs it?' the manager of a particularly run down guesthouse told me one afternoon in late October.

His place was desperately in need of a complete overhaul. It had a great location. With careful investment he could more than double his business. I said so.

312

'You want to take it over?' he asked back.

I was about to answer when General Manager Li drove past. He slowed and shouted across to me.

'Come and have dinner tonight, House 62, five o'clock sharp!'

Before I could reply or think of an excuse he had driven away. The man who wanted me to take over his guesthouse waited for me to turn back to him then carried on where he had left off. I only half heard him. I was wondering what I had done to earn a dinner invitation from General Manager Li.

Over the past few days several local officials and managers had come into the Lodge in the early evening, rolling drunk from too much *bai jiu*. Boozy dinners seemed to be an end of season ritual.

Did General Manager Li's invitation mean that I now qualified as a local manager? I was touched if that was the case but I had only just had lunch and it was approaching four in the afternoon. I did not want to eat dinner at five. Nor did I particularly want to get drunk so early in the day either.

I said farewell and 'I'll think about it' to the guesthouse owner and carried on up the steps towards our house.

For the past few days I had been meaning to chop logs for firewood for the coming cold weather but had kept putting the chore off. I was getting into my swing with the axe when my mobile rang.

'Mark! Where are you? We're waiting for you at House 62.' It was Pan Guang Lin.

I looked at my watch. Four forty-five Jesus.

'I'm at home Pan Guang Lin,' I said.

'I'll come and pick you up,' he said and rang off.

I dashed into the shower, put on some clean clothes, grabbed four packets of cigarettes and belted down the steps to the road. Pan was already there in his blue pick-up van.

'General Manager Li and the others are waiting for you,' he whined. 'What kept you?'

'But it's not five yet,' I complained back at him.

'Exactly. You're late. We can't start eating till you get there.'

Pan was wearing his smartest brown jacket, a clean shirt, and his hair was neatly brushed. He looked smart, more than I did in my fleece jacket with its hole made by a spark from a recent bonfire. I climbed into the cab and jammed my knees against the dashboard.

We drove along and down the ridge road, through Yin Shan Jie, and down to a bend above the gully that leads to the Sword Pool. Pan pulled over, leapt out of the cab and slammed his door with a clang. I unwedged my legs and followed.

'Come on,' he said, 'this way.'

He led me down some steep steps past a house under renovation. It had recently been rented by a Beijing businessman who was paying forty times the price which the last tenant had paid. Our destination was right below it.

Number 62 was the summer home of Jian Yujie, of the Nanyang Tobacco brothers. A new English language signpost on the path below calls it the 'Baccy Villa', which makes me smile. Apart from some cheap furniture and the white tiled bathrooms the rambling villa is filled with a charming aura of genteel decay and innocent neglect, like a modest stately home before the National Trust has taken charge of it. It is large and roomy, has a long servants' corridor to its rear that reminds me of school and the exterior has not been defaced by aluminium windows. Outside there is a wide and long garden, mostly paved over and shaded by Japanese maples. The garden's stone entranceway is so far from the house itself that people rarely step through it to walk up to the front door. It is the epitome of an overlooked, neglected jewel, like Moganshan itself.

The place is managed by a loveable rogue with a drop-dead gorgeous girlfriend. His name is Yao Xing and his official position is deputy manager of another rundown hotel that belongs to his aunt. Yao looks and acts like a thug thanks to his close cropped haircut, round face, beady eyes and the way he throws his words at you with a flick of his head. But he is a charming thug. Over the summer he had often come up to the Lodge for a quiet beer after closing time. I enjoyed his company.

His girlfriend is called Wawa, Chinese for 'Baby'. The name suits her. She is Cindy doll perfect in looks and figure and despite the sweet way she pretends not to, which makes her even sweeter, she knows it. Wawa has one of those smiles that make a man's day.

For General Manager Li's dinner Yao had set up a long table under the largest tree on the terrace. The sound of the stream rushing down the gully right below us leant an air of Arcadia to the setting.

Pan presented me like a bounty hunter bringing in a fugitive.

'Ah, you've come!' General Manager Li shouted and stood up. Then he pointed to my place at the far end of the table. 'That's your bottle! *Yi Li Te*. You like it?'

'My favourite brand of *bai jiu*, General Manager Li,' I replied, not entirely truthfully. Everyone at the table had a bottle in front of them.

'Then let's have a drink! You are behind already,' Li said.

I took my place and twisted the top off the bottle. I looked for a small glass. There was only a large one.

'In the beaker!' Li shouted. 'Half full! *Gan Bei!*' In other words: give yourself a proper drink and down it in one with me. Now!

He smiled an impish smile as I poured, then stretched his glass down the table. I stood to meet it. Everyone did the same.

'*Gan Bei!*'

I have a problem in situations like this. I like *bai jiu*. Ninety per cent of my foreign friends in China hate it. It tastes foul to the unacquired taste, has a kick like a camel and does serious damage. But it also produces the happiest drunks I know. I have never tried Ecstasy but from what I hear of its effects, *bai jiu* is Ecstasy in a bottle. Everyone at the table becomes your best friend. At a Chinese banquet the most common declaration after '*gan bei*' is: '*Women shi hao pengyou!*' – We're good friends. Some of the best parties I have ever been to are Chinese banquets where the *bai jiu* flows freely. It breaks down barriers, as well as chairs and, on one spectacular evening in Shanghai, an entire restaurant. But that is another story.

It was five o'clock however, time for tea and biscuits not hard alcohol. The sun was still high in the sky. If the dinner party carried on the way it was starting off I would be lucky to see it set.

As our host, General Manager Li was at the head of the table. Beside him sat Mr He, manager of the Moganshan Spring Water Factory, and opposite him the driver of the water factory truck, a young man called Wang. I had been

316

given the place of honoured guest at the other end of the table from Li. On my right was Pan Guang Lin and on my left my old friend and nemesis Mr Ge. He gave me his trademark lopsided smile but this evening it seemed to be angled in my favour, as if to say: 'Well, Mark, we had our fun all those years ago and you're still here, so I am going to show you tonight that I actually like you.' Or something like that. I was pleased to see him.

I had barely put down my glass and was grimacing from the body blow of the hard liquor when Pan Guang Lin thrust another full one at me.

'Fill up again and drink a fine for being late,' he said.

'That's not fair,' I replied. But I followed his orders. The second hit was easier to swallow. I smiled at Pan.

As I feared, the last thing I remember clearly that evening was indeed the sun going down. It must have been about six-thirty. By then Mr Ge and I were joking like old neighbours and Pan Guang Lin was teasing me about almost burning down the cottage. He reminded me how I had woken him up and screamed down the phone to bring an axe. He told me that I had got the tones wrong, which is why he brought a crowbar.

I gave it back to him about the useless chimneys and we were both laughing. There was food at some stage but I had difficulty reaching it because we were sitting at a long table, covered in bottles, not a round banquet one as usual. I was already on my second half litre of *bai jiu*. A plate of peanuts landed beside me so I scoffed the lot, remembering my manners well enough to try not to let my hosts see me use my hands. A voice in my head was urging me to fill my stomach with solids. Pan poked me with cigarettes and patted

317

my knee. I forced a Malboro into his mouth. We laughed some more about Joanna's temper.

The last sober conversation I had that evening was with Mr Ge, I think. I asked him if he had drunk the whisky I gave him at my first Moganshan banquet, the one Joanna and I hosted four years ago.

'Ah, the whisky,' he said. 'Yes.' He paused and looked at me. 'It's in my cabinet at home. I still haven't opened it.'

For the first time ever, Mr Ge smiled a straight smile at me.

'Cheers, Mr Ge!' I raised my glass.

Then, as often happens with people of my dinner companions' generation when the *bai jiu* is flowing freely, talk turned to the bad old days and the Cultural Revolution. The Chinese call it 'to eat bitterness', *chi ku*. Everyone over the age of forty in China has eaten a lot of bitterness. The topic inevitably crops up in dinner conversation the same way that our parents reminisce about the 'good old days'. In China the good old days are only just beginning.

The men told me stories of families struggling to survive through harsh winters, house fires that killed young siblings – Pan caught my eye at that, he looked completely sober for a second, and sad – suicides by the dozen, many in Du Yue Sheng's old villa where the roof beams were well placed for hanging, and 'struggle sessions' during which young Red Guards tormented the simple country people whose crime had been to work for foreigners. Someone reminded me that our landlord at the Song Liang, Mr Wang, or rather his family, had lost everything and then been singled out for special persecution thanks to the family fortune founded by the Ice King. I discovered that there had once been an artisans' workshop on Yin Shan Jie that was famous for its wooden carvings of Buddhist icons. The place had been sacked and demolished by the Red Guards. This was the first time I had heard the sadder side of Moganshan's history.

Li brightened up and changed the subject.

'So, Mark,' he said, 'What's it like to be the first foreigner back in Moganshan?'

He looked genuinely curious. I imagined that I could sense a nostalgia for the really old days, the ones he only knew from his parents, the heyday of Moganshan that had brought upon the innocent locals the repercussions that my dinner companions had just described.

I spoke about the village and its early history – which by now I knew a fair bit about – and how foreigners like me loved the place for special reasons, difficult ones for Chinese to understand.

I tried to explain them. I talked about the village in the Welsh mountains where I was brought up, the rain and mist, the busy summers and quiet winters, the sense of community. I think I even told them about old Vyrnwy Jones getting plastered every New Year's eve and falling out of his boots when he tried to pull them off in the snow while he went first footing. The way we were drinking it seemed appropriate. I must have made little sense thanks to the *bai jiu* and the convoluted concept but that was all right because everyone else was drunk too.

General Manager Li responded with another toast. He was having difficulty getting his words out straight. Pan Guang Lin and I were getting physical. We hugged and swigged in turns. Yao Xing, who had been entertaining some guests of his own inside, came to join us with the beautiful Wawa who sat right beside me. The conversation switched into the local dialect so I just smiled, at Wawa mostly. Occasionally I said something inane and then smiled some more.

The party broke up at seven-thirty. Everyone was legless. Pan offered to drop me back at the Lodge.

'I am driving past there anyway,' he said.

He was so drunk he could hardly walk. But we stumbled up the steps and climbed into his blue van. He swerved up the narrow mountain road, solid stone wall on one side and precipice on the other. The van turned into the parking area in front of the Song Liang Hotel. I protested to Pan that it was unnecessary to drive me to the door of the Lodge but he insisted. It is a narrow space for a car and turning round there sober and in daylight is enough of a challenge.

Pan braked sharply. I opened the door and fell out of the cab. I crawled out of the way and stayed on the ground while Pan made a ten point turn. Like a spectator at a close fought boxing match I cringed while I watched him almost reverse into the hotel and then almost drive over the low top of the retaining wall, five times each. At last the van jerked back the way it had come.

When Joanna came out to see what was going on I was lying on my back, staring at the stars and singing nonsense.

'll walk 'ome,' I slurred at her, pulling myself up onto my elbows. 'ber m'up.' She was smiling. That was a relief.

Then, according to Joanna, I kissed our new Labrador puppy full on the mouth.

Apart from a daylong hangover, I came away from General Manager Li's dinner with the feeling that I had been accepted in Moganshan. It is hard to tell these things in any alien society and especially China, where secret resentments can burst to the surface after years of apparent goodwill. But it seemed as if I had been treated as a Moganshan resident, an insider for the first time. I was definitely not 'one of them', never could be, but my hosts that evening had been open and generous in a way I had rarely experienced in China. Then again, it might just have been the *bai jiu*.

My alcohol-fuzzed imagination was not entirely groundless however. Some days later I was told that the chief of the Administration Bureau, Mr Yang, had said some good things about Joanna and me during his end-of-season debrief. We were attracting more foreigners to Moganshan. He was happy with us being here.

It was good to hear that we had received official blessing. It was also important. It is a fact of life in China that you need friends in high places.

During the first months of our life in Moganshan, soon after I had lost the magazine business, I had been nervous that my erstwhile friends in very high places in the propaganda system – now my enemies – would come after me. They had blackened my name in Beijing and Shanghai, made me an outcast and labelled me a potential terrorist. It was not impossible that they really would chase me out of China.

I had been careful in Moganshan not to talk about what had brought me here, especially with the officials. If one of them asked too specific a question I would reply that I had 'finished my business in Shanghai'.

As time passed I relaxed. I began to feel safe. My enemies might be able to ensure I never worked again in the Chinese media industry, but they could not stop me working in my wife's coffee-shop, writing books and gardening.

I was still a thorn in their side however. There was one

battle left to fight, one last thing I could not put behind me, not just yet.

That November the trademark case was given a hearing at the high court in Beijing. It was the final appeal and I was dreading it. I had lost the first round, an appeal in the Beijing middle court to overturn the Trademark Bureau's decision to cancel my rights to my trademark. The judge had apologized when she gave her verdict.

'You should appeal,' she said, quietly, outside the courtroom. 'You might have a better chance.' Her loaded words had given me hope, so I pursued it. Once every few months I had been dragging myself away from Moganshan to visit my lawyers in Beijing. Together we went over the history of my business in excruciating detail.

The lawyers were convinced I *should* win and like the middle court judge they thought our chances much better in the high court. But first I had to help them collect more evidence.

The key to the case was to show that our opponents, the State Council Information Office, the highest authority in Chinese media, had fabricated evidence, which they had. Proving it was not going to be easy. My best hope lay in persuading the man who had helped the government create the fake evidence, my one-time supporter in Yangzhou, to tell the truth. The trouble was: he was an official in the city's News Office and his ultimate 'leader' was the State Council Information Office. I was going to ask him to go against his superiors. That's an awful lot to request of a Chinese official.

It was difficult, but I did it.

Mr Sun Xiao Feng of the Yangzhou People's Government News Office even agreed to appear in the high court in person as a witness. Mr Sun is a good and brave man.

On 13 November 2006 I caught a bus to Yangzhou and from there Mr Sun and I took the overnight train to Beijing. I was leaving nothing to chance. If he realized that I was, in effect, escorting him Mr Sun was polite enough not to show it. We spent most of the evening in the restaurant car talking about old times.

I was impressed by the high court. The building was brand new, very large and very empty, as if to emphasize that not many people reached this ultimate stage in the Chinese legal system. It seemed that ours was the only case being heard that day. The court room itself was small and narrow. There were no spectators or press. The haven I had made for myself in Moganshan seemed like a distant dream.

The presiding judge was a woman again. On either side of her sat her panel, two other judges. They were significantly older than the ones at the middle court. Across the room from us was the defendant, the State Trademark Adjudication Bureau and beside them my real opponent, a lawyer acting for the State Council Information Office, the Chinese cabinet's pet propaganda unit. In effect, if we had been in London, you could say I was suing Alasdair Campbell for libel and he had appointed the judge, and the jury was stuffed with his best friends.

I shall skip the details. But we knocked them for six. The harrowing effort we had made to prepare my case paid off in spades. I noticed the presiding judge cringe with embarrassment on my behalf at one point. That was a good moment.

It did not take her long to reach a decision. Less than a month. My lawyer took the call. The clerk of the court told him to come and pick up the decision and also, he added, the deposit we had paid for the hearing. You only get your deposit back if you win. We prepared to celebrate.

The next day, one hour before the appointment at the courtroom, when my lawyer was stuck in a traffic jam somewhere on Beijing's third ring road, he received another call from the clerk of the court.

'Don't come,' he was told. 'There have been some new developments. The decision has been postponed.' And the clerk hung up.

My lawyer immediately rang the judge.

'I am not in a position to comment,' she said.

And that was that.

I was gutted. More than the victory that had been snatched from us at the last minute, I had desperately hoped for finality, that the hearing would have brought my battles to an end. If we had lost the final appeal there would have been nothing more we could do. I would have been free to get on with my new life in Moganshan in the knowledge that I had done everything possible to tie up the loose ends of my last one.

And I had almost done it. That made it harder to bear.

I heard the news when I was back home. Christmas was a few days away. My lawyer said he had been looking forward to giving me a surprise present but, alas, we'd lost. We had a good party nonetheless, although Joanna took the news quite badly.

The court case will probably still be unresolved when you read this. Things looked up in April 2007 when the high court suggested to the State Council Information Office that they settle out of court, to save face all round. The Information Office mentioned a number to my lawyer, in passing as it were, and brazenly admitted it was based on how much they could squeeze through their books without having to apply for funds from the central government. Mr Sun Xiao Feng and I asked for more and a proper offer in writing. Nothing happened . . .

Oh, I forget. Something did happen. While we were waiting to hear, the Information Office launched a campaign to destroy Mr Sun's career. He is coping well.

Jane McCartney, the London *Times* correspondent in Beijing, spent a weekend in Moganshan soon after that offer was made by the State Council and she wrote a story. For the first time in more than fifty years an English-language newspaper ran a report with the dateline 'Moganshan'. That made me smile after all the 'from our Mokanshan correspondent' lines I had read in the *North-China Daily News*.

On Boxing Day 2006 there was a heavy snowfall. The mountain, all the way down to the ticket office on the steep front road, was coated by a couple of inches. If I was looking for a metaphor that told me to block out the past, start again on a clean white sheet, then this was it.

We took the children for long walks, had snowball fights, and waited for them to walk under a bamboo tree whose feathery branches were laden with snow. Then we pushed the trunk so Isabel and Tristan were covered in the fine white powder.

'Look! It's snowing again,' we shouted.

We were happy.

I did not know it at the time, but that was why I was in Moganshan, and why I was not as angry as I should or could have been about the court case.

Soon after the western New Year, Joanna prepared to leave for Guangzhou with the children to spend time with her parents. The water would be freezing in the pipes any day now and it would be impossible for the family to live in the house. I was to stay on until the end of January, to keep the Lodge ticking over and to look after the few guests who were coming to stay in the cottage. I'd get water from the spring in the garden and I could always use my paint-stripping heat gun – purchased specifically for the purpose – on the pipes if I wanted to get water into the house for a day. I sealed the windows with insulating tape and spent my afternoons in the woods looking for firewood.

Cutting trees for firewood is illegal in Moganshan, but everyone does it, within reason. I conscientiously limit myself to typhoon-damage and trees which are clearly dead or dying.

I have to be careful not to get caught at it so I walk deep into the woods, which means down the hill. It is good exercise lugging the lengths back home. If you know where to look there is plenty of potential firewood lying or leaning about.

I have only once been intercepted by a forestry worker, an old man from the valley. Every day he climbs two thousand feet in cloth slippers, whatever the weather. His patch is the side of the mountain above his village.

'What are you doing here?' he asked.

With an axe and bow saw over my shoulder it would have been churlish to lie.

'Chopping wood,' I replied. 'But I only chop dead or dying trees.' I stepped up to one and put my hand on it. 'Like this one.'

'That's illegal,' the man said.

'But it's dead,' I replied.

'Chopping any wood here is illegal. Doesn't matter if it is dead or not.' The man looked strict. 'I should report you to the forestry department office.'

'Ah, to Mr Wu,' I name-dropped. 'I know him well.'

326

The man's eye flickered with acknowledgement. Then he came back with an awkward question: 'So he gave you permission then, did he?' Damn.

I went back to basics.

'Smoke?' I asked, pulling out my Malboro Lights. 'They're foreign. Ever tasted one?'

The man took one and looked at it. 'Your foreign cigarettes are too strong,' he said.

'No, they're not. Go on, try it.'

He put it in his mouth and I lit it for him. There was hope now. He looked less stern.

'Anyway,' he said. 'This old stuff makes terrible firewood. Look, it's totally rotten.'

I had deliberately given him a decoy, one that I knew perfectly well was useless. A less dead tree and my intended target was right behind him.

'There you are, see,' I jumped at the opportunity. 'No one else will want a tree like this.'

He took a drag of the cigarette and puffed the smoke into the air. He watched it float away and disperse. Then he spoke again, severely.

'I am responsible for this section. You understand that if you get caught here,' I thought that was happening right now, 'then I will be in big trouble.' I nodded. 'There are plenty of dead trees right behind your house, on Zhong Hua Shan. Why don't you chop them?'

'Actually they are good trees up there,' I said, secretly pleased to hear he knew who I was and where I lived. That was a good sign.

'Oh, there are some that are sure to die soon. You just have to look for them.' I had, without success. He was looking for an excuse to get me off his patch. That much was obvious.

'But what about these ones?' I pointed to the dying ones near by. Their bark was falling off, which makes them easy to spot.

'Hm,' he muttered, then changed tack. 'Whatever you do, please do not come back here tomorrow.' The important word seemed to be 'tomorrow', my opportunity to give face.

'I understand,' I said. 'I promise. I will not come back. Tomorrow.'

He smiled and looked at the sky. 'Still half an hour before it gets dark,' he said.

'Yes. You're right.'

'See that tree over there?'

'Yes.'

'It'd make good firewood.' He was looking at a tall tree in the woods some distance away. 'Dying too.' He looked up again at the sky. 'I guess you should just have enough daylight today, since you are not coming back *tomorrow*.'

And he turned and walked down the hill to his village without a backward glance.

That particular tree made excellent firewood.

I was secretly looking forward to Joanna and the family leaving me alone on the mountain for a few weeks. I would have time to write, watch black-and-white movies, and sit in peace by the smoky fire. There were some nice people coming to stay in the cottage and I always had the Lodge to play with when I got bored.

The day before Joanna left I was down there looking after things while she stayed at home and packed. In the evening she brought the children down for supper. We were eating up surplus supplies from the freezer. Tonight was homemade fish pie.

While the children were watching cartoons in the coffee-shop's snug, Joanna crossed the corridor to stand in the kitchen doorway.

'There was a strange man outside the house this afternoon,' she said.

Joanna never wastes time on preambles. 'He walked up and down the steps outside the kitchen window a couple of times and he kept looking inside. Do you know who he was?'

'Er, no.'

'It was as if he was preparing to break in or something.' She looked at me. 'I was scared. I don't think he knew I was in there.'

My mind started working. 'Did he look like a country type, maybe a local government driver? Or was he a city man?'

'He wore black. Looked like a guy from the city.'

I could picture him. He sounded like a government goon, a driver too perhaps. Or could he have been someone more sinister? Ideas raced through my head. More than a few of my friends had once again been wondering out loud about my personal safety after the fuss I had kicked up in the international media when the trademark case appeared in the high court. I had taken on the Chinese government and made it public, and I was a single individual, not a big corporation. And I lived alone with my family in an isolated house on a mountain.

I kept insisting that the repercussions my friends imagined did not happen in China. But sometimes I could not help wondering.

My research on Moganshan had only recently brought me to the website about R. J. Felgate. The story was fresh in my mind: a dispute between a local and a foreigner, a break-in and a murder. It had taken place during the early hours of 7 January 1912. Today was 3 January 2007.

It was the anniversary bit that got my imagination going.

I had bitter experience of my enemies' fondness for anniversaries: the trademark dispute was registered on my birthday in 2004 and lost precisely one year later. The high court appeal date had been set four days later than usual, four days after my birthday, but only because my lawyer had got the court to postpone the hearing so I could stick to my fortieth birthday plans.

I thought back to how the authorities used to spoil my Christmas Days when I was running the magazines. It was convenient for them that we went to print on the 25th of the month. Every year I took a call on 25 December. One-time it came as I was giving Joanna her first ever Christmas stocking. I would be presented with an impossible problem, like a party game, and have to solve it before I could open my presents, or sit down to Christmas dinner.

My enemies like to spoil my day and they loved an anniversary. I would have put the mysterious intruder down to coincidence if I had not known them so well. Besides, I do not think getting buggered about every Christmas Day for five years and three birthdays in a row is a coincidence.

(We always got the January magazines out on time. It was fraught but we did it. And my fortieth was a blast.)

In three days time it would be ninety-four years to the day since Felgate was murdered. I was going to be alone at home and the only foreigner on the mountain. To round it

330

off, ninety-four is one of the worst numbers on the Chinese superstition scale, it implies: 'Go die'.

I do not generally suffer from paranoia. I like to think I am a calm and reasonable individual and have a modicum of courage in me somewhere. I enjoy the occasional horror movie, even on my own in the house. In fact Joanna and I had made it a tradition to watch *The Shining* every year when the snow started falling.

So I did not set too much store in the silly ideas which were beginning to rattle around my head.

Then a couple more coincidences added themselves to the list.

The Friday after Joanna and the children left I had a drop-in visitor at the Lodge. He was a German up for the day from Hangzhou where he worked for the Chinese government. He arrived with a colleague and his girlfriend. They stopped in for a cup of coffee then went to wander the mountain and returned for a late lunch.

Rolf was bursting with questions about Moganshan. Once we had covered the usual ground, he came to a particular concern.

'I would be scared,' he said.

He was leaning over the bar, staring straight into my eyes.

'I am sorry. What do you mean?' I asked.

'Security,' he said in his clipped English, his voice slightly high pitched and slow like a black-and-white-horror-movie bad guy. 'I would not feel safe living here alone.'

He held my gaze. 'Is you house safe?'

'Absolutely,' I replied. 'Never worried about anything like that.' I lied through my teeth.

Listening with a bemused smile to Rolf's fears, I did feel braver in a way. I had mentioned the cottage to him. He

331

explained that it was staying there that worried him.

'If you are worried about the cottage, I live right next door,' I said. 'You would be perfectly safe up there. I have a dog too.'

Rolf looked at me for a few seconds. I thought he was searching my eyes for a flicker in my confidence. Then, in that slow and deliberate horror movie voice he said: 'You heard about the German family in Nanjing, *ja*?'

'The one that was murdered a few years ago?' I said. It was old news. 'Yes. I know the story. They were killed by robbers who panicked, weren't they?'

Rolf nodded. 'That's what everyone says,' he paused. 'But did you know that the guy was about to reveal his Chinese partner's corruption to his bosses in Germany and the press?' Rolf smiled as a storyteller does when he reveals a twist.

'The robbers were set up to it.' Another pause, and then a very German: 'Possibly.'

I laughed with Rolf and told him he was making things up. But I wished he would go away.

'We see each other again,' he said. 'Maybe.'

Rolf and his friends climbed into the taxi I had ordered and disappeared with a cheery wave.

That Friday was 6 January. The weather was cold and dry, the mountain seemed more than usually quiet. No one was at the cottage that night. I shut up the coffee-shop and hurried home once Rolf had gone. There was a tree I had been meaning to cut down for ages. It was one of the last of the 'weed' trees on our patch and blocked out the light on one side of the cottage. Now seemed as good a time as any to chop it down. It would only take half an hour with my new electric chainsaw. The extension cable would reach from the cottage's kitchen.

I changed into some old clothes, grabbed my work gloves and the chainsaw, the light machine oil that had to be kept topped up, the extension cable, and went up to the cottage. I was looking forward to the distraction of physical labour.

Five minutes later the tree came crashing down. I had cut through the main trunk at shoulder height so I could saw logs off it one by one. I made short work of the branches, carrying the thin ends over to the bonfire heap and laying the good lengths to one side. They could dry out while I was in Guangzhou for Chinese New Year with my family and in-laws and then the UK for the rest of the winter. I would have a good stock of wood when I came back early in March to set everything up again before the children and Joanna came home.

Then I set to work on the remains of the trunk. The wood was solid, bright and pale. The sawdust flew out of the side of the tree and formed a neat pile on the ground. I meant to cover it with brown leaves when I had finished. No one would know I had cut a perfectly healthy tree down. I would store the timber on the first floor balcony of our house, out of sight and safe from scavengers.

Just as I was finishing the final and thickest slice at the lowest part of the trunk, an army officer in uniform appeared at the top of the steps from the house. He was one of the Hangliao men. Thanks to the chainsaw I had not heard him coming. He was new and I did not know his name.

Damn, caught red-handed again, I thought.

Charlie, our Labrador puppy, ran towards him and he backed off a bit. I dashed over behind her. I was much taller than the officer and danced around right in his face, flapping my arms in a pretence of shooing the dog away. It was a futile attempt to block his view of the ex-tree behind me. I must have looked like I was doing an impression of Basil Fawlty, not that he would know.

'You're busy,' he said.

'Er, yes, um, just cutting up some firewood.' There was a remote, ridiculous chance he would think that I was chopping logs up as opposed to a tree down.

'Is there anything I can do for you?' A stupid question but I had to stop him talking about the tree.

'No,' he said.

'Maybe you've come to check the water tank?' The army often came up to look into the tank at the far end of our garden in the woods. It supplied water to several of their properties.

'No.'

'The electricity then?'

'No.' He looked around the garden for a few seconds, at the cottage and then over his shoulder at the house below. 'I was just wondering if you were still here, that's all. You all alone? Family gone?'

Jesus Christ. Not funny any more. If I was the target of a coordinated scare campaign it was succeeding brilliantly. Without another word the man turned and walked back down the steps. He had shown no interest in my blatantly-illegal tree chopping.

I sat down on one of the logs, pulled out a packet of cigarettes and lit one. I needed to calm down. But instead of thinking of something else, I added up the coincidences:

Local officials making sure I was alone? Check. Man in black casing our house a few days ago? Check. Have I pissed off someone powerful, who plays dirty, and has a fondness for anniversaries? Check. Apparently completely coincidental conversation with German fellow about foreign whistle-blower getting murdered by Chinese? Check. When is the ninety-fourth anniversary of the Felgate murder on the mountain? Tonight.

And, by the by, what had a highly poisonous pit-viper been doing behind my house last summer? And was it normal wear and tear that destroyed the car's brakes before it had done twenty thousand kilometres?

I really was getting paranoid.

As dusk fell, I walked into the woods. I was looking for a hiding place. Perhaps the water tank at the end of the garden? It was flat and there was a tiny overgrown path from its rear, down the hill to the back road, which I could use as an escape route if necessary. Or maybe in the trees on the ridge overlooking the houses? I went up to the attic and dug out my sleeping bag. The evening was fine and there was no sign of rain. Roughing it in the woods, I would be perfectly comfortable. But then I wanted to be close enough to see who might turn up. I wanted evidence, for my sanity if nothing else.

By the time it was dark I had stored the remains of the weed tree on the upstairs balcony of the main house. I made a wall out of the logs at the far end. I was thinking about hiding behind them in my sleeping bag. From there I was sure to hear someone breaking in and it was an unlikely place to look for me. But if they did find me there was no escape apart from jumping off the balcony. I could hardly leave the ladder below me.

I stopped and poured myself a strong whisky. By now it was pitch black and cold outside. I sat at my desk in my study, put on some quiet music and lit a cigarette. The idea was to calm down, but while I drank I couldn't help thinking of Felgate.

On the website, the author describes in detail her great grandfather's last night alive in Moganshan. Her main source was the report on the murder by the British Consul in Hangzhou, but she has embellished the facts with some perfectly acceptable and realistic conjecture.

I had saved the pages on my laptop. I poured another stiff drink, lit another cigarette and clicked on the mouse.

'That night when Robert retired to bed he went through his usual routine to secure his house. The front door was locked and the security pin removed. The dogs were shut under the stairs, the oil lamps put out, and, candle-stick in hand, Robert left the dining-room by the staircase door. After locking the door behind him he carried his candle upstairs to his bedroom, entered, and locked that door as well. He got ready for bed as usual, placing his revolver under his pillow, and checking that his other guns were within easy reach. Then he blew out the candle and settled down to sleep.

About midnight he was awakened by a noise. He knew instantly that something suspicious was going on, and he scrambled hastily out of bed. He lighted his candle and pulled a jersey over his head. Then he seized his revolver and unlocked the bedroom door . . . Tense with suspicion, he made his way cautiously downstairs, unlocking doors as he went. Every instinct told him that strangers were in his house, and as quietly as he could he opened the dining-room door. As he stood there, peering across the flickering light of his candle, a hand smashed down on the little flame, plunging the room into darkness. Arms seized him, and as he opened his mouth to let out a yell, a black cloth was wrapped round his head, muffling his cries. With a crash he was flung to the ground, and his hands and feet were tightly bound . . . Hands at his feet and head dragged him out of the house, bumped him down the porch steps and dropped him on the icy ground outside. He struggled violently and tried to call for help, but swift blows to his head silenced him. His cries became moans, and he drifted into unconsciousness.

[One of the robbers] hauled a bundle of bedding from the house which he threw over the body to conceal it from chance passers-by.

Satisfied that their captive was no longer a threat, the men lost interest in him and went back into the house to turn it over from top to bottom . . .

Outside, Robert lay unheeded on the ground, his life ebbing away through the deep cuts on his head. In the small hours of the night shock, loss of blood and the winter cold brought his life to an end . . .

. . . Doors. There were no locks on the doors. I had to secure them. Of course there were locks on the front and back doors but they were not strong enough. I needed to jam them shut. And I needed a weapon.

Then I would sleep in the bedroom. It suddenly seemed necessary, to prove I had not gone crazy, that I slept in my own bed. If I could barricade myself into the house, then an intruder would be sure to disturb me. I would not walk into an ambush with a candle in my hand. I'd lie in wait and give him what for. The whisky was working.

I took a tape measure from my desk and went around the doors, front and back, balcony and the bedroom. There weren't any in between the bedroom and the outside of the house. That was a let down. No matter.

I measured the distance from the door handles to the foot

of the nearest solid object, a wall, a heavy cupboard or a bed. Then I picked up my bow saw and went out on to the balcony. I cut poles from the tree I had felled that afternoon and took them inside to make the final adjustments. I placed one end of each pole against the door handles and the other along the floor and against whatever was solid. Once I had cut off an inch or two the improvised jams worked well. I tested them by pulling on the door handles from the inside and the doors did not budge. Thanks to the handle in the bedroom being so close to the bottom of our heavy bed, I used an extra stout pole for my final line of defence. I was beginning to feel safer.

Finally I collected my hatchet, my full-sized axe, and a beautifully made bamboo and leather cosh that I had inherited with a great uncle's Triumph Dolomite, years ago in the UK. I propped the big axe against the wall and lay the hatchet and cosh on the bedside table. I was ready. Let them come.

Then I went downstairs for a final whisky.

Before I undressed – remembering to keep a pair of shorts and a T-shirt on so I would be ready to spring out of bed – I picked up the hatchet and made a few practice swipes, just inside the door where I pictured a man's hand fumbling for a light switch. The big axe was for back up, the heavy artillery. Then I tried with the cosh at head height. I used to fence a fair bit, sabre, so I practised a couple of feints too. They were awkward with the hatchet but the cosh was light and easy to stop mid-swing. I put them back down on the bedside table, handles towards me, and lay down.

I claim I was trying to hold on to my sanity by sleeping in my own bed. The truth be told, I think I lost it that night.

There are plenty of stories of foreigners being driven crazy by China. The first one I heard was when I was a student in the eighties. A Frenchman had been working on a deal for years and thought he had finally secured it. At the last minute he found he hadn't. So took his clothes off and ran naked through Tian'an Men Square.

One of my best friends, whom I have mentioned before but had better not identify, rang me up one evening in Shanghai and said: 'Mark, you free for a drink later?' I said yes. 'Good, can we go somewhere quiet where I can say cunt a lot?' I suggested a bar. We met. We drank, but not to excess. And if Dudley Moore and Peter Cooke were at the next door table, they would have said, 'All right, chaps, that's enough of the C-word.'

The Chinese go crazy too. In fact, if we foreigners think the country is driving us mad, we do not know how lucky we are. We can always leave.

One Chinese New Year in Guanghzou with Joanna and the family we called on my father-in-law's stepmother. She lives in a bare concrete grace-and-favour apartment in Foshan, the next door city. Her late husband had been a middle ranking official in the fifties. While we were sitting around the edge of the room on school chairs eating fruit, waiting for more relatives to arrive so we could go out to lunch, step-grandmother-in-law's elderly widow neighbour burst in and started making a circuit. One by one she told us that the President of Taiwan was hiding from assassins in her apartment upstairs. His wife was with her too.

Someone ushered her out gently and everyone smiled. The old woman had lost her wits in the Cultural Revolution.

That's how they do things in China. They are subtle. They

do not, as I reassured my friends, put a bullet in your head like Russia, or imprison you like an African dictatorship. They send you mad, over the edge. Now they had done it to me.

I must admit I have never been so scared as that night in Moganshan. The words of my friends: 'Aren't you concerned for your own safety?' kept running through my head.

I added up the coincidences again and lost count when I thought of more, like the debilitating liver infection I caught from the water in our spring that summer when I was writing the story of the magazines. I had never had a problem with the water, yet there I was, laid out for ten days on my own by an illness I have never experienced the like of before, or since.

It was tempting to call one of those friends and say, 'Yes. You were right. I am concerned for my own safety. In fact I am scared shitless. Please get out here fast.'

I didn't.

I was also tempted to drive down the hill and find a hotel for the night. Again I didn't. For all the fear and the paranoia, there was a stubbornness inside me that wanted to prove I was wrong. I agreed to torment myself, for my own good, as Joanna and I did with *The Shining*. It was not an act of bravery, in spite of my whisky fuelled fantasies of chopping burglars to bits with an axe. It was stubbornness and alcohol that carried me through and put me to sleep, eventually.

I wish I could say I saw the ghost of Felgate that night.

I slept like a baby.

Chapter Sixteen
Still Here

I am still here. My family is still here. In Moganshan. In China. Often, very often, I sit in the garden of our cottage with a glass of cold beer, my feet up on a tree stump, and wonder: why?

It is very pleasant, the garden. Over the years I have cut back the surrounding bush and trees to let in the light and create a sensation of space, of being on the top of our mountain. We arrived in the middle of a wild forest. Now we have a large lawn with flowerbeds along its sunnier edges.

Around the lawn we have planted hydrangeas, rhododendrons, roses, azaleas, bulbs, and whatever else I can find locally that will survive. A garden on the top of a small conical mountain is never going to be a reservoir of earthy richness. The plants that do thrive, like the azaleas – our own cuckoo flowers – bloom only briefly. On my way up and down the mountain I watch their cousins in the valley come out first, then the colour makes its way uphill like a rising tide until it reaches our cottage last of all. They shrivel and fall in reverse order, first ours, then the village, then the valley. We must have a happy cuckoo. The garden serves its purpose. It is a flat space where children can run around and in the evening grown-ups can lounge on bamboo chairs and stare at the setting sun and the stars.

It is also the perfect place to sit and ponder.

I am often asked what am I doing here, why did I come to China in the first place. It is a standard question from friends in the UK. Long-term China hands who know something of my story ask me the more awkward one: 'Why are you *still* here?'

Good questions.

Why leave home, friends, family, the familiar environment and lifestyle that brought you up, that your education prepared you for, and take off to live in an alien country and culture? And China of all places, a particularly alien country and culture that outsiders have been struggling to understand and adapt to without success for centuries? What is it about China? And why, for heaven's sake, stay here when you have been so completely shafted?

In the UK, as if to help me out, people say: 'How brave you are.'

The implication is that it takes a special kind of courage to make a life here. 'And how impressive to speak the language,' they carry on, noting my awkwardness. 'It must be so hard doing business with the Chinese. Everyone knows how inscrutable they are.'

The answer I would like to give the well-meaning aunts and uncles and old friends is: 'No. I am not brave. And learning a foreign language is not that difficult or impressive, even for a Brit. And as for the Chinese being excellent and inscrutable businessmen, you don't want to get me going on that subject.'

They don't want to hear it.

'You're the brave ones,' I should be saying. 'You had the guts to stay at home, to make a life there and something out of it. That takes far more courage in my opinion, to have to find a job, pay for a house, a mortgage and expensive school fees, save for retirement, look after your ageing parents, deal with your awkward relatives, vote for a government, buy a car, life insurance, a lawnmower. You are far braver than I am. I'm escaping all that, dodging my responsibilities, fleeing a life that I thought I couldn't cope with. In actual fact, I am a coward. That's why I am in China.'

I am a coward because I turned my back on my obligation to be British and live like it.

I think we are all cowards to some extent, the foreigners who have come to China to make our lives. We copped out. We like to think of ourselves as opportunists, pioneers, ground-breakers and all those good things, but we're yellow really. Expat general managers on well-paid postings that'll end in a couple of years, having padded the family savings, are not included. Nor are professionals like journalists and diplomats. I am talking about people like me who came and stayed for reasons we cannot quite explain or face up to, not if we think hard about them. Shanghai is a notorious refuge for runaways. It always has been.

Many of my foreign friends and acquaintances in China are entrepreneurs. We claim to be making a new life in China, doing something 'different'.

We are not making a new life. We are running away from an old one. And it is easy to do something 'different' in a place where you are 'different' to start with.

I have entrepreneurial friends in the UK too. They are far braver than I am and my China-based gang of merchant adventurers. They face fierce competition, enforced reg-ulations, taxes that get collected, a mature and established market. In China, where such irksome problems exist they most often only do so on paper. Of course we face challenges of a different sort, as I know only too well. But when my magazines were declared illegal, I was not sent to jail or deported. I only had to pay someone off.

Sometimes I cannot help thinking of Lord Jim, Joseph Conrad's tragic hero. That's not to say I imagine myself his real-life counterpart. But like Jim I ran away, deserted my post and have tried to make up for it ever since. The tribal chief I served to the best of my ability was the Chinese Communist Party Propaganda Bureau. The battle I fought on its behalf, hamstrung by misunderstanding, was to make foreigners feel at home and happy in a few Chinese cities. It took guts to fight off my enemies, inside and out, and hold on to my integrity. I produced something good too, something that is remembered. But then I overstepped the mark, made a move I thought was right and that I could explain to my masters but which in hindsight was a mistake, and I was shot down by my adopted chief – metaphorically speaking.

No one is writing a novel about me, or making a film for that matter, but they are erecting my statue. It will not have my name on it but it will be me nonetheless. The Administration Bureau has finally come round to the idea of commemorating the foreign founders of the village. The statue is for *Fu Lijia*. I think they are referring to Revd J.W. Farnham but there are no bilingual records to verify the match. Nor are there any surviving photographs of him. So they have used me as a model.

When Joanna suggested, quite rightly, that they tried a little harder to find out what he looked like, she was brushed off with, 'Oh, just so long as he looks foreign. That's all we care about.'

Naturally, I said yes. I hope my grandchildren will come and see it one day. And even if it does not have my name on I am still going to dine out on the fact that after all the trouble the Chinese government has given me, they put my statue up. The head is already done and according to the Administration Bureau's office cleaner who has seen it, it looks exactly like me.

Leaving aside the facts that my wife is Chinese and that China is my children's mother country, it is Moganshan that keeps me here really. I love the village with a passion that has not dimmed one jot from when I first found it. And it is a wonderful place to bring up children. We live in the heart of China but we are not in the thick of it. Moganshan is the best of both worlds. Ask my contemporaries in the glass towered corporate sweat shops of Shanghai and Guangzhou, and Beijing, or Hong Kong even. In fact you do not need to ask them. They will tell you without prompting, the minute they set foot here, even the ones who say I must have gone cuckoo to still be in China after everything that happened to me. I heard it second-hand from a local hotel manager the other day, too.

'Hey, Mark,' he said, 'my foreign guests at the weekend kept telling me how lucky you were. They were very jealous.' He laughed, probably to cover his confusion.

And although it might be mistaken for it, life in Moganshan is never dull.

It is the small things I notice most: a new fence around a chicken coop, a tiny flowerbed along a path where there was none before, a tree in the woods which has collapsed under the Russian ivy.

Then there is the ever changing scenery. The views over the surrounding country are like impressionist paintings. At different times of day, in different seasons, they are barely recognizable from the last time I looked. Even hazy days are different from each other, and when the atmosphere is clear, distant hills that yesterday looked as if they were in the next province seem so close you could touch them. The changes can occur within an hour, especially in the summer when the sun comes out after a downpour. Once the steam has risen to be recycled into the next thunderstorm the hills appear so green they look like they have been spray painted.

I make regular rounds, covering the hillsides by section. A fire watcher might have made his summer home at the little hut in the woods where I like to sit and drink a cold beer. Or a typhoon has brought down a tree in such a visible place that I must be quick to get it home before anyone else does. Or a new gap in the trees beside a recently opened path gives me a glimpse of a piece of rock which might make for good climbing. It will take me a few forays until I find the best route to its top or bottom.

An inevitable consequence of living full-time in Moganshan is that I am gradually getting to see more of the limited wildlife – unfortunately including close encounters with poisonous snakes. I have had a wild civet cat investigate me so closely I could have shaken hands with it, got to know a hedgehog who lurks round the back of the house, just as the toad does at the front, and Charlie our Labrador has put up hundreds of Chinese bamboo partridge and chased countless squirrels.

And at long last I have seen a wild boar.

After all the stories I had heard about them, the 'wild boar specials' on Moganshan menus, the gristly knobs of meat I chewed at the Hans' place, the traps and three-legged dogs, the tracks I crawled along and the holes the animals dug with their snouts, I was determined to see one in the forest. Only then could I call myself a local. Most people I know in Moganshan have only seen a wild boar once in their whole lives, if that.

It happened like this. I was on a long hike. My aim was to find a route through the hills towards the Tianmu Mountains, almost a hundred kilometres to our south-west, and I meant to find it by sticking to old mountain paths as much as possible. In my rucksack I had a tent, sleeping bag, and food for three days.

As dusk fell on the first day I was desperately trying to find my way over a high ridge. I had passed through Geling that morning and was heading deep into the wilderness. The last small village was far below and behind me. Every vertical path I struggled up turned into a dead end.

Eventually I accepted defeat and pitched a rough camp in a bowl at the end of a trail in the bamboo. I could see no way out. I resigned myself to retracing my steps the next morning and finding a long way round the ridge.

After an exhausted night's sleep and breakfast cooked with the last of my water, I set off back the way I had come, down into the valley. But in the full daylight I could now appreciate how well made the apparently dead end path was. It must have been made centuries ago. It had to go somewhere. No one built a path like that to nowhere.

I turned back yet again and, just above where I had camped, noticed a faint switchback heading towards the crest of the ridge. I dropped my rucksack and scrambled up it. At the summit the path was overgrown and it almost disappeared. But it crossed over.

On the far side the trail was even fainter, but I skipped down through the bamboo and collected my rucksack.

Beyond the ridge was one of the strangest valleys I had ever stumbled into. The sparse bamboo had been flattened in patches by a typhoon, and where it had been cut by man had been left to rot. It was a mess. There was also litter. Not much, but enough to give me the haunting impression that whoever had been there had left in a hurry.

The sides of the valley were steep and close, and the bamboo only rose for about twenty metres either side of the valley floor before running into thick bush. Thanks to the mist and cloud it was dark and wet. Even on a clear day I doubt much sunshine reached into its depths.

As I made my way down from the ridge I picked up a path made of large stones. They were not just broad; they were big, square and smoothly cut, like an avenue of ancient corner stones. As I was slowly climbing down a particularly steep section I heard something moving about ahead of me. I stood still and waited.

The animal came into view and climbed the opposite slope, barely thirty metres in front of me. At first sight I assumed it was a dog, something like a German shepherd. It was large but the rump was low, the shoulders sloped the right way and through the mist the colour seemed about right. I expected to see a bamboo cutter appear any moment, or hear a man's shout at least.

Then it grunted. Like a pig. A deep throaty grumble. I realized I was watching a wild boar, a big one. I held my breath. He was magnificent. And he showed no sign of sensing my presence.

In his own time the beast strolled upwards across my

front, a perfect shot if I had been a hunter. He seemed so confident that I decided to go for my camera, no matter if I spooked him. He would be gone soon anyway. But he was so close – if I *did* spook him, would he charge me, or flee? In any case, getting my rucksack off would not be a bad idea if he decided to charge just for the hell of it. I looked around for a retreat. There was none. I reached for my belt.

The animal's head went up and froze, looking straight ahead. He stayed that way for a mere second, although it felt like an eternity, and then he seemed to see me through his right ear. With a snort he bolted, away from me, thank God. He thundered into the bush, stopped out of sight, and let out a loud grunt. I assumed he was mustering his family. There were a series of heavy crashes and then silence.

I stayed where I was, my hand still on my belt, and let the awe of what I had seen sink in. It did not matter that I had missed the chance to take a photograph. Like Lao Gao's flute playing in the night, the experience in itself was more than enough, one that I did not feel the need to share, or prove to anyone. I will never forget it.

Less thrilling than a once-in-a-lifetime boar sighting but still stimulating enough to keep us on our toes are the big changes back in the village, big for us at least: a new tenant in a villa, or a switch in management at one of the guesthouses or restaurants. The tenant manager of the villa at the bottom of the steps to our house has changed three times since we have been here. Lao Han has cannily maintained his position as caretaker. He now looks after four guesthouses in total. Most days he comes by the house and sits on the terrace for a chat or plays with Isabel and Tristan. I think he is a good neighbour.

Joanna disagrees. 'He's always on the make,' she says. I start defending him. Joanna is still getting used to village life.

Two years ago the house next door to the Hans' old place was taken over by a *nouveau riche* from Shanghai.

Mr Zhou has taken a perfectly charming, slightly shabby villa and turned it into a pretentious art gallery. He has bricked up the ground floor windows, torn out the wooden heart of the house, tiled the ground floor, put in a central staircase better suited to a Shanghai office block and hung enormous and garish oil paintings on the walls. Any trace of the original house: the wooden windows and shutters, the quaint porch, the wooden floored corridors, its charm, all have vanished. For good measure, while the neighbours and I looked on aghast, Mr Zhou had the exterior varnished from top to bottom.

When I walk past the monstrosity Mr Zhou grabs my arm and drags me inside to be impressed by his latest piece of cheesy art. He tells me with glee how much everything cost, furniture and pictures.

I have nothing personal against Mr Zhou, let me stress, apart from him being Shanghainese. He is just not my type.

After two years of haggling the Hangliao have got around to restoring the ruined Hans' place, where my love affair with Moganshan began. Like Mr Zhou's place next door, aluminum windows have replaced wooden shutters and the interior has been tiled and whitewashed. To complete the sad desecration, because the army could not be bothered or did not want to pay up to finish the job, they stuck a roof on top of the surviving stone walls without building them back up to their original height. So the house has one and a half floors. The bricked-in upstairs windows are cut in half by the eaves of the new corrugated iron roof. It is a sad sight. The other day I heard the Hangliao had changed their minds and were going to restore it again, but only up to two floors, not the original three.

Rumours about major renovation projects fly around the village like the injunctions from the Hangliao against fires and Falun Gong used to when we first arrived.

In the early winter of 2006 when I was in his office Mr Yang, the head of the Administration Bureau, showed me the blueprints for the development of Yin Shan Jie. He must have been to Shanghai on a recce. The drawings and artist's impressions he laid across the desk bore a striking resemblance to Xin Tian Di, 'New Heaven on Earth', a pedestrian complex of boutiques and restaurants in the heart of old Shanghai, developed by a Hong Kong property company in the early 2000s and itself a direct rip off of Covent Garden. I know so because I was shown the artist's impression in my publishing days. They included photographs of Covent Garden and the Marais in Paris.

'Moganshan's Xin Tian Di!' Mr Yang declared.

There was already a 'Xin Tian Di' down the road in Hangzhou and they are cropping up all over China now that the Shanghai one has taken off.

The pictures showed an anonymous, boxlike collection of shops and restaurants which could have been Anytown on a hill. Stick figures walked up and down with their heads in the air, admiring the faux rustic getaway, or looking into the windows of Gucci and Louis Vuitton.

I said what I thought Mr Yang wanted to hear without praising the project directly. I had a feeling that what I saw would never become reality.

It almost has. The bureau has opted for a compromise, a halfway house. Some old but not original shops and one restaurant were demolished at the end of 2006 and the rubble left undisturbed through the winter. The following April, a week before the season began, work started on the site. Two brand new buildings went up, one either side of the Yong Li Restaurant. It is one of the best in the village and somehow survived demolition. It is also the restaurant where Crystal and I had our first meal in Moganshan.

Apparently the still empty new building at our end of the street, which we overlook from the Lodge, will one day be a boutique restaurant complex with a coffee-shop inside. When I was explaining to anyone who would listen that I welcomed competition, someone told me that it was to be ours, a branch of the Lodge.

'What?!'

'That's what the Administration Bureau is saying,' was the answer.

It seems that in a rural community in a Communist country you can still have your life centrally planned for you.

I guess I will not be the only foreigner here for much longer. There is no point trying to resist that. Besides, I would rather take part in the process. Playing the role of village mascot, a walking talking museum piece, can be trying.

Sometimes I feel like the resident ambassador for all things foreign. Earlier this year a French family had an unsatisfactory – to put it mildly – stay at a local guesthouse. They came and complained to me. It was our fault because we had listed the guesthouse on our website.

'You must do some'sing abou'teet!' the irate, verging on hysterical, Madame shouted at me.

352

When she had left, the guesthouse owner came and complained too. It was our fault because we had encouraged the French family to come and stay in the first place.

'I don't want any more of you foreigners coming!' he shouted. 'You are too much trouble!'

He took in another big group the next weekend, this time Germans, and everyone was happy.

Another weekend a gang of American students turned down the rooms they were shown in the guesthouse above the Lodge. They wanted to check out other options, as you do. The owner came down the steps and into the Lodge in a whirlwind of words. He demanded that I explain what he had done wrong. I hadn't a clue what he was talking about.

Joanna also has to endure a perverse prejudice on my behalf. Chinese visitors walk into the Lodge and ask to see the boss.

'That's me,' she replies correctly. The business is in her name.

'No, not you, we mean the foreigner,' her fellow countrymen say.

'Sophisticated' Shanghainese have not only refused to speak to her, they even insisted on speaking English as if to prove how necessary it was that they were served by the foreigner, me. She deals with them, I think the word is, peremptorily.

Those hassles are a small price to pay for our life here. We have brought them on ourselves anyway. And we are making modest progress at changing a few small things for the better.

For example, at last I have persuaded our maid at home, Xiao Xie, to carry our rubbish down the steps to the bins and not throw it in the bushes across from the house below us.

'But that's where I used to throw rubbish when I looked after that house,' she explained. 'And then,' she carried one, 'when they did the renovations, the builders threw their rubble on top and my rubbish was buried. All we do is wait for the next time they do some building work and then your rubbish will be covered up too.'

'When did they renovate, Xiao Xie?'

'Last year. You remember.'

I wanted to ask her when she thought they would renovate again, which was bound to be many years hence. That particular tenant was a notorious miser, one of the reasons Xiao Xie was now working for us, not him. I thought better of it.

'Xiao Xie,' I said, 'the problem is that my foreign friends can see the rubbish.' Not entirely true. They would have to look for it but it was not impossible that they might stumble on it.

'And my friends, like me, hate rubbish being thrown into the woods. They'll think I did it.' It was clearly a foreigner's rubbish. No one else in the village eats Marmite and drinks fresh milk. I delivered my argument winner: 'Xiao Xie. I lose a lot of face.'

'Oh, I see,' she said.

She started lugging the rubbish down to the bins from that day on. The Moganshan Summer Resort Association would have been pleased.

My happiest contribution to the improvement of Moganshan so far has been with Mr Wang, our landlord for the Lodge. He was so overrun by foreigners last year that

354

he completely renovated his hotel during the winter, and he did it properly. He came to have a chat first.

'You should try to make the place more cosy, Manager Wang,' I said. 'Repainting, new floors and bathrooms are one thing, but it's the small details that count, the furnishings for example, the little touches.'

I have the *Time Out Guide* to weekend breaks from London on our bookshelves. I flicked it open and came to a photograph of a classic small country hotel bedroom.

'Here you are,' I handed it to him. 'Look at this picture. See those? Bedside table lamps. Much nicer than the wall-fitted reading lights you have now. Those are for a business hotel, not a country escape.'

'But . . .' Mr Wang started 'bedside table lamps are cheaper. That can't be right.'

'Just because something is expensive does not make it right,' I tried to explain. 'You have to create a certain feel.'

He was looking at the picture closely. 'Hm, like curtains instead of blinds?'

He was getting it.

When the renovations were finished a few months ago, Mr Wang took me on a tour. He'd done a good job. The wall lamps had been replaced with new ones, but also beside each bed was a small table and on it a bedside lamp. And he has put DVD players in every room. We have a large collection of English-language movies in the Lodge. Mr Wang is not stupid.

This year his investment is paying off. The descendants of the Moganshan Ice King are prospering from the spiritual heirs of his customers. Where they used to complain about the ice going soft, now they complain about the beds being hard, but otherwise the foreigners are pleasantly surprised, especially the ones who have spent some time outside Shanghai.

Our daily life has fallen into a comfortable routine. Joanna drives the children to the kindergarten in Yucun while I walk Charlie down the hill to the Lodge. Instead of 'Going to market?' the greeting is now: 'Going to work?'

'Going to work,' I reply to Han the Street.

When I reach the road I cut straight across and down the steps, as I used to for the market. Halfway down I bear off to the right through the bamboo on a dirt path that leads to Lao Gao's perfect little house. I keep track of his tidy life. The wood pile is stacked like a supermarket display apart from the log of the week which he is gradually working through for his stove. The floor of his goose pen is caked in mud and goose-shit. It looks like polished concrete that has been swept out every morning. The handmade fence around it, made from tops of the hairy bamboo, could sell by the yard in B&Q. There is not a trace of litter below Lao Gao's house, the vegetable patch is immaculately ordered and the building well-maintained. The Mokanshan Summer Resort Association would be pleased again.

Below Lao Gao I follow a path through the bamboo that passes the back door of a villa where several old couples live. The simple method they have used to keep their backyard tidy has been to lay an old carpet across it. The original colour has faded to a dark grey. An old lady is usually sitting on a stool inside the door, brushing her teeth after a breakfast of rice porridge.

'Going to work?'

'Going to work.'

Then downhill again through the bamboo, past a spring inside a stone arch like a Roman ruin and into the yard of a ramshackle villa used as a dormitory by General Manager Li's workers.

The terrace in front of the house is full of junk, organized by type. Old washbasins, doorframes, bamboo scaffolding, a stack of window panes leant up against a wall, a rusting motorbike, piping, planks, trestles, a circular saw, a pile of bricks, firewood for the stove. On sunny days washing is hung on lines between the sycamore trees: grey Y-fronts, tattered blue Mao jackets, nylon socks, a pair of carpet slippers, a couple of bras and sensible women's knickers. The hillside around and below is covered with trash.

'Not bad but must try harder,' the Mokanshan Summer Resort Association might have said.

The men will be at work by the time I pass and the women washing clothes in the spring or tidying the kitchen. On both sides of the house and behind it the men have built brick and cinder block shacks like a small shanty town. One of them has been waiting for a roof for two years now. Tiny passageways with dirt floors wind through them, narrowed by communal washbasins.

At the far side of the builders' yard I come out on the steps that lead from Ridge Road down to the Lodge. Directly above the Songliang Hotel, the lowest house on the ridge that belongs to the Hangliao is waiting for its new tenant to start restoration. He is a Shanghainese, another Zhou *nouveau*. He told us that he would be using the house as a holiday villa for his company. Joanna and I quietly hope he will forget the whole idea. It is unnerving to have uphill neighbours in Moganshan. You never know what they might drop on you.

357

Opening up the Lodge first thing in the morning is one of my favourite tasks of the day. I make a strong cup of coffee, take it outside in the sunshine and sit in a bamboo chair by the wall to watch the village go to work. The bus arrives and unloads the bureau workers, the street sweeper starts and stops, chambermaids emerge from the Songliang and hang up bedding to air, and Mr He drives up to the spring water factory in his Volkswagen Santana. If he spots me on my perch he'll hoot his horn and wave. Someone might point out a squashed snake on the road below me.

When the caffeine has kicked in I open up the wooden shutters, give the Lodge an airing and prepare for the breakfast customers. I slice fresh bacon and half cook some tomatoes if we are expecting a crowd.

I am prepared: to cook, pour coffee, and answer questions. People are always asking questions. It never ceases to surprise me that the first one is rarely, if ever, 'Are you open yet?' or 'Do you have breakfast?' It is: 'How long have you lived here?'

Sometimes they ask it as they walk in the door. It is the first thing out of their mouths. I find that rather intrusive but you get used to it. Moganshan does make people curious.

Now and again someone will insist on knowing how I ended up here and I will give them a brief synopsis of my business career.

'So you're that poor guy, are you?' an American said once, when he made the connection.

'Yes. I suppose I was,' I replied. 'But I'm not any more.'